3.50

Mildred B Lynch

DOMINICAN LIFE

DOMINICAN LIFE

By

F.-D. JORET, O.P.

With a Foreword by
Father Bernard Delany, O.P.

THE NEWMAN PRESS
WESTMINSTER, MARYLAND

AUTHORISED TRANSLATION OF
NOTRE VIE DOMINICAINE
BY F.-D. JORET, O.P.

Reproduced in Great Britain by photolithography
by Lowe & Brydone (Printers) Ltd., London, N.W.10

FOREWORD

A RELIGIOUS Order is assuredly not one of " the Creeds," as is sometimes imagined by those not of our faith, nor is it a " Religion " except in a restricted meaning of the word, as St. Thomas explains thus : " Every Christian at baptism when he renounces Satan and all his pomps is made a partaker of the true religion. But religion has a second meaning, namely the obligation whereby a man binds himself to serve God in a peculiar manner by specified works of charity and by renunciation of the world." Only in this secondary sense of the word can the Religious Orders be ever described as "Religions." A Religious is first a Christian and a Catholic ; but secondly he is a Catholic who has taken his Catholicism and Christianity a step further and renounced not only sin but also the world, and by the three vows strives to live solely for God in the work in which he has dedicated himself to God's service.

Hence when we hear enthusiasts speaking about " Dominicanism," " the Dominican Life," or " the Dominican Way " we must not associate with these expressions any sectarian intent. The Dominican Life is a particular way in which a Catholic Christian seeks union with the Divine Will through Jesus Christ Our Lord. The Dominican Order is one family within the City of God, a cell or a member of the Mystical Body, a branch of the True Vine. Under God's providence St. Dominic brought it into being at a definite moment in history in order to fulfil a definite function in the Church. The children of this family of St. Dominic, forming themselves on the traditions and examples of seven centuries, are bound together within God's Church by ties that transcend differences of race and tongue and are more enduring than the bonds of earthly kinship.

This book, written especially for members of St. Dominic's Third Order, is intended as a guide and manual to teach them St. Dominic's spirit. They are to remember that they are truly his children and should bear his family likeness. They are to dismiss from their minds the error that all religious Orders are much of a muchness, only differing because their members happen to wear different habits. Each Order has its character, its function, its special technique and way of approach to God. The Tertiary must learn about his Order and absorb its spirit. The present Holy Father in his glorious Apostolic Letter, *Unigenitus Dei Filius*, reminds us that Religious Founders created their Orders *in obedience to the inspiration of God.* " Therefore all who would reproduce in themselves the stamp and character of the religious family to which they belong should look to the origins from which it sprang. They should, following the examples of the best children of their common founder, glorify their Father by keeping his Rule and Precepts, by imbibing his spirit ; indeed they can only be regarded as faithfully doing their duty when they follow steadfastly in his footsteps. ' And their children for their sakes shall remain for ever ' (Ecclus. xliv. 13)."

This book, although written specifically for Tertiaries, will prove instructive and useful to all members of the three great branches of St. Dominic's Order. God grant it may lead all to love more and more our common heritage and always to rejoice in " the religion of Dominic, which is a delightful garden, broad, joyous and fragrant."

It only remains for us to express our gratitude to an anonymous Tertiary, first for translating this book and secondly for generously applying all the profits of the work to benefit Father Bede Jarrett's foundation at Oxford.

BERNARD DELANY, O.P.

September 1937.

THE AUTHOR'S PREFACE

THIS book is intended for you, dear Brothers and Sisters of the Third Order, who share our Dominican life, though you are living in the midst of the world. My earlier pages are addressed directly to you. And they are preceded by the Rule which has been drawn up for your guidance.

But afterwards, when I am trying to treat more particularly of the spirit of our religious family, that spirit which we speak about so much and which we certainly feel, but which we find great difficulty in defining clearly, I am in hopes of being of service to my other brothers and sisters in St. Dominic, notably to the sisters of the regular Third Order.

Whether we belong to one branch of the Order or to another, we are in duty bound to take account of the whole of that great family which is our own, to be at one in our devotion to our great Patriarch and to be imbued with his spirit.

We ought all to know where to look for the well-springs of our life as well as the traditional way of drawing upon them, and we must know, above all, how a Dominican should pray.

Each one of us must set upon his whole life the seal of truth. *Veritas !* That magic word which is emblazoned on our shield sums up the whole of our rule of conduct.

In setting before you the life of the First Order, in which the Dominican spirit is realized with special fulness, I run no risk of failing to interest our Tertiaries. To quote from an address delivered by one of themselves to a gathering of his brethren : " It is not so much the Third Order which has to be explained and commended to would-be postulants. It is the First Order itself, it is St. Dominic, his example, his life, his acts, his spirit. Could we not describe the true Tertiary as a really Dominican soul, the soul of a Dominican religious who is prevented by certain reasons, circumstances or insuperable obligations from observing the Rule of the First Order ? " [1]

May this little book contribute to winning recruits for our beloved Third Order and may it also enable me, in a modest way, to help all our brothers and sisters in St. Dominic to live in the spirit of our common Father.

PASSE-PREST,
    7th March, 1936.

[1] Paul Jamot, T.O.P., in *L'Année Dominicaine,* June, 1932.

TABLE OF CONTENTS

ix

Rule of the Brothers and Sisters of the Secular Third Order of St. Dominic

CHAPTER I

THE NATURE AND OBJECT OF THE THIRD ORDER

1. THE secular Third Order of the Friars Preachers, or the Order of Penance of St. Dominic, also known as the Militia of Jesus Christ, is an association of the faithful living in the world, who, sharing in the religious and apostolic life of the Order of Friars Preachers through the observance of their own Rule approved by the Holy See, strive under the direction of the Order to attain to Christian perfection.[1]

2. The object of the Third Order is the sanctification of its members or the practice of a more perfect form of Christian life, and the salvation of souls, in conformity with the condition of the faithful living in the world.[1]

3. The means of attaining this end are, besides the accomplishment of the ordinary precepts and the duties proper to one's state : the observance of this Rule, especially assiduous prayer—as far as possible liturgical prayer—the practice of mortification, and apostolic and charitable works for the Faith and the Church according to each one's particular state or condition in life.

4. The assemblies into which the Third Order is divided are called Fraternities or Chapters.[2] One may, however, for a special reason, be received into the Third Order without being incorporated in any particular Fraternity.[3]

5. Chapters cannot lawfully be erected without the

---

[1] *Cf.* Canon 702, 1.
[2] *Cf.* Canon 702, 2.
[3] *Cf.* Canon 703, 2.

consent of the local Ordinary.[1] As far as possible the Brothers and Sisters should have distinct Chapters.

6. Whatever is said in the Rule concerning Tertiaries, though expressed in the masculine gender, applies equally to women as well as men, unless the contrary is evident from the context or from the nature of things.

7. The erection is also desirable of Chapters of secular priests who, under the direction of a Dominican Father, aspire to a more perfect apostolic life.

CHAPTER II
CONCERNING THOSE TO BE RECEIVED AND THE CONDITIONS REQUIRED

8. In the first place, since the spiritual prosperity of this Order depends generally on the reception into it of well disposed persons, no one shall be admitted into the Third Order unless, in the prudent judgment of the Director, he has been proved, after careful investigation and sufficient test, to be a Catholic of devout life and good repute, sincerely desirous of striving after Christian perfection, and gives good reason to hope, especially if he be young, that he will persevere in his good resolution. Moreover, as a true spiritual son of St. Dominic, he must strive to be an ardent and zealous promoter of the truth of the Catholic Religion, and exemplary for his loyalty to the Church and the Roman Pontiff.

9. All, therefore, of both sexes, whether married or single, ecclesiastics or laity (except, however, Religious and lay people who already belong to another Third Order) [2] who are thus well disposed, can be received into the Third Order of the Friars Preachers, provided that they have completed their eighteenth year, or, if the Provincial for a just reason should so permit, at least their seventeenth year. Married persons, however, are not to be received ordinarily without the consent of the spouse, unless there be a just motive for acting otherwise.

[1] *Cf.* Canon 703, 2.
[2] *Cf.* Canon 704, 1, 705.

10. Those who have power to admit aspirants to the Third Order are :

(*a*) The Master General of the Order, or the Prior Provincial within the limits of his jurisdiction :

(*b*) The lawfully appointed Director of a Fraternity of the Third Order or a Father delegated by him in each case for his own Fraternity :

(*c*) Any priest delegated by the Master General of the Order or by the Prior Provincial. He may not, however, in places where a Fraternity is already erected, use this faculty without the consent of the Director of that Fraternity, or the special permission of the delegating authority. The delegation given by the Master General is for life, but the delegation granted by the Provincial requires the confirmation of his successor.

11. For the reception of anyone into a particular Fraternity of the Third Order, the consent of the Council of that Fraternity is required as well as that of the Director.[1]

CHAPTER III

THE HABIT OF THE BROTHERS AND SISTERS

12. The entire habit of the Third Order, made of plain woollen material, consists of a white tunic, a leather belt worn round the waist, and, for the Brothers, a black mantle with capuce, for the Sisters a black mantle with veil and linen coif.

13. The Tertiaries ordinarily, however, wear instead of the habit of the Order a small white woollen scapular under their secular dress.

14. At public functions, Tertiaries, with the consent of the local Ordinary, may wear the full habit of the Third Order,[2] or some particular insignia, according to local custom. But, if they take part collectively, they shall have their distinctive insignia, and walk after the cross of the Fraternity.[3]

---

[1] *Cf.* Canon 694, 1.
[2] *Cf.* Canon 703, 3.
[3] *Cf.* Canon 706.

this Order, nor may they without a just cause pass to another Third Order.[1]

CHAPTER VI

THE RECITATION OF THE OFFICE

28. Tertiaries shall recite daily either the ancient Office which is the *Pater noster*, or the Little Office of the Blessed Virgin Mary, according to the Dominican rite, or the fifteen mysteries of the Rosary. When unable to satisfy the above obligation, they may recite any one of the Little Offices approved in the Order, or even a third part of the Rosary.

29. If they recite the ancient Office of the *Pater noster*, they shall say : for Matins twenty-eight *Paters* and *Aves*, for Vespers fourteen, and seven for each of the Little Hours. They shall also say the Apostles' Creed at the beginning of Matins, before Prime and at the end of Compline. Matins may be said in the evening for the following day, or on the morning of that day ; the Little Hours before mid-day ; and Vespers and Compline towards evening. The Office, however, may be said at any time of the day, provided that the order of the Hours is regularly observed.

30. Priests and those in Sacred Orders satisfy this obligation by the recitation of the Divine Office ; but once a day they shall say the Responsory *O spem miram* with the versicle and prayer in honour of St. Dominic.

31. Tertiary priests may with the permission of the Master General of the Order use the Dominican Breviary and Missal, and the Calendar of the Order.

CHAPTER VII

CONFESSION, COMMUNION AND OTHER PIOUS EXERCISES

32. The Tertiaries shall, unless legitimately hindered, approach the Sacraments of Penance and the Holy

---

[1] *Cf.* Canon 705.

Eucharist at least twice each month. But if they do so more frequently, and even daily receive the most Holy Body of Christ, their devotion is to be commended.

33. Tertiaries should make every possible effort to assist daily at the most Holy Sacrifice of the Mass, and piously and attentively unite with the priest who is celebrating. Likewise, they should devote themselves to mental prayer and works of piety in conformity with the spirit of the Order.

34. Let them be particularly and lovingly devoted to the Blessed Virgin Mary, most faithful Patroness of the whole Order, to her Spouse St. Joseph, to the Blessed Patriarch Dominic, to St. Catherine of Siena, Patroness of the Third Order, and to all the Saints and Blessed of the Order.

35. Let them behave with great reverence in Church, especially during the celebration of the Divine Offices, and be an example to all the faithful.

36. It is greatly to be desired that in each Fraternity a Retreat of not less than three days be made at least once a year.

CHAPTER VIII

·FASTS

37. In addition to the fasts and abstinences prescribed by the Church, the Tertiaries, who are not impeded from doing so, shall fast on the vigils of the feasts of the most Holy Rosary, our Holy Father St. Dominic and St. Catherine of Siena. Moreover, in accordance with the penitential spirit of the Order and the prescriptions of the ancient Rule, it is laudable that they fast on all the Fridays of the year, and perform other penitential works with the advice of the Director, or of a prudent Confessor.

CHAPTER IX

THE AVOIDANCE OF WORLDLINESS

38. Tertiaries should abstain from frequenting places of worldly amusements. They should not, for instance,

go to dances or frivolous entertainments. But if it is impossible for them to abstain from these things, let them learn to make a virtue of necessity and, if time permits, let them seek permission from the Father Director, or at least inform him.

CHAPTER X
REVERENCE TOWARDS PRELATES AND CLERGY

39. Tertiaries should show the greatest reverence towards their Bishop and Parish Priest, and faithfully accomplish their duties towards them in accordance with local laws or customs. Let them hold in esteem the other clergy also, according to the dignity and official position of each.

CHAPTER XI
APOSTOLIC AND CHARITABLE WORKS

40. Following the example of the Apostolic Patriarch Dominic, and the Seraphic Virgin Catherine of Siena, Tertiaries should be animated with an ardent and generous desire for the glory of God and the salvation of souls.

41. Mindful of the traditions of our forefathers, the Tertiaries should labour by word and deed for the truth of the Catholic Faith, for the Church and the Roman Pontiff, proving themselves their valiant defenders in everything and always. Let them also assist in apostolic works, especially those of the Order.

42. They should devote themselves, under the direction of Superiors, to works of charity and mercy, either singly or collectively, according to the circumstances of the time and local necessities, and as far as their condition and capacity will permit.

43. They should also help the Parish Priest in the pious works of the parish, and particularly, where it is necessary, in giving religious instruction to boys and girls.

CHAPTER XII

VISITING AND ASSISTING THE SICK

44. Let visitors of the sick be appointed in the Fraternity, who, according to the wish of the Director, may charitably visit the sick brethren and endeavour to assist them spiritually and temporally.

CHAPTER XIII

DEATH OF THE BRETHREN AND SUFFRAGES

45. The death of a member of the Fraternity shall be announced as soon as possible to the other members, who, unless lawfully prevented, should personally attend the obsequies for the deceased.

46. Moreover, within eight days from the receipt of the notice of the death, each member of that Fraternity shall recite a third part of the Rosary, hear one Mass and apply one Holy Communion for the soul of the deceased.

47. Each Tertiary shall daily say one *Pater, Ave* and *Requiem* for the living and dead of the whole Order.

48. Besides, each Tertiary shall annually have celebrated, or at least assist at, three Masses for the welfare of the Brothers and Sisters, both living and dead.

CHAPTER XIV

THE SUPERIORS OF THE THIRD ORDER

49. The Order of Friars Preachers is placed under the direction and correction of the Master General of the Order, to whom as a consequence both Fraternities and individual Tertiaries as well as all the Directors are subject in all matters that pertain to their manner of life in accordance with the Rule.

50. Besides the Master General of the Order, Provincials also within the limits of their own Province

have, by reason of their office, pastoral care of the Third Order.

51. The Master General of the Order and Priors Provincial have the right to visit either personally or by delegates each Fraternity once a year or even oftener if necessary. Whatever it may seem good to them to decide whether by way of counsel, admonition, ordination or correction, even including the deposition of an official, should be accepted by each and all cheerfully and humbly.[1]

52. Tertiaries who are not members of any Fraternity shall regard as their Superior the Master General of the order or the Prior Provincial ; while those who belong to a Fraternity depend also on the Director and the other Superiors of that Fraternity.

53. The appointment of the Director of a Fraternity erected in a church of the Order is reserved exclusively to the Master General or the Prior Provincial. In the case of churches not belonging to the Order the consent of the local Ordinary is also required.[2]

54. The Director is appointed for three years, on the expiration of which he may be re-appointed.

55. During his term of office, the Director, as such, can discharge those duties which concern the training and spiritual direction of the Brethren. As to preaching sermons to them, the laws of the Church shall be observed.[3]

56. Directors who are secular priests must send to the Provincial once a year an account of the state and progress of the Fraternity entrusted to their care.

CHAPTER XV

THE OFFICIALS OF THE FRATERNITY

57. In every Fraternity there shall be a Prior, Subprior, Novice Master, and other Officials and Councillors.

---

[1] *Cf.* Canon 690, 2.
[2] *Cf.* Canon 698, 1.
[3] *Cf.* Canon 698, 2.

58. The Council of the Fraternity may not exceed twelve in number. The Prior, Subprior and Novice Master are, by reason of their office, members of this Council.

59. On the erection of a Fraternity all the Officials are appointed by the Provincial ; and also on the dissolution of the Council, which happens automatically as often as the whole Council or even the majority of the Councillors from any cause whatever retire from office.

60. The Officials and Councillors hold office for three years ; but each year a third part of the Council shall be renewed by the Director and the remaining Councillors. In the year, however, in which the Officials are to be renewed, the Council must first be completed, and then the Director with the whole Council shall select the Prior and other Officials. In case of disagreement between the Director and Council, recourse must be had to the Prior Provincial.[1]

CHAPTER XVI

THE OFFICE OF PRIOR AND OF THE OTHER OFFICIALS OF THE FRATERNITY

61. The office of Prior is carefully to see that the Rule is observed by all the members. He should also diligently note whether in the movements, comportment or dress of any member of his Fraternity anything occurs which might be offensive to the eye. If he notice any of the members transgressing or even negligent, let him charitably admonish and correct them ; or, should it seem to him more expedient, he may report the matter for correction to the Director of the Fraternity.

62. In the absence of the Prior the Subprior takes his place.

63. The other Officials shall accomplish their respective duties according as particular customs and the needs of each Fraternity may best determine.

[1] *Cf.* Canon 697.

64. The Council shall be summoned by the Director, who presides at it, as often as the vote of the Council is required according to the Rule, or when any important matters according to its particular statutes have to be transacted.[1]

CHAPTER XVII

THE MEETINGS OF THE BRETHREN

65. Once a month, on a fixed day and hour, the Brethren of the Chapter shall assemble to hear a sermon from the Director, and to assist at Mass if the hour be suitable.

66. The Director shall read and explain the Rule to the Brethren, inform them of the matters to be discussed and point out and correct such negligences as he thinks fit before God, and in accordance with the Rule.

67. Let the suffrages for the living and the dead be said also, and absolution given from the faults committed against the Rule.

CHAPTER XVIII

THE CORRECTION OF THE BRETHREN

68. Should anyone be found guilty of a notable fault, and, after having been admonished by the Director, fails to amend, let him be corrected according to his condition and in proportion to the gravity or levity of his fault. He can even be temporarily excluded from the meetings of the Brethren ; or even perpetually, with the consent, however, of the Fraternity, if after one or two admonitions he does not amend ; nor can he be again admitted without the consent of the Council of the Fraternity.[2]

69. Only the Master General of the Order or the Prior Provincial may, for serious reasons, expel a member from the Third Order ; and this, in case of grave scandal, even without admonition.[2]

---

[1] *Cf.* Canon 697, 1.
[2] *Cf.* Canon 696.

CHAPTER XIX
DISPENSATIONS

70. The Master General of the Order has full power to dispense from any precept of this Rule. Likewise, the Provincial within the limits of his jurisdiction, or even the Director in his Fraternity, or their delegate, can dispense their Tertiaries in special cases and for a reasonable cause.

CHAPTER XX
THE NATURE OF THE OBLIGATION OF THIS RULE

71. The precepts of this Rule, except those which are divine or ecclesiastical, do not oblige the Brothers and Sisters under pain of sin before God, but only to the punishment determined by the law or to be imposed by the Prelate or Director in accordance with the prescriptions of Chapter XVIII. Mindful, however, of their Profession, let all the Brethren observe the ordinations of this Rule by the help of the grace of Our Lord and Saviour Jesus Christ, Who with the Father and the Holy Ghost liveth and reigneth, God for ever and ever. Amen.

APOSTOLIC DECREE APPROVING THE ABOVE RULE

Our Holy Father, by divine Providence Pope Pius XI, in an audience given to the undersigned Secretary of the Sacred Congregation of Religious on 23 April 1923, approved and confirmed, in answer to the petition of the Most Rev. Fr. Master General of the Order of Friars Preachers, the Rule of the Brothers and Sisters of the Secular Third Order of St. Dominic, long ago approved by the Supreme Pontiffs Innocent VII and Eugene IV, now brought into harmony with the needs of our time and revised by the Sacred Congregation as it is in the present copy, the original of which is preserved in the Archives of the said

Sacred Congregation, and without prejudice to any of the prescriptions of the Sacred Canons.

Given at Rome, from the Secretariate of the S. Congregation of Religious, 23 April 1923.

C. CARD. LAURENTI, *Prefect.*

MAURUS M. SERAFINI, Abb. O.S.B.,

Secretary.

CHAPTER I

THE THIRD ORDER

SECTION I. THE AIM OF THE THIRD ORDER.
1. To Lead to Perfection.
2. Perfection to be found in Union with God by Charity.
3. The Duty of realizing Perfect Charity.

SECTION II. THE TERTIARY PROFESSION.
1. It is a real Profession.
2. The Obligation Contracted.
3. Risks and Spiritual Advantages.

SECTION III. A RELIGIOUS STATE.
1. The Sacramental Character and the Virtue of Religion.
2. The Virtue of Religion and the Theological Virtues.
3. The Virtue of Religion and the Moral Virtues in the Religious State.

15

FIRST SECTION

THE AIM OF THE THIRD ORDER

I. TO LEAD TO PERFECTION

CANON law commends those of the faithful who join the associations which the Church has either founded or approved (Canon 684).

These associations are of different kinds, according to the object which they have in view. If they have been instituted to further particular pious practices or works of charity they are generally described as " pious associations " or " sodalities " and some of them are entitled to call themselves " confraternities " (Canon 707). So we get such organizations as the Association for the Propagation of the Faith, the Confraternities of the Rosary and of the Blessed Sacrament.

Above these associations, in a completely separate category, the Church places the secular Third Orders. " Secular Tertiaries," she states, " are those faithful who, living in the world under the direction of a religious order and according to its spirit, strive to attain to Christian perfection in the secular life through following rules approved for them by the Holy See " (Canon 702).

The difference is obvious at once. In this case it is no longer simply a question of devoting oneself to some charitable or pious work—of furthering by alms and prayers the propagation of the Faith, of reciting the rosary once a week, of adoring the Blessed Sacrament at certain times. These are all laudable works in which a Tertiary also may take part, but the motive for his entrance into a Third Order is desire for perfection. He hopes by that means to strive more effectually to attain to Christian perfection.

A person remains in the world. One day, maybe, he will be able to leave it to enter a religious order where the attainment of Christian perfection will be made easier for him : that is his aspiration. Possibly, however, hindrances of some sort, such as chronic ill-health or " insuperable obligations," will definitely and finally preclude him from ever realizing his ambition.

Sometimes that aspiration is wholly lacking, and all that is desired is to be attached to some special Order, to follow its direction and to imbibe its spirit whilst continuing to lead a secular life in the world. Candidates for a Third Order may, and indeed do, differ widely in these and many other respects, but they must be at one in regarding it as their chief object in life to become perfect.

The Rule of the Brothers and Sisters of the secular Third Order of St. Dominic sets forth that aim in the very first paragraph. It returns to it with more detail in the second. " The object of the Third Order is the sanctification of its members or the practice of a more perfect form of Christian life." Before anyone can be admitted into a Fraternity or Chapter, it must be proved and established " in the prudent judgment of the Director " that the postulant is sincerely desirous of striving after perfection (II. 8).

If, however, it should come to pass that someone is admitted into the Third Order for some less worthy reason, in a wave of enthusiasm or under the influence of a feeling of sympathy, all hope is not lost for him and for those who have charge of his soul. Such souls may derive encouragement from what St. Catherine of Siena writes in her *Dialogue* [1] about those who have thus entered religion.

" The important point," she remarks, " is for them to practise virtue and to persevere until death in so doing. (Yes, what is important is not so much to begin well as to end well.) . . . Not a few there are who have pre-

[1] *Dialogue*, Ch. CLVIII.

sented themselves after having kept the commandments perfectly, but who have subsequently looked back or have remained in the Order without advancing in the way of perfection. The circumstances or the dispositions with which they took passage in the ship are prepared and willed by Me who have called them in divers ways." (God is speaking.) " But it is not from these preliminary conditions, be it said once more, that one can judge of their perfection : that depends entirely upon the interior spirit with which they persevere in real obedience, once they are within the Order."

We are, all of us, very imperfect beings, lacking in many things, and we are confronted with the life-long task of completing and perfecting ourselves.

Exterior works, such as discovery and development of the world about us by means of the sciences, the arts and crafts, are all very well. It is also good for us to understand, maintain and improve that physical matter which is so closely joined to us as to form one body with us : our health is important. Sports may be encouraged and the laws of hygiene should always be respected. But before any of these things, I am entrusted by God with the paramount duty of developing myself morally, and of bringing to its appointed end the being that I intrinsically am, my own true self. By constant and progressive effort I ought to be fashioning myself " in such wise that at length eternity may change me into myself."

This, then, is to be my aim, my only aim, to become perfect and eventually to blossom forth into that of which I am at present only a germ. Left in the hands of my own counsel with this object in view, I have it in my power to deviate from my right course. If I do so, I shall be nothing but a failure : I shall have failed to fulfil my destiny.

God conceived my being and set it in the world willing

that it should fulfil itself, that it should even surpass itself in supernatural beauty. Reason and grace, whereby I personally participate in the idea and will of my Creator, urge me to realize this perfection in spite of all opposing tendencies which tempt me to evil. The deep voice of my conscience enjoins what is right. Be what you are !

We shall see presently what it is that constitutes this perfection ; but for the moment let us grasp the one great principle which underlies and dominates everything in our Tertiary life, as indeed in every truly moral life.

It is not a matter of adding other practices to those we already have, and of making out for ourselves a list of meticulous observances. No, dear Brothers and Sisters of the Third Order, what is all-important is to gain a clearer and stronger conception of our final goal, to have a greater anxiety for perfection.

II. WHERE IS PERFECTION TO BE FOUND ?

Let us now consider what we mean by perfection. For although, absolutely speaking, there is only one perfection, there are a great many relative perfections, even in the moral and spiritual order.

A man is described as being perfect in his manners, as having perfection in his art : he may be lauded for the perfection of his science, or he may be proclaimed the perfect theologian. What is implied is that on such and such a point he is deficient in nothing, he is accomplished, he has reached the limit of possible development as far as courtesy, art or some branch of science is concerned.

But what does all that amount to, if we contrast it with the absolute perfection which is the consummation of what constitutes our essential self ? Everything else, even to being an excellent artist, a man of great learning, an eminent theologian, is mere child's play compared to that perfection which alone deserves to be called perfection pure and simple.

Of that perfection it is important to form a correct notion. We Christians ought not to speak as if it meant only the realization of a purely imaginary ideal which the greatest and most enlightened men have conceived for others. This view is not entirely false, and we shall return to it by and by. But let us fully apprehend and boldly affirm that the end we have to pursue is not a mere ideal. Our goal is a concrete Being Who existed before us, from Whom we proceed and to Whom we must return. Our supreme end is identical with our first cause. Someone exists Who made us entirely and claims us entirely. " It is God Who has created me," said Blessed Osanna of Mantua, " and to Him only I must belong." [1]

We cannot possibly complete ourselves unless we return to Him Who is the source of our being. *Mihi adhaerere Deo bonum est.* It is good for me to cleave to God. I shall be perfect when I attain to that.

Now it is charity which unites us to God, the charity whereby we love God with all our being and above all things. That is where perfection lies. Apart from that, there is nothing as far as the spiritual life is concerned. Other perfections count for naught. [2] " If I should have prophecy and should know all mysteries and all knowledge . . . and have not charity I am nothing," says St. Paul. [3] Blessed Osanna of Mantua was only six years old when, as she wandered on the bank of the Po, she heard a voice which murmured : " Child, life and death consist in loving God."

It is indeed through charity, and through charity alone, at least actually, that we cleave to that Pure Spirit,

---

[1] M. C. de Ganay, *Les Bienheureuses Dominicaines*. Other quotations are taken from this book and from the great *Année Dominicaine* which has been re-edited by the Fathers of the Province of Lyons and contains in twelve volumes notices of all the saints, and of the blessed or venerable persons who have adorned our Order from the thirteenth to the eighteenth century. It must not be confused with the monthly review of the same name which appears in Paris and to which I shall also have occasion to refer.
[2] St. Thomas, *De perfectione spirituali*, Ch. I.
[3] 1 Cor. xiii. 2.

to that Being of infinite perfection. The day will come
when it will be by our intelligence that we shall see Him
and shall possess Him for all eternity. The result will
be an immense love which will finally establish us in
beatitude. But here below, so long as we are without the
light which reveals the divine beauty, our heart goes
further than our mind, our love already lays hold of
that God of Whom we can only form a limited conception. Thanks to charity we possess within us our God,
together with the assurance that we shall see Him when
the right time comes. "He that abideth in charity
abideth in God, and God in him." [1]

What has been said above respecting the arts and
sciences holds good also with regard to moral virtues :
they only give us relative perfection. Yet here, at any
rate, these relative perfections are none the less requisite,
since it is not permissible for a child of God to be intem-
perate, profligate, treacherous, etc. It is also desirable
for him to have, as far as possible, some artistic and
scientific culture. It is a good thing for him to develop
himself physically. But even the still more relative and
secondary perfections of which these things admit can
be derived, in due order, from the charity in which dwells
absolute perfection. Charity is the first principle of that
harmonious blossoming forth of our whole being. It
implies all the other virtues which together form the
Christian and human ideal, and which appear as so
many manifestations of its profound life. " Charity is
patient, is kind," says St. Paul, " charity envieth not,
dealeth not perversely ; is not puffed up, is not ambitious, seeketh not her own, is not provoked to anger,
thinketh no evil, rejoiceth not in iniquity but rejoiceth
with the truth : beareth all things, believeth all things,
hopeth all things, endureth all things." [2]

[1] 1 John iv. 16.
[2] 1 Cor. xiii. 4–7.

Elsewhere the same apostle, after enumerating sundry virtues, such as mercy, benignity, humility, etc., concludes by saying : " But above all these things have charity, which is the bond of perfection." [1] It binds all the other virtues into a perfect unity. [2]

Still more true would it be to say that charity is the mother of the other virtues. There is not one of them which is not generated in her womb by the desire to act aright for God Who enjoins them all, each one in its particular sphere.

And that is why St. Augustine could write : " Love—and do as you will." "" Peter, lovest thou Me ? " That is the only question Jesus put to St. Peter, and if He interrogated him a second and a third time, it was only to repeat the same query.

" Dearly beloved brothers," said St. Dominic as he lay dying, " this is the inheritance which I leave to you as my true children—have charity."

III. THE DUTY OF REALIZING PERFECT CHARITY

The anxiety for perfection which must inspire us will lead us on to charity, because in charity dwells the essence of spiritual perfection. We ought then to take pains fully to realize charity in ourselves. We are all the more bound to do this because God has made it the subject of His great precept : " Thou shalt love the Lord thy God." To love God as much as He is lovable is beyond our power. That is a perfection to which God alone can attain, for He alone is capable of infinite love. The only perfection which is within the reach of a creature is to love God with all the power with which God has endowed him. In telling us how that should be done, Holy Scripture enumerates our various faculties. " Thou shalt love the Lord thy God with thy whole heart, and with thy whole soul, with thy whole mind and with thy whole strength." It piles up the words which express

---

[1] Col. iii. 14.
[2] St. Thomas, IIa IIae, q. 184, a. 1, *sed contra.*

our powers to let us know that not one of these powers is exempt from the obligation to love God. Moreover, each one must be wholly employed in this duty, and no part of any one is entitled to shirk it. In short, everything in us must be consecrated to divine love. There is no exception : there is no measure.

As regards the goal at which we are aiming and which dominates and directs all our interests, how could there be any measure ? The physician does not put any limit to the health which he is attempting to restore to his patient. He certainly limits his remedies and he measures them with a view to the cure he is hoping for. But it is an absolute cure that he purposes. If any element of compromise enters in, that is because he is not solely a physician ; the ordering of health does not monopolize the whole field of his conscience. Health is not the supreme end. Where it is only a subordinate end, it becomes just a means. That is why Blanche of Castile, who loved her son with all a mother's love, nevertheless said to him : " I would rather see you dead than guilty of a mortal sin." Mortal sin is the ruin of charity : it is renunciation of the supreme end. Anything rather than that ! To live in charity is our absolute duty. We will strive to do it without measure or limitation.

Does that mean that we ought to give God our love so completely that we shall be uninterruptedly occupied with Him alone ? Well, yes ! the precept goes as far as that, but it does not oblige us to succeed forthwith. Actually that will be possible only in Heaven. Nevertheless, our duty is to strive after it henceforward and keep ourselves in the way which leads us to that goal.

We must, at the very least, refuse to take pleasure in anything which is absolutely repugnant to God. The greater part of the divine injunctions which are appended to the great commandment is directed to a prohibition of all sins which destroy charity. But if one can say that this is, strictly speaking, sufficient, it is only on condition that whilst we are realizing this elementary form of perfection we are still straining towards that total perfection which will be consummated in heaven.

Total perfection does not come simply at the finish like a gift which will be presented to us without our having to give it any thought. It is the object which we must be always striving for and towards which all our life must be directed. The end and object of life must not be confused with its mere termination. That is the mistake made by those people whose whole spiritual life is negative, and who think that all they need do, to keep themselves in a state of grace to the end, is to avoid all the mortal sins. As though all we had to do to make our way home was to avoid falling into precipices ! The object must be constantly before us as a focus of attraction, like a magnet. We must not be indifferent to it : we have to *will* it quite positively.

This positive determination must and does express itself through action. We must advance actively towards the goal. No one is free from that duty. But as to the exact manner in which it is to be done, no cut and dried general direction can be given. The programme changes according to the individual, and even for the individual it may change from one day to the next. The negative precepts we have recently dealt with are clearly defined, they are the same for all and are always the same. But the great positive commandment of charity ever retains its flexibility, and is diversified in its exactions. It says to each soul : " Thou shalt love as much as thou canst in thy present state." [1] But that state varies.

It varies externally according to the conditions in which we find ourselves providentially placed. The marriage to which we are pledged ; the sacred orders we have received ; the charge of souls we may have

[1] St. Thomas, IIa IIae, q. 186, a. 2, ad 2.

assumed ; the religious vows we have taken ; the Profession we have made to follow the Rule of the Third Order : these and countless other less important circumstances differentiate our state of life and thereby diversify the positive schedule of our duties. In addition to the duty which is incumbent on all the human race, there are particular differences according to the different states of life in which men are placed. Dominican Tertiaries, for instance, constitute one of these states.

And in each state, however lowly it may be, there are still as many differences as there are individuals—differences which arise primarily from the interior condition of each one. In every soul, when grace reaches a certain level, and when love attains a certain strength, they tend by virtue of their actual vitality to produce acts corresponding to their power. If I fail to perform these acts when the occasion presents itself and I have no reasonable motive to justify their omission, I am to that extent escaping from the pursuit of the supreme goal, I am withdrawing a little of my life from the attraction of the great end, I am ceasing to concentrate upon it as I ought. Even if the act set before me is to be regarded as of counsel rather than of precept, I must not disregard it, once my conscience shows me that it is right for me in the state in which I am at the present time. " Quench not the Spirit," says St. Paul.

Individual duty may be modified from one day to another. An omission which was formerly justifiable, and was consequently not a venial sin, might be culpable to-day because my heart has grown larger. I am like a traveller who started out on his journey when he was still a child. Naturally enough, he covers more ground when he has grown to manhood. He advances in proportion to the length of his legs. I must love God with all my heart. And if my heart is more capable of love than in the past, it ought to love more and give evidence of that increased love. Of course, the stain of sin does not attach to every act not inspired by the fulness of the love of which we are capable. Progression increasing with perfect regularity is practically impossible. Moreover, acts which fall short of our capacity for loving do sometimes mysteriously prepare the way for a future more perfect act which will lead to an increase of power. Nevertheless, it happens only too often that these acts remain on a lower plane through our negligence, and of that we are guilty.

Let us be high-spirited souls who keep on rising under the inspiration of the great goal. " Oh, dear Jesus," said Blessed Osanna of Mantua at the close of a very beautiful prayer, " enable me to grow increasingly in Thy love, to advance in it with firm and steady steps : so that my heart may be inebriated and inundated by it. Ah ! far from fearing to be submerged in it, I long for it with all my might, and my one wish is to be engulfed in the depths of the abyss."

When Sister Adelaide of Rheinfelden was praying one night after Matins at Unterlinden, a soft voice whispered in the ears of her soul : " I am thy last end," and she understood the words to mean : " I have so attracted thee, thyself, thy whole life and the impulses of thy heart, I have so effectually and irrevocably welded thee to Myself, I have made thy will so conformed to My own that very soon, thy earthly trial over, thou shalt be united to Me, thy eternal end, without delay, without hindrance, immediately and for ever."

SECOND SECTION

THE TERTIARY PROFESSION

I. IT IS A REAL PROFESSION

A GOOD Christian performs day by day such acts of virtue as befit the station in which Providence has placed him. What more could he do if he were a Tertiary? . . . Take another such Christian, one who belongs to a Third Order, is he any better?

Let us avoid comparisons between individuals. God alone is judge. Let us only consider the aforesaid good Christian and compare his present condition with the state in which he would find himself if he became a Tertiary.

Two things would certainly place him in a more favourable position for striving after Christian perfection. In the first instance, his condition on entering the Third Order would receive a new direction which would regulate his duties and extend them. Then he would be under a stricter obligation to fulfil those duties and would be less liable to omit them. His profession would consequently give him a twofold aid towards the acquisition of greater merits.

A term consecrated by the Church characterizes at the same time this more favourable position and this more binding obligation. By the very fact of his Profession, the Tertiary is introduced—is fixed—into a " superior state of life." Although it falls short of the state in which those who take the triple vow of religion are established and settled, nevertheless it imitates that state in its quality and duration.

In view of the perfection which he is bound, like any other Christian, to strive for amid the duties of his secular

life, the Tertiary has at his disposal special means which
are well proved and which have been long since canonized
by the Church.   They are the Rule and way of life
required by the Third Order of which he forms part.
" Besides the accomplishment of the ordinary precepts
and the duties proper to his state " there are definite
observances prescribed for him, " especially assiduous
prayer, as far as possible liturgical prayer, the practices
of mortification, and apostolic and charitable works for
the Faith and the Church, according to his particular
state or condition in life " (I. 3).

The ordinary Christian may, of course, in a moment of
fervour make like resolutions, impose upon himself
similar penances, perform identical religious exercises,
and devote himself to the same apostolic or charitable
works.   But in his case the acts will be more or less
spasmodic, at the mercy of chance and the impulse of
the passing moment : sooner or later circumstances or
instability of character are likely to lead to their being
dropped altogether.   The Tertiary, on the other hand,
by a choice long considered and really personal, by a
decision taken when he was completely master of himself,
has made profession to lead this life until his death.

Far be it from me to liken the simple Christian
who is concerned with his perfection to a man who is a
law to himself or who plays fast and loose with the
spiritual life.   But the Tertiary is undoubtedly admitted
into a training school of spirituality and makes a profession of Christian perfection.   If he is fully conscious
of his Profession, if he takes quite seriously its emblems
which he wears, I was going to say its badges which he
displays, he will continue unremittingly to strive after
perfection according to the principles and the practice
of his school.   " The Brethren of the Third Order, after
their Profession, which is for life, are bound to persevere
in this Order, nor may they without a just cause pass to
another Third Order " (V. 27).

Still more strongly is it prohibited to " return to the

world," as the ancient rule expresses it. "We give order," it says, " that no brothers or sisters of this Order or Fraternity should be allowed, after their Profession, to leave the Order or to return to the world. It is permitted, however, to pass over to one of the approved religious Orders where the three solemn vows are professed."

In such a case, ascent is made to a still more perfect condition of life, to which one is bound still more closely by the vow of religious obedience, which is a promise made to God. In the Third Order there is no promise to God, but a word of honour is given. And that is a great thing. Even in the world the breach of such a pledge is very severely judged. Moreover, this particular undertaking is, like the above-mentioned vow, made in public : it is regulated by the Church and officially accepted by her. It is therefore weighty. One must not lightly bind oneself in that way.

"No one shall be admitted into the Third Order unless, after careful investigation and sufficient testing, he gives reason to hope that he will persevere in his good resolution." *Maxime si sit juvenis.* If he is young, particular circumspection is necessary (II. 8). Moreover, no one must be inscribed in the Third Order before the completion of his eighteenth year. Only with the sanction of the Prior Provincial, given for adequate reasons, is it allowable to receive a postulant at the age of seventeen (II. 9). Finally, before being admitted to their profession, novices must apply themselves for a year to study the Rule under the direction of the Master of Novices "in order to acquire a knowledge of their obligations, and strive to assimilate the spirit of our Holy Father, St. Dominic" (V. 21).

I can, at any rate, understand the mentality of Blessed Osanna of Mantua, who, after having entered the noviitiate of the Third Order at the age of fourteen (it was permissible in those days), deferred making her Profession for forty years. But I can find no excuse for those

persons who, after undertaking these solemn engage-
ments, come in the course of time to disregard them
altogether. One does not leave a fraternity as one might
cease to attend a salon. And the fact of having lost sight
of the religious who received one's Profession does not
give a dispensation from a contract which was binding
" until death."

II. THE OBLIGATION CONTRACTED

The Tertiary has solemnly promised " that henceforth he will live according to the Rule and manner of
the Brothers and Sisters of the Order of Penance of St.
Dominic " (V. 25).

These words of profession comprise the sum total of
the observances that it is intended to practise : they
express the desire to live by the Dominican Rule. They
also formulate the exact nature of the obligation incurred :
they pledge one to this Rule.

Now the Rule of the Third Order of St. Dominic
closes with a very important notice : " The precepts of
this Rule, except those which are divine or ecclesiastical,
do not oblige the Brothers and Sisters under pain of
sin before God, but only to the punishment determined
by the law or to be imposed by the Prelate or Director
in accordance with the prescriptions of Chapter XVIII."

Do not run away with the idea that this regulation
implies anything derogatory to the Third Order : do we
not find the same thing in the Constitutions of the Friars
Preachers and their Sisters of the great Order ?

At the Chapter of Bologna (as we learn from Bl.
Humbert of Romans), St. Dominic declared, for the
consolation of the timorous, that the actual rules were
not binding under penalty of sin. St. Thomas also
writes in his *Summa Theologica :* " There is a form of
religious life, that of the Order of Friars Preachers, in
which transgression or omission does not in itself involve
any fault either mortal or venial and is punishable only
by a fixed penalty. The reason is that they have bound

themselves in this way to the observance of those kinds
of regulations." This enactment which St. Dominic
originated and which St. Thomas regarded as so very
wise has since then been extended by ecclesiastical law
to all religious families. Of course, the matter of the
three vows is on an altogether different footing, and so
is the case of a formal precept imposed on anyone who
makes a vow of obedience. But these things do not
affect Tertiaries. On the other hand, what follows in
the text of St. Thomas does apply also to them. "They
may, however, sin, either venially or mortally, if their
conduct proceeds from negligence, passion or contempt." [1]

Is it then possible for them, by breach of rule, to commit
mortal sin? Yes, in the case of contempt. Total and
wilful disregard of their Rule, which is an authorized
form of Christian perfection, approved by the Church
and voluntarily professed, is direct opposition to the duty
of seeking perfection : it is an offence against Holy
Church and it is the attitude of an apostate. But contempt of that sort, St. Thomas considers, is rare, even
amongst those who often fail to keep the Rule. "An act
of transgression or omission," he says, "implies contempt when the will of its perpetrator rebels against the
precept of the law or of the rule, and when it is this
rebellious spirit which makes him act in opposition to
the law or the rule. But when it is a particular motive,
such as concupiscence or anger, which induces him to
infringe the law or the rule, he is not sinning from contempt but from some other motive—even should the
lapse recur frequently for the same motive or one similar.
St. Augustine also states that every sin does not originate
in contempt. Nevertheless, constant repetition of a fault
predisposes us to contempt."

If there is no contempt, the sin can only be venial :
it will never be mortal, and this should reassure over-
timorous souls. Nevertheless, some measure of venial
sin, slight though it may sometimes be, is always entailed

[1] IIa IIae, q. 186, a. 9.

by the voluntary and unreasonable infringement of the Rule.

Why—seeing that the Rule does not bind under penalty of sin ?

What is prescribed in the Rule does not of itself bind under penalty of sin, it is true. But my conduct must always conform to what is enjoined by my reason, the reflection in me of the eternal order. I must not make myself responsible for any action or omission which my reason could not fully justify in view of my last end. In order the better to direct my life towards its supreme goal I made profession of this Rule and I am bound constantly to take it into consideration. I may indeed happen to have an adequate motive for not observing some special practice and then I do right to omit it. But if I omit it under the influence of some passion, I am sinning against the virtue which ought to have controlled that passion and to have brought rational order into my conduct. If there is not passion, there may have been simple negligence. I omit a prayer pre-scribed for me by the Rule through carelessness, or I say it without proper attention. In all such cases I am culpable, because I have not conformed my conduct to the order of my reason.

Furthermore, a Tertiary must perform the penance which the Rule or the Superior imposes for faults. It is sometimes asserted that this, at least, is binding under penalty of sin. Why ? Is it not an article of the Rule like any other ? Not more than the rest does it bind us under penalty of sin, seeing that we are not told that it forms an exception. This is the teaching of Cajetan, who is a great authority on the question.[1] But here again a voluntary omission brought about by negligence or passion is not free from sin. And here there would be more likelihood that the sin might become mortal,

---

[1] In IIam IIae, q. 186, a. 9, VI. *Cf.* I. M. Tonneau, O.P., *L'obligation* " *ad poenam* " *des constitutions dominicaines* in *Revue des Sciences philosophiques et théologiques*, February, 1935.

because systematic refusal to perform penances imposed
for faults would be very apt to lead to contempt.

We are now in a position to understand the sense and
the implications of the last paragraph in the Rule of the
Dominican Third Order. After stating that its injunctions do not bind under penalty of sin against God, but
only bind us to the penance fixed by the Rule or laid
down by the Director of the Chapter or Fraternity, it
adds : " Mindful, however, of their Profession, let all
the Brethren observe the ordinations of this Rule by the
help of the grace of Our Lord and Saviour Jesus Christ."

In order to observe faithfully the Rule which they have
embraced, Tertiaries should re-read it from time to
time.   Perhaps on the day of their Profession they heard
themselves addressed by the Director of the Dominican
Fraternity in the terms of an ancient formulary.   The
words only state the exact truth : " Receive, Brother,
this Rule as a lasting record and memorial of the promise
you made to-day.   Know that it will be shown to you
at the Last Judgment by the holy angels for your glory
and security if you have kept it ; if, on the other hand,
you have neglected it, it will be turned against you by
your accusers to your despair and shame.   Take it therefore with your hands, embrace it with your mind, that
embracing it in deed, it may profit you unto life everlasting."

III.   RISKS AND SPIRITUAL ADVANTAGES

The Tertiary's " order sheet " is therefore one which
is calculated to reduce to a minimum the spiritual
dangers to which he is exposed, whilst at the same time
providing him with enormous advantages.

Risks there are, undeniably.   It stands to reason that
if we have placed ourselves in a state which entails more
claims upon us, we shall have more opportunities for
failure.

However, the sins to which we become liable *as
Tertiaries* will only be venial.   I shall never commit

more than a venial sin by omitting to perform an act prescribed by the Rule, but not commanded by God or the Church. As we have said, only in the case of contempt is there mortal sin, and contempt is rare. Moreover, I may assure you that it is not confined to Tertiaries. The ordinary Christian, anyone, in fact, who absolutely despises a precept, reduces his soul to a state of anarchy which is deadly to him.[1]

Undoubtedly, in giving way to such contempt, the Christian would be more guilty of ingratitude than an infidel, and the Tertiary still more so. Similarly, the sin of a Tertiary may afford more matter for scandal than that of the ordinary Christian, and for that reason may be charged with special gravity.

The above, then, constitute all the risks incurred by those who make their Profession. In practice they are very slight.

The advantages, on the other hand, are immense and far more than compensate for any possible drawbacks. Who would venture to condemn as evil all modern means of rapid transit, on the ground that they sometimes give rise to accidents ? To reach the distant spot to which I wish to go, I consider the railway preferable to a journey on foot. So also I shall find in the Rule of the Third Order a superior way which will more satisfactorily lead me to my last end. Moreover, it carries with it an insurance policy against accidents. To the Tertiary may be applied a great proportion of the remarks which St. Thomas makes about the Religious : " His sin, if it is a light one, is to some extent covered by his numerous good deeds. And if he should chance to commit a mortal sin, he recovers himself more readily, primarily because his intention which he usually directs towards God, but which has deviated for a moment, springs back almost spontaneously . . . as happened in the case of him who said : ' I know not this man,' and who shortly afterwards, when the Lord had looked at him, began to

[1] St. Thomas, IIa IIae, q. 105, a. 1.

weep bitterly. . . . Besides, his brethren help him to
rise, as it is written, ' If one falleth, another will support
him.' But woe betide the solitary who falls : he has no
one to come to his help." [1]

Let us not be amongst those timid souls who can see
nothing but the possible risks. St. Thomas, in the
passage just quoted, speaks of the good deeds which
absorb the sins to which one is exposed. He who has
made a profession, albeit without religious vows, participates in proportion to the stability of his profession
in the advantages derived from permanent vows. There
is more certainty and more merit attached to his performance of good deeds. More certainty, because he has
pledged himself to do them and consequently is less
liable to omit them.

But is there really more merit ? Is it not more
meritorious to offer work to God spontaneously with
one's liberty unfettered ?

Let us consider this point. You are not acting under
compulsion when you act on the strength of a promise
freely made to God. And, by the very fact of your having
offered to God in perpetuity your power of action, you
have subjected yourself to Him far more fully than if
you were only to offer Him a series of acts. Is not the
man who makes a present of the tree more generous
than he who makes annual offerings of its fruit ? Moreover, when, after serious consideration, I have made
profession to do good at all times, my will works with a
stronger attraction to that good than if I act on impulse
as the result of passing emotion. If a good disposition
prevails, the vow itself does not preclude continual self-
surrenders to God in joy. Even at times of temptation
and weakness, a certain sense of satisfaction is felt at
being bound by past promises. It is rather like a patient
who is not quite sure of himself and allows himself to
be tied down to undergo a painful operation.[2] Finally,

[1] IIa IIae, q. 186, a. 10.
[2] IIa IIae, q. 88, a. 6 ; q. 189, a. 2.

in addition to the merit of the particular virtue I practise in performing a good act, the virtue of penance, for instance, when I fast, there is the yet higher merit of obedience. For here the great advantage of this kind of profession comes in. By breaches of the Rule one does not sin against obedience, and by observing it one acquires the merit of obedience. If its precepts do not serve to increase our danger of sinning they hold good to help us to win merit, and such great merit ! As St. Thomas teaches, the merit of an act of virtue consists in the fact that a man despises a creature in order to cleave to God. After the theological virtues, which definitely lead us to cleave to God, there can hardly be a more meritorious moral virtue than obedience. Does it not make us despise the best of our created possessions, our will, simply to enable us to cleave to God ? [1]

I cannot find anyone to whom I can better compare our Tertiary than to a son who works for his father. The father does not force him ; but is that going to make the son neglect the good of the house ? Such conduct would indeed be folly : it would prove him to be an unworthy son and would display the mind of a hireling or of a slave. As a rule, the son will do more than a servant, whilst his work is performed with the ready alacrity of a volunteer. Nevertheless, he is acquiring the full merits of obedience. His obedience is all the better for being steeped in love, based on his affection for his father and his interest in the good of the house.

[1] IIa IIae, q. 104, a. 3.

THIRD SECTION

A RELIGIOUS STATE

EVERY Profession places us in a certain state. In this respect the Tertiary Profession resembles all the others ; but whereas most men, in virtue of their profession, are established in a secular state, the Tertiary is fixed in a religious state.

What do you mean by a religious state, I shall perhaps be asked. Are not those who bind themselves by the three great vows the only ones to enter upon that state ? If, on the other hand, you stretch the meaning of the word, ought you not to say that all men on becoming Christians are brought into a religious state ? What special place is reserved for Tertiaries between ordinary simple Christians and those to whom the name of religious is usually restricted ?

I should like to answer these questions, not categorically, but by expounding the principles which give a key to the problems.

Actually each Christian from the day of his baptism is placed in a religious state. He belongs for ever to that religion of which Our Lord Jesus Christ is the supreme pontiff.

From the moment of His conception Our Lord was ordained priest. By the very fact that the Person of the Word assumed a human nature, that human nature was set apart from other men, entirely dedicated to God for all eternity, and furnished with power to draw up to Himself the homage of the human race and to make the divine benediction descend upon us.

It is by the sacrifice of the Cross that the religion of Jesus Christ is fully expressed. As the sacrifices of old

were but the figure of that sublime sacrifice and a preparation for it, so also the sacrifice of the Mass is its
commemoration and its extension throughout the world
until the end of time. Now it is one of the purposes of
the sacramental system to place Christians in a state in
which they can take part in the eucharistic worship
which constitutes for them the centre of true religion.
That is effected more particularly by the three Sacraments which imprint an indelible character upon the
soul.[1]

I. THE SACRAMENTAL CHARACTER AND THE VIRTUE OF RELIGION

The sacramental " character " or seal gives us something like a reflection of the priesthood which His hypostatic union conferred upon Jesus. From our baptism,
and increasingly up to the highest point in Holy Orders, ·
we are set apart by this " character," we are dedicated
to Christian worship and we are endowed with powers to
take part in it.

Thus distinct from other men, the Christian is established in a state which he will never leave. He has not
received just a nominal, external, revocable charge.
Even as in olden times slaves and soldiers were branded
with the effigy of their master or their chief, his soul
bears an impression which will never pass away. Grace,
which also affects the immortal soul, may be lost
through sin. But no sin, however great, can efface that
character. For whereas grace is a personal thing, the
possession of which is subject to the fluctuations of the
free will, the character participates in the immutability
of the priesthood of Our Saviour, of which it is the reflection in ourselves. Priest for ever, Christ holds us henceforth in His hand, as beings placed at His service and
qualified by the character to be His instruments.

If there is a state of the soul which truly deserves the
name of " state " it is surely this one. Where else can

[1] *Summa*, IIIa, q. 63.

such stability be found ? It is a religious state. By the
sacramental character which has been imprinted for
ever upon her, the soul finds herself really consecrated
to God, following Christ Himself. She bears in her
intelligence a power resembling that possessed in its
plenitude by the Sovereign Priest of the Christian religion. In the Cenacle He spoke the words that anticipated the great Sacrifice of the Cross which the Mass
perpetuates. " This is my Body . . . given for you :
this is my Blood . . . shed for many."

" Do this for a commemoration of Me," added Christ.
And the apostles, thus chosen to act as He acted, repeated
His words while reproducing His gestures. Thanks to
the sacramental character which they had received from
the Saviour, they entered as it were naturally into His
great priestly activity—always real though unseen.
They could be observed to adopt His attitude, they could
be heard to pronounce His words and they re-enacted
the same sacrifice under His influence as the one High
Priest. Every Christian priest continues this apostolic
function. Even when he is not actually engaged in
performing the essential rite of the Christian faith, he is
qualified to offer to God the homage of men and to
impart to them the divine grace which flows from the
various sacraments and even from the simplest of his
blessings.

If the priest has received the sacramental character or
seal in its plenitude, every baptized Christian has received
a measure of that power, which is strengthened by
Confirmation. Are we not participating in Our Lord's
priesthood when we enter intelligently and devoutly
into the sacred rites which are being celebrated by those
who direct our Christian worship ? In the great religious
society, priests are, so to speak, authorised by Our Lord
to act in His stead : but every baptized soul is at least
a shareholder in this spiritual society and is entitled to
his portion of the good things amassed by Christ Jesus
for the common weal.

But when Christians, and particularly priests, have been thus set apart from the rest of men, it is of vital importance that they should maintain this distinction in every way, that their souls should rise to the height of the consecration they have received, that they should be worthy of their title, and make good use of the powers with which they are endowed.

The sacramental character calls for the virtue of religion. This virtue becomes more and more necessary as we rise higher in the hierarchy and are more deeply stamped with the image of Christ. It does not suffice to play a part in the Christian religion : we must have the spirit of the part. We must become closely conformed to Him Whose gestures we copy and Who throughout His life honoured His Father. Ought we not to be living always as persons who lately, this very morning, celebrated or attended Mass and who will shortly do so again ?

All men, even the least logical among them, are naturally astonished when a priest or even an ordinary Christian has not the sanctity required by his religion. Worldly men are indeed over severe in their censure of those who, like themselves, are only human beings, and who have to struggle against the same obstacles caused by sin. Those very critics, when it suits them, declare the obstacles to be insuperable. Here also they exaggerate and run to the other extreme. With the grace of God we can triumph over sin. If we recognize those difficulties we also know that the sacraments, in consecrating us to Christian worship, bestow upon us the grace of virtues and of gifts, and so perfectly adapt this grace to our needs that it can cure all the ills that result from sin.

Certain masters of the spiritual life, who have closely followed the counsels of the divine Master, have laid special stress upon the great virtue of religion, which is strengthened particularly by sacramental grace, and they have striven to make their disciples proficient in this virtue, to the end that sentiments conformable to

their religious character should continually fructify in
their souls. Moreover, as this virtue of religion occupies
a truly central place in the spiritual life, as it receives
the direct influence of the three theological virtues and
holds sway over all the moral virtues, it must necessarily
be the means by which the whole of life can be perfectly
organized.

The history of religious Orders proves the excellence
and the fruitfulness of this conception.

II. THE VIRTUE OF RELIGION AND THE THEOLOGICAL VIRTUES

The virtue of religion teaches us to turn to God ; it
does not unite us directly to Him, like the theological
virtues that have God Himself as their object, but directs
to Him certain interior and external acts which we
accomplish in order to express our recognition of His
incomparable excellence and to assume the attitude of a
servant before His beneficent authority.

Through faith we cleave to God's truth, through
hope we rely upon His power, and through charity we
love Him in Himself and for Himself. Thus, by the
exercise of the theological virtues we embrace God, we
live in Him.

The virtue of religion finds its material scope outside
God, but it engages itself therein only with a view to
Him. Its immediate aim is to offer Him worship, to
do Him honour. Because of this character, which distinguishes it from all other moral virtues, it comes near
to the theological virtues. Being concerned with presenting our homage to God, it comes more directly
under their influence, and it even mingles with those
high virtues by instilling the note of religious respect
into the acts of our faith, our hope and our love.

In the very first article of his treatise on religion, St.
Thomas, under the pretext of etymology, stresses, without
seeming to do so, this close connection between the three
theological virtues and religion.

He says that religion, according to Cicero, comes from *relegere*, which means to re-read. Religion makes us re-read continually, as though in a cherished book ever open before the eyes of our soul—re-read and meditate upon God Himself.

" In all thy ways think on Him," the Wise Man advises in the Book of Proverbs. " I set the Lord always in my sight," said David. " The Lord is in this place and I knew it not," exclaimed Jacob in a great outburst of religious feeling.[1] As the result of continually thinking of God by faith we become like Moses, of whom the Epistle to the Hebrews says that he seemed to see the unseeable.

Since the days of Moses a wonderful grace has been given to the world. The Word became flesh. The great divine book has been translated into our human language, with the illustrations we needed to make us understand it and savour it. Men have had a tangible revelation of what God is. " We have seen, heard and touched the Word of life," wrote St. John. " I am Who am . . . think of Me always." Our Lord, in speaking to St. Catherine of Siena, used the same description of Himself that God had given to Moses. But to-day we are impressed with the conviction that a great tenderness, an encouraging sympathy, shines in the divine glance which rests upon us and in which we read the thought of our Creator and Redeemer—His idea for our life.

When she was six years old, St. Catherine of Siena saw Our Lord in the sky above the Church of St. Dominic. Clad like the Pope, He was looking at her and blessing her. All her life long she kept before the eyes of her soul that first page of the divine book which symbolized all that God expected of her. It was to be her vocation to dedicate herself to the service of Jesus in the person of the Sovereign Pontiff, the head of the Church, through the medium of the Order of Preachers.

In that upraised Godward glance, expressive of

[1] Prov. iii. 6 ; Ps. xv. 8 ; Gen. xxviii. 16.

sovereign respect, together with absolute dependence, in that meditation on God, religion acts under the immediate influence of faith. But we shall see that it is no less intimately linked with charity.

St. Augustine thought that the word " religion " was derived from *reeligere,* to re-elect. And since God is always the subject-matter of religion, it is God Whom our religion makes us continually re-elect. After having chosen Him in the first instance as the One Being, beloved above all else, we choose Him again every time we discover a fresh or a deeper motive for our love : we also choose Him again with a keen sense of regret and new resolution when we have neglected to seek Him, or when, through serious sin, we have turned away from Him. " Father, I have sinned against Heaven and before thee : I am not worthy to be called thy son : make me as one of thy hired servants." " Thou art still my son," replies the father. But the son will be only all the more eager and affectionately desirous to serve One who wishes to be both his father and his Lord. That alacrity for the service of God is devotion—the fundamental act of the virtue of religion which the fervour of charity increases more and more.

Like the son who had strayed away from God, but still more surely, will the son who has remained faithful find his devotion increasing as his filial love grows stronger.

In response to the action of some secret spring, both brothers will feel themselves impelled to be constantly watching for what is pleasing to God : they cannot do enough to honour Him and to carry out His will : " Always ready to serve Thee, dearest Lord ! "

Joined to the interior sentiment which realizes the essence of religion in spirit and in truth, will be found, at the proper times, those various outward gestures through which the body expresses the disposition of the

soul and pays its own tribute of worship. Some men make
an offering to God of the material possessions which they
could have used, and even sacrifice things that they
greatly cherish. Others again not content with presenting their offerings day by day, pledge their future
beforehand by vows.

These are very noble acts of religion, instigated by the
love of God, by charity.

If we accept an alternative etymology, also suggested
by St. Augustine, religion would appear to come from
religare—to bind. Our religion does actually bind us to
Almighty God. Conscious of our own weakness and of
our great need of help, we attach ourselves to Him, we
seek to be allied to Him above any other. And we do
well, because He is the indefectible first principle, the
immovable support, thanks to which we shall never
succumb. " It is good for me to adhere to my God, to
put my hope in the Lord God." [1] The work of the
theological virtue of hope is to bind us to God, just as to
re-read Him is the office of the virtue of faith, and to
re-elect Him the function of the virtue of charity. And
here its immediate outcome will be the practice of
assiduous prayer.

Next to the devotion described above, prayer occupies
the most prominent place amongst the acts of religion.
Whereas by the former our will was devoutly submitted
to God, now it is our intelligence which subjects itself
to Him, imploring the help required. Prayer is a religious act, but it is one directly inspired by hope.

Through the sacraments also, provided they are
received piously, as well as through prayer the soul has
recourse to divine Omnipotence, the great motive of
our hope. Frequent use of the sacraments belongs, as a
primary essential, to the practice of religion.

Thus the virtue of religion is enabled by its proximity

[1] Ps. lxxii. 28.

to the theological virtues and their influence to carry out
perfectly the acts that are peculiar to it.

III. THE VIRTUE OF RELIGION AND THE MORAL
VIRTUE IN THE RELIGIOUS STATE

Apart from the acts which strictly belong to it and are
spontaneously generated by it, the virtue of religion,
taking precedence of the other moral virtues, can make
a perpetual liturgy of all the acts of our life—whatever
they may be. " Whether you eat or drink, whatsoever
you do, do all for the glory of God."

The term " religious " might conceivably be applied
to any man who periodically worships God by approved
acts, such as assisting at Sunday Mass. Nevertheless,
the name of Religious, St. Thomas tells us, is confined to
certain men who devote their whole life to the worship
of God and, in order to do so, detach themselves from
worldly entanglements.[1]

The name of " religious " is eminently suited to them :
in them is realized the true type of the " religious."
For they are not content with taking part, perhaps every
morning, in the sacrifice which our sovereign Priest
renews at the altar, nor yet with supplementing it occasionally by some particular offering or even some particular vow. They offer themselves as a holocaust to
God, reserving nothing for themselves either for the
present or for the future. Whatever they may possess is
sacrificed to Almighty God. What can possibly be left
to one who has completely abandoned for God all earthly
possessions, all bodily enjoyments and even his free will ?
Here we have the three vows which are the foundation
of the religious life in its full sense. They constitute in
themselves a twofold outstanding act of the virtue of
religion : a sacrificial holocaust in which the victim is
completely consumed, and vows which pledge all the
rest of life. They offer up all for ever.

---

[1] *Summa Theologica*, IIa IIae, q. 81, a. 1, ad 5.

Thanks to this offering which withholds nothing, thanks to this promise which pledges the whole life, all acts from that time forth are invested with a religious character. They are religious from their very source, the will, which has been consecrated by the vow of obedience and which controls the whole.

To the vows is added an organized system of regular life, in order to ensure their practice and perhaps even their perfection by separating the Religious more entirely from the world and by allocating every part of his day to the service of God. It is a system which has ripened slowly under monastic tradition, and which has been modified by every Patriarch to suit the Order he has founded; the habit, the enclosure, silence, choral office, study of sacred science, works of penance, modes of eating, of taking recreation, of going to sleep. These things are called "observances," and to grasp the true import of the word we must realize that originally "observance" was synonymous with "respect." It is not a question of carrying out, willy nilly, a string of orders, but of doing it to give honour to God. Correctly speaking, the term "observance" is applicable only to the injunctions of a religious law. They are "observed" out of consideration to the Omnipresent God in order to give Him tokens of our attention, our reverence or our dependence. In that way everything, even the silence, becomes, in the words of the Dominican Constitution, a beautiful liturgical ceremony.

The Dominican Tertiary shares "in the religious and apostolic life of the Order of Friars Preachers." That is the consequence of the profession he has made "in honour of Almighty God, Father, Son and Holy Spirit." If this profession does not entail vows, it does, nevertheless, place the one who has made it in "a sacred order." He becomes subject to superiors and must follow a rule. The rule contains a set of observances which have been specially selected with a view to permeating the secular life with the spirit of the religious state.

"I wish the Rule of the Order, which is signed by my superiors and will be found in my travelling bag, to be placed beside me so that I may carry it to the grave." These words were written in the will of the Duchess of Alençon, who was burnt alive at the Charity Bazaar and whose exemplary life is still remembered by the Tertiaries of St. Dominic. She never departed from the Rule of the Third Order, even when travelling. This Rule, along with the instructions of her Superiors, had served during her novitiate to prepare her for her Profession, and she had clung to it ever afterwards, that she might shape her life religiously according to its precepts.

The Tertiary, like the Religious of the First Order, recites the divine office " seven times a day," and perhaps " rises in the middle of the night " for that purpose. He even receives and is bound always to wear " the most important part of the Dominican habit." " By creating the Third Order," says Père Lacordaire, " Dominic brought the religious life into the midst of the domestic hearth and to the nuptial bedside."

St. James tells us that " to keep oneself unspotted from the world " is a part of true religion. It is, of course, in the first instance the work of temperance or of similar virtues. But the virtue of religion uplifts this operation to the level of its own dignity.[1] It impels us to exclude from our life all that is ugly, all that is frivolous, all that is vain,[2] and to fill it instead with that honourable integrity which God, in Whose presence we stand, wishes to find there that He may glory in it.

There is a variety of moral virtues which help to moderate the inordinate impulses of our passions, to give us courage in the face of our fears and to regulate our relations with our neighbours. Above the virtues of temperance, fortitude and justice reigns prudence,

---

[1] *Summa*, IIa IIae, q. 81, a. 1, ad 1.
[2] Comp. Ch. IX of the *Rule of the Third Order*.

which decides and enjoins the acts that ought to be performed in every Order. But the great virtue of religion rises even higher than this governing virtue, which it impregnates and through which it diffuses itself into all our other moral actions.

The honour of God, which religion has always in view, inspiring in the soul an unremitting concern for it, is a powerful incentive to the formation of reasoned decisions and to perseverance in keeping resolutions. Respect for the divine presence—what a curb upon the passions ! How much the thought that God could be proud of us should encourage us to strive after a high ideal and pursue it disinterestedly ! Under the animating influence of charity the virtue of religion repeats constantly, in the ears of the soul, St. Paul's cry : " All for the glory of God." And it is ever urging us on to heights to which we should never otherwise aspire.[1] In a life so ordered all works of renunciation or devotion, such as those mentioned by St. James—the bridling of the tongue and the care of orphans—become indeed " a religion clean and undefiled before God and the Father." [2]

Compliance with the commandments of God is not sufficient. We must follow eagerly in the path of the evangelical counsels. The Tertiary, though he does not pronounce the three vows, so far imbibes their spirit as to be able to make sacrifices of a similar nature. God is so infinitely preferable to riches, pleasures or independence ! For His sake, to do Him honour, we detach ourselves from earthly goods.

No longer that excessive anxiety about the future, doubly excessive because it means that we rely too little upon God and too much upon money. Less and less shall we be eager for gain, and yet no time will be lost in useless occupations. We shall be the better able to spend for the benefit of all when we realize that property has been given us by God for it to be turned to good

---

[1] IIa IIae, q. 81, a. 8, c. and ad 1.
[2] James I, 26, 27.

account and not to be kept selfishly for ourselves. We must be prepared to give away what is superfluous. And if we should come to run short of the necessaries of life, we shall accept with good grace the real poverty which comes to us providentially.

Furthermore, we shall accustom ourselves to an austere life, in which joy is kept under restraint, not passionately sought or gloated over, but merely tasted when God gives it, not asked for, scarcely even desired.

Finally, we shall so thoroughly understand that God is our Master, we shall so completely keep ourselves in subjection to His suzerainty that we shall always obey His authority underlying that of our visible superiors. And if it falls to our lot to give orders to others, we shall do it in a spirit of obedience to His commands.

St. Thomas tells us that religion thus understood is identical with sanctity, because it not only provides for the due performance of the functions strictly related to worship, but it also embraces the whole life and organizes it to perfection, being the fittest instrument the virtue of charity can use for that purpose.[1]

[1] IIa IIae, q. 81, a. 8, corp et ad 1.

CHAPTER II

A RELIGIOUS FAMILY

SECTION I. A REAL FAMILY.

    1. The Order of St. Dominic.

    2. Dominican Solidarity.

    3. Life in a Fraternity.

SECTION II. THE VENERATION DUE TO OUR PATRIARCH.

    1. St. Dominic, by his greatness, deserves the respect of all.

    2. St. Dominic our Law-giver has a right to our obedience.

    3. St. Dominic our Father claims our filial piety.

SECTION III. THE SPIRIT OF ST. DOMINIC.

    1. What is the Spirit of a Religious Order ?

    2. Where is the True Spirit of our Order to be found ?

    3. What constitutes the Dominican Spirit ?

FIRST SECTION

A REAL FAMILY

I. THE ORDER OF ST. DOMINIC

THE child who is born into the world is not merely the offspring of the union of a father and of a mother ; he is the product of a society long established and surrounding him. As he once lived by the substance of his mother, so he continues to live in the bosom of this human group. When, after a few years of relative un-selfconsciousness, the conception of his individuality gradually asserts itself, it will not lead him to isolate himself from his fellows ; otherwise he would merely vegetate bodily and spiritually. He must, on the contrary, accept and realize this social life, the necessity for which is obvious to his reason. To develop himself fully and to attain happiness the human individual must remain united to his fellow-beings. " It is not good for man to be alone," the Creator has said.

Now it is man, such as he is normally constituted, whom God has taken to raise to the supernatural state. In the institution of this new order God could not, without being inconsistent in His designs, contradict the natural aspiration which He had implanted in the heart of His creature and refuse to respond to the needs which that creature feels. So the Catholic Church is nothing else but a social realization of religion, expressly willed and prepared by the divine Founder of Christianity Himself. Whatever Protestants may say, the whole gospel corroborates this fact. And, in reading the many passages in the Epistle where St. Paul speaks of Christ's mystical body, it becomes clear that he is referring primarily to that particular assemblage of men into one well-organized

corporation where they must help one another, fulfil
their special duties according to the place they occupy
and all collaborate for the common weal. It is understood, of course, that each one separately lives by the
grace of the Head. But St. Paul is more particularly
concerned with the community of this participation,
with the solidarity of all the members of Christ and with
the help they ought to render one another. Because the
Middle Ages were truly Christian, as well as profoundly
human, the social spirit was then universally cultivated.
In civil life it found expression in the guilds and cor-
porations which, as we all know, were then so flourishing.
It was cultivated also from the religious point of view,
and the Order of St. Dominic was one of the noblest
outcomes of that movement. In his own country a man
belonged to this or that corporation, according to the
particular form of service to which he gave himself.
Our Order is a spiritual corporation in which some
members of the immense society which is the Church
are drawn together into a more intimate community.
They do not wish to leave the Church, outside which
there is no salvation. They do not pretend to rise above
her. They remain in her bosom. Only they have
formed themselves into a specially homogeneous group
which may be compared to a family in the midst of a
great city. And the Church herself can only profit by
possessing such families, families which are the more
vigorous as their members are more closely united one to
another.

  The more souls are linked together, the better are they
armed against their individual weaknesses and rescued
from the discouragement which overtook them when they
remained in relative isolation. Even if they only find
other weaklings like themselves, their wills, united in
sympathy with others, gain support and strength. Better
still will it be for them if they feel themselves surrounded
by energetic souls who point out the way and draw them
in their wake. Instructed and urged on by their leaders,

encouraged and supported by brotherly emulation, they
will give of their best. Why should I not do what my
brothers and sisters are doing ? Yes, I can. My religious
superior or my religious director tells me so and shows
me how to do it.

Union has the further advantage of facilitating division of labour. Individuals, working as members of a
group in which each one devotes himself to some particular part of the common task, achieve a better result
than could be reached if each one attempted the whole.
This was a dominant consideration with St. Dominic
when he was planning his Order, the various branches of
which supplement one another ; and the same principle
was carried into the organization of individual priories
and convents.

Amongst Dominicans no provision has ever been made
for isolation—even occasional isolation such as is practised
by other religious like the Franciscans and the Carmelites.
Dominic took up his residence in the midst of a populous
town, and he made his household of Preachers a true
city, not a conglomeration of individuals. In his view
the perfect convent is not one in which everyone carries
out separately all that the Rule requires. Their object
is attained by collective action. The apportionment of
the various duties is provided for by the Constitutions
and arranged by the Superior, who gives to each the
particular dispensations necessary to enable him to
carry out more efficiently the special work expected of
him.

The whole Order forms, as it were, a great city in the
universe. From the time when it first took definite shape
in the district of Prouille, its scope was clearly outlined.
Under the term " holy preaching " it included the devotions of a convent of contemplative nuns, in the vicinity
of which the friars had their headquarters. The constant
prayers of these sisters and their sacrificial life supplied

what the friars, so frequently drawn into the bustle of the world, were unable to perform. It was a counterpoise on the contemplative side to balance the mixed life of the Preachers.

But something similar was required on the active side, in which the friars could take but a limited part if they wished to remain faithful to the monastic, canonical and scholastic observances prescribed by their founder. As early as the year 1206 certain laymen banded themselves together, at the request of our blessed Father's friend, Bishop Foulques, under the title of " Militia of Jesus Christ." They were truly knights wearing the white tunic and the black cloak, and pledged themselves to fight in defence of the faith, the rights of the Church and all Catholic interests. This knightly body had the direct benefit of St. Dominic's direction. Introduced into Lombardy, it became very flourishing, and in 1235 Pope Gregory IX advised St. Dominic's successor, Blessed Jordan of Saxony, to make careful provision for its spiritual direction. The " Militia of Jesus Christ " is commonly regarded as the original form of the Third Order, on the strength of a statement to that effect in Blessed Raymund of Capua's life of St. Catherine of Siena.

But the Dominican Tertiary life was also, and much more certainly, inaugurated by those other of the laity, men and women, who, heart-stricken at the relaxation of morals in the world, formed themselves into groups of so-called " penitents " or " continentes," attached themselves to the Preachers' churches, followed their religious observances and assisted them with their friendship, their influence and temporal goods. The spiritual help they received in return, the authorized counsels and the example of virtues, enabled these pious souls to render ten times more efficacious the works of mercy undertaken by the Friars. After the " Militia of Jesus Christ " had ceased to be required as a military order, it allowed itself to be absorbed into these Fraternities of a somewhat different nature to fight evil and promote good by spiritual weapons only.

When the Master General, Muño de Zamora, St. Dominic's sixth successor, decided to give a definite constitution to the Third Order in 1285, all he had to do was to unify and revise the rules which had long been in force in those brotherhoods of penance linked from an early date to the Dominican Order, by having placed themselves under the guidance of the Preachers.

Groups of a very similar kind had sprung up also under Franciscan influence. In the petition against the Friars Preachers and the Friars Minor which the clergy of England addressed to King Henry III in 1255, we find the complaint : " They have invented new confraternities into which men and women enter in such great numbers, that it is hard to find anyone who is not a member."

Of course, this was somewhat of an exaggeration. Other fraternities were being organized which were quite independent of the Friars. But, over and above the spiritual benefits which all such penitents could derive from forming themselves into local groups under the shadow of a chapel, the particular Fraternities we have just seen criticized on such inadequate grounds, and specially the Dominican Fraternities, obtained the additional advantages of belonging to an Order like that of the Preachers. It is a " sacred Order," animated by a spirit which the Church has always recognized as being soundly orthodox, whereas certain other groups, organized with the same good intention, were soon suspected of heresy, incurred the censure of the Church and perished miserably. Highly privileged indeed are we who belong to those Dominican Fraternities which have triumphantly survived the trial of seven centuries : we are drawn along the road to Heaven by all the saints who have gone before in the fervour of that same spirit, and we see ourselves upheld by a multitude of fathers, brothers and sisters still with us upon this earth.

II. DOMINICAN SOLIDARITY

When belonging to an Order like that of St. Dominic, one is entitled to the advantages which all associations naturally confer on their members. I need not dwell further upon the division and specialization of labour which enable the Order to fulfil its enormous and complex task.

I will only remind my readers of the moral support which groups of brothers can give one another by their example, as well as of the courage and the light they derive from the instructions of authorized directors who preside over and direct their spiritual life, and of the incomparable inheritance left upon earth by the venerable ancestors whose sons they have become. What a magnificent patrimony the family has been able to amass during so many centuries !

Consider, in the first place, all the books that we read with as much profit as pleasure—those which describe the origin and the history of our Order, the lives of the saints who have adorned it, the thoughts of the doctors who have enlightened it. All we need do to nourish our soul is, if I may say so, to eat our own home-made bread and to drink the wine of our own vineyard.

To us also belong those noble works of art which depict the features of our blessed founder and the greatest of his sons and daughters. What a wonderful portrait gallery they make ! We shall do well to surround ourselves with these pictures which will help us to be less unworthy of our past. Great indeed is our good fortune in having had a Fra Angelico to paint those beloved faces, to represent our saints as taking part in those great gospel scenes which we must re-enact after them, and as entering with the angels into the beatitude of paradise, where we hope some day to join them.

But I wish to remark certain effects in the supernatural order which can be brought about only in a

religious Fraternity like ours. Within it we can truly
merit for each other, we can pray efficaciously for one
another, and we can make rigorous satisfaction for each
other's sins. Even death itself does not put an end to
this beneficent intercourse which the Church calls the
communion of saints.

Profiting by the merits of others means very much more
than drawing from the study of their good example a
psychological impulse to follow them : it means that
the excess value, so to speak, of the good works they
accomplish is shared in by us. It is true that everyone
must labour for himself to obtain an increase of supernatural life ; just as fruit comes only to the tree in which
the sap rises, so knowledge comes only to that mind which
has applied itself to study. The acts of others cannot
formally dispose my soul to the inflowing of sanctifying
grace.

But there is another kind of merit—inferior indeed, but
nevertheless very real—which *can* be communicated.
God is naturally inclined to extend to their friends the
favour with which He regards those who love Him. It
seems only just that He should grant the desires of people
who live only to do His will. Do these not wish with all
their heart for the sanctification of all other members of
their spiritual family ? God takes that desire and makes
it His own. For their sake He imparts to those souls
who are united to them actual assistance which, if they do
not resist it, will lead either to conversion or to greater
holiness.

By that means charity, while increasing the life of the
soul which is practising it, does also tend indirectly to
the perfecting of that soul's neighbours. As members of
the same mystical body of Jesus Christ, and especially as
cells still more intimately connected, we can and we do
profit by one another's good work. It is not even essential that we should formulate a definite intention to that
effect, although it is advisable as an incentive to our
efforts and as a means of allocating their fruit.

Blessed Stephana was the daughter of an excellent Christian, a Tertiary of our Order, and her father used to take her with him when he went to consult his spiritual director, Blessed Matthew Carreri. Her after-life shows the profit she derived from the merits of these two souls. Blessed Matthew told her that she would one day be his heiress. She did indeed inherit his burning charity and his participation in the sufferings of Our Lord. He bore on his body the sacred stigmata : she participated every Friday in the Saviour's sacred Passion.

The intention we form of gaining merit for others can be supplemented by prayer, which gives additional value to merit. Merit relies on the justice of God : prayer appeals also to His mercy, asking Him to bestow the alms of His grace.

In letters addressed to Blessed Diana and her daughters of the convent at Bologna, Blessed Jordan of Saxony called upon them in all confidence to pray for the Order that the brethren might increase in numbers and in virtue. Shortly afterwards he congratulated them upon the magnificent result of their prayers. " Rejoice and give thanks a thousandfold to the Father of all Goodness. . . . Disappointed at realizing that I had been preaching for a long time with little or no result to the students of the University, I was contemplating departure when suddenly God deigned to stir the hearts of a considerable number of them, and to fertilize the ministry of my word by the outpouring of His grace. Ten have already taken the habit." At a later date he writes : " Your prayers and those of the sisters have been wonderfully answered : our friars are multiplying throughout the world and increase in number and in merit."

Theology rightly teaches that our prayer is infallible only in the case of ourselves. It is our own self which is placed by our humble trustful and persevering prayer in a condition to receive the gifts of God. But the people whom we are now considering are of our own body, belong to the same spiritual family, have entered it and remain in it with the same sentiments. Very rarely indeed do they put any obstacle in the way of the graces which we ask for them as well as for ourselves.

According to the measure of the pains we take with our prayers and our good works they acquire a third value, known as "satisfactory," and this can be transferred to others without being diminished or modified. It is literally true that we can bear, instead of our brothers, the penalty of their sins. We substitute our acts for theirs, we pay for them ; and the divine Creditor is satisfied. St. Thomas even asserts that God is less exacting when the penalty is offered for another than if the culprit is paying for himself, because the charity from which the main value of the satisfaction is derived is usually greater when one is willing to suffer for others.

I wish I could quote at full length a touching form of words used in some Fraternities on the occasion of a Profession. In the name of the Apostolic See and of the Most Reverend Master General, the director of the Fraternity solemnly declares that the new brother will in future have a share "in the good works done before God, exercised and practised in our Order, no matter who does them or what they may be. May you thus profit by the sacrifices of all our priests, by the prayers of all our brothers who sing God's praises night and day, and of those apostolic men who are evangelizing heretics and idolaters within Christendom and outside it : by their labours, their pilgrimages and journeys : by the trials of the young, the vows of virgins, the works of lay brothers. . . ."

Not satisfied with bestowing upon the new brother the spiritual blessings which come to him from the living

members of the Order, the Director goes on to call down
upon the newly professed brother the graces earned by
all the blessed souls in Heaven, invoking by name the
most illustrious—first our Patriarch, then the martyrs for
the faith, the great bishops, the saintly confessors, the
glorious virgins and the innumerable company of those
whose feast we celebrate on the Dominican All Saints'
Day.   They still remain in the Order of which we have
become members.   Death only cuts off from our body
these members whom it surprises in a state of mortal
sin.   But the saints whom God has received into beatitude belong to us more than ever.   They are concerned
with their brethren upon the earth, they intervene on
their behalf and pray for them.   And God blesses us in
consideration of their merits and their prayers.

When our Father St. Dominic was dying, he said :
" I shall be of greater service to you above than I have
been here below."   *O spem miram quam dedisti !*   What
marvellous hope you have thus given us !   Father, assist
us by your prayers . . . *Pie Pater Dominice, tuorum memor
operum* . . . O, dear Father, plead your merits for us
before the Sovereign Judge !

The biographies of Dominicans who have been
favoured by authentic visions make profitable reading
for us.   The object of those favours is to manifest that
which for us remains invisible.   Sometimes St. Dominic
appeared to them accompanied by one or more of our
saints.   In many cases he came to fetch these holy souls
at their last hour.   Occasionally—notably in the cases
of Blessed Catherine of Racconigi and Lucy of Narni—
the visions preceded their entry into the Order which
they were destined to sanctify.   A very consoling instance
is that of Blessed Antony Neyrot.   From the apostacy
into which he had lapsed amongst the Mussulmans, he
rose to martyrdom, thanks to St. Antoninus, who had
formerly clothed him with the habit in the Convent of
San Marco and who appeared to him in full glory to
exhort him to repent.

Every year, we sinners recite in the Office of All Saints' and particularly on the feast of the saints of our Order, a very beautiful responsory which ends with the words : " May their merits assist us who are fettered by our sins. May their intercession excuse us when our miserable actions accuse us ! And Thou, Lord, Who hast granted them the victor's palm, refuse not the pardon of our sins that we may at length be their companions on high."

Several times a year a general absolution is given to us, either in Chapter or individually in the confessional, to complete the work of pardon for our sins by the remission of the penalties they have deserved. We owe that absolution to the saints in Heaven. They did so much penance here below, even though they required so little expiation themselves, that they heaped up an inexhaustible treasure available in the first place to those who are admitted to their family.

If, despite all, Purgatory awaits us at the close of this earthly life, our brethren in Heaven and on earth will still assist us by that marvellous co-operation which is revealed to us in the doctrine of indulgences. Our Holy Mother, the Church, counting upon the treasure of the saints, has attached to certain prayers, to certain acts, plenary or partial indulgences which those on earth may apply to the departed themselves. This fruitful means of assisting them is additional to all the works of satisfaction which we can offer as well for them as for our living brethren, and also to the Suffrages formulated by the Rule. Let us bestow this noble alms upon them. Others will some day render us the same service.

III.   LIFE IN A FRATERNITY

Even if we could only be isolated Tertiaries, attached to no Chapter and without a Director selected from among the Friars Preachers, we should, nevertheless, derive great benefit from entering the Order of St. Dominic, because we should acquire all those supernatural bless-

ings and good things that have been specified above.
Separated though we might be from any Dominican
centre, we should still be in communion with the great
invisible life of the Order.

That is why the Rule prescribes that one may be
admitted into the Third Order without forming part of
any particular Fraternity. Even in these circumstances
reception of the habit at once confers " participation in
all the spiritual goods of the Brothers and Sisters of the
Order " (IV. 19).

Consequently, a person who resides in a place where
no Dominican Fraternities are established may take
advantage of the passing visit of a Friar Preacher to
obtain admission to the Third Order of St. Dominic.
Another, who lives within easy reach of a Fraternity,
may have some special reason for not belonging to it.
It is the duty of those who have received the powers of
Superiors of the Order to judge of the validity of this
reason. Permission to receive the habit is left to their
discretion, as is also permission for the final Profession
after the period of probation (V. 23).

But anyone who voluntarily remains an isolated Tertiary when he could easily enter a Fraternity can have
no adequate conception of what the Third Order actually
is. In the Code of Canon Law it is defined as " an
association of Christians." We have only to read the
Rule to see what it enjoins in that connection. Those
particular Christians who have formed themselves into
groups in order more readily to attain perfection place
themselves under the guidance of the Order (I. 1).
This means that they are normally in touch with the
neighbouring Priory of Friars Preachers, from whence
comes the direction they need. They have a Director
who generally belongs to this Priory. Professions are
made before this Director, who takes the place of the
Most Reverend Master General.

The Master General and the Prior Provincial have the
right personally or by delegation to visit each Chapter

once a year, or even at shorter intervals if necessary.
" Whatever it may seem good to them to decide—whether
by way of counsel, admonition, ordination or correction,
even including the deposition of an official—should be
accepted " by the Fraternity and by each of its members
" cheerfully and humbly " (XIV. 51).

The Director appointed by the Master General or
the Prior Provincial can, by virtue of his office, " do
everything that concerns the training and spiritual
direction of the Brethren." Once a month there should
be a meeting of the Chapter to receive his instructions,
his explanations of the Rules, his reprimands, such punish-
ments as he deems fit, and also dispensations and absolution from faults. Corporately all attend Mass, recite the
Office, pray for the intentions recommended to them and
recite the Suffrages for the departed (XIV, XVII–XIX).

The Director is assisted by a Council, which comprises
a Prior, a sub-Prior and a Novice Master, whose institutions and functions are provided for by the Rule. All
must collaborate, each one doing his part to edify the
members of the Fraternity (XV, XVI).

The solitary life, says St. Thomas, is suitable only for
the perfect. Being perfect, they suffice to themselves.
But others will derive the greatest benefit from coming
together to hear or receive the instructions, the examples
and the corrections so useful to him who would attain
spiritual perfection.

Is it because he is perfect that this or that one abstains
from attending the Chapter ? Is it not rather that he
does not fancy whoever is in charge—because Father X.
is no longer Director ? Surely such an attitude is a very
clear indication of imperfection.

That particular Father is no longer Director ! But
what matter whether it is " Peter, or Paul, or Apollo " ?
Only God, Our Lord Jesus Christ and St. Dominic
matter—all the others are only their delegates. St.
Catherine of Siena used to kiss the footprints of passing
Friars Preachers whoever they might be.

These people " rub you up the wrong way ! " Make
the sacrifices which Christian charity demands, here as
elsewhere.   Go to the meetings, and when you have
devoutly attended Mass and prayed together you cannot
continue to cherish those unkindly feelings towards one
who is your fellow-communicant in the same Christ,
who is invoking in the same terms the same Father, St.
Dominic, and who received from you the kiss of peace on
the day of clothing.

In these family gatherings we learn the modes of thought,
of prayer and of action which constitute the spirit of our
Order.   We assimilate its memories, its traditions, its
customs, and that venerable lore which the elders trans-
mit to their juniors.   We communicate to each other
interesting items of current news, and we realize, as did
the Psalmist, what a good and pleasant thing it is to
dwell together in fraternity.

It is there that we learn the various requirements of
the great Dominican family, for which of its intentions
we ought specially to pray, and how we can best give it
our assistance.   Each one offers his devotion ;   each
works to the best of his abilities.   Some can give services
of an intellectual nature :   they may even do apostolic
work, as, for instance, catechizing an adult convert.
Others take care of the sacristy, humbly knit stockings,
organize a charity sale, etc.   The personal element does
not enter into true devotion of this kind.   The work is
not done for Father So-and-So :   it is for the Priory,
for the Novitiate, for the Province. . . . And if our
labours pass unnoticed we shall modestly accept this
lack of recognition, content to have been able to express
to St. Dominic the gratitude to which he is entitled from
us.

If some day inexorable circumstances should separate
you from the Fraternity, should preclude your attendance
at the Chapter meetings and deprive you of the counsels
of the Father who directed you, you will echo the words
Henry of Cologne wrote to Jordan of Saxony, reminding

him of their intention to remain together. (*Stemus simul !*) "What has become of our 'let us keep together'? You are at Bologna and I am in Cologne. . . ." Nevertheless, like these two saints, you will remain in spiritual communion with your absent friends and you will derive real consolation from being so. You will resemble Blessed Villana dei Bottis in her attachment to the Dominican Church of Santa Maria Novella, where she had dedicated herself to God and where she had spent long hours of prayer. When she could go there no longer, she would climb to the summit of one of the turrets of her palace to gaze at the campanile in the distance. So will you likewise look back frequently in spirit to that Priory Church from which the light of the Dominican life first flowed and continues to flow into your soul.

SECOND SECTION

THE VENERATION DUE TO OUR PATRIARCH

To illustrate the various points we have been considering. I have purposely selected my examples from our own religious family : the subject-matter itself is such as is applicable to all Third Orders. The time has now come for us to cease generalizing, and to set ourselves to ascertain what it is that distinguishes from others the religious family to which we belong. We must arrive at a clear conception of the special characteristics of the Dominican Third Order.

St. Dominic is its Patriarch. There is the fundamental principle to which we must return again and again in order to learn what spirit must be ours. Is it not the spirit of our Blessed Father that must animate us ? But we must first consider St. Dominic in his function of Patriarch and pay him the honour due to him in that capacity.

Honora patrem—honour thy father, says the fourth commandment of the Decalogue. This precept inculcates the respect due to all greatness—especially when it is holy—the submission due to every superior, especially where a solemn promise of obedience has been made, and the filial piety due to a father, particularly to a spiritual father. Is not all that applicable to St. Dominic ? He is a very great saint, he is the superior to whom we have promised obedience, he is the father of our soul. On these grounds we owe him respect, submission and filial piety. May we take delight—in this case very great delight—in obeying the fourth of God's commandments !

I. ST. DOMINIC, BY HIS GREATNESS, DESERVES THE RESPECT OF ALL

He was great amongst men. What was the nature of his greatness? Greatness of temporal power? Greatness of intelligence and genius? Greatness of virtue and sanctity? To which of these three orders of greatness which Pascal has taught us to distinguish does the greatness of St. Dominic belong? Temporal power descended to him by right of birth. On the summit of Caleruega his grandfather had built a fortress for the protection of the countryside against the raids of the Moors. The Señor de Guzman ruled the village which grew up at the foot of this castle. Dominic might, like his father, have sallied forth at the head of his men on a crusade against the Moors, who were ravaging the south of Spain, or he might have imitated his friend, Simon de Montfort, the commander of the crusade against the Albigenses who infested the South of France. There were actually some religious amongst those who shared with Simon the direction of the crusade. Several of them were advanced to bishoprics. Powers and honours of this kind Dominic refused consistently to the end, in spite of much pressure. After he had founded his Order he attempted more than once to pass on to another his office of Superior General. He despised " worldly greatness," and all that resembled it.

Dominic is great with that higher greatness which is greatness of spirit. Before he was born, his future was foreshadowed to his mother, Jane of Aza. In a vision she seemed to see that she had given birth to a dog, which proceeded forthwith to run about with a torch in its mouth to give light to the world. As a young man he one day appeared to his mother with a bright star shining in his forehead. Others, especially Sister Cecilia, afterwards saw that star, and it became a tradition. Fra Angelico, in his representations of our Father, never failed to place the star on his brow as his special attribute.

How fully these portents were realized, history can tell us. Pierre Larousse in his great dictionary describes St. Dominic as having been the first European Minister of Public Instruction. It is indeed a fact that, by his own efforts and by those of his sons scattered over Europe and even beyond its borders, he made provision for the instruction of the world.

Only it was primarily religious knowledge that he was concerned to impart, at a time when Christendom was foundering on the shoals of ignorance and heresy. Others trusted only in the force of arms to bring the Albigenses back to the Catholic truth. He tried to do so by reasoning in public conferences and private interviews. The first time he met a heretic, in the person of the innkeeper who was his host at Toulouse, he spent the whole night convincing him of his error. When the sun arose, another light had risen, dispelling darkness from that soul. In that famous night the vocation of Dominic was revealed—his vocation as a Preacher and as founder of the Preachers. The spiritual sons he was to form to his own likeness were to be " champions of the faith and the lights of the world "—according to the prophecy of the Pope who approved his Order.

The most magnificent eulogy ever pronounced upon our Patriarch was delivered by the Eternal Father Himself to St. Catherine of Siena, and may be read in her celebrated *Dialogue.* " Dominic," said God the Father, " has taken on him the office of the Word, of My only-begotten Son. . . . He was a light which I gave the world through the intervention of Mary." On another occasion God told her : " I have two sons : I have begotten the one by the generating act of My nature and the other by a free and loving adoption." And in one of her visions the saint beheld St. Dominic emanating from the heart of the Eternal Father as the Word proceeded from His lips. . . . She was able to contemplate them both. St. Dominic's very face resembled that of Our Lord. No doubt it was not the bodily face of the Holy Patriarch, now in his tomb, that St. Catherine saw, but the countenance of his soul, if I may so express myself. By a special divine favour, the spiritual features of the holy Patriarch were revealed to her in a manner calculated to impress her imagination. " My only-begotten Son," said the Eternal Father, " devoted His whole life, all His acts, His teaching and His example to the salvation of souls. Dominic, my adopted son, had directed all his mind and all his efforts to saving souls from the snares of error and vice : that was the chief object which led him to plant and to train his Order. Therefore I tell you that in all his acts he may be compared to My Begotten Son."

Indeed I do not know that any man has ever come nearer than St. Dominic to the greatness which is manifested in the life of the Incarnate Word. Read the sworn deposition supplied for the process of his canonization. I will give a few verbatim quotations selected from amongst them. *Zelator animarum, zelator maximus animarum*—that is how one witness after another describes our Blessed Father. *Zelator salutis generis humani*, says William of Montferrat, one of those who had been admitted to his special intimacy. His burning zeal extended to the entire human race. His charity embraced the faithful, the unbelieving, and even lost souls, said Brother Ventura. As he thought about them, he shed many bitter tears. Their sins tortured him—*peccata aliorum cruciabant eum.*

Nearly the whole night long he used to pray in church *pernoctans in oratione*, and at times would utter cries of agony which recalled those of Gethsemane. " Saviour, have pity upon Thy people ! " " What will become of sinners ? " On their behalf he scourged himself till the blood ran, after he had used the discipline for himself : and then he would return to the charge and lash his body a third time for the souls in Purgatory. Afterwards he would resume his prayers, leaning his forehead against the altar when sleep overtook him.

Daily in the Convent he delivered moving exhortations to his brethren. Every tempted soul found a consoler in him. When he was amongst strangers, either as the guest of a humble household or in the palace of some prelate or prince, his conversation always turned upon the love of God and the vanity of the world. To every person he met as he tramped the roads he longed to convey the gospel message. One day, when he had as fellow-wayfarers foreigners whose language he did not know, his missionary zeal was rewarded by a celestial miracle which enabled him to make himself understood by all. Even while he was walking he would study the Sacred Scriptures which he carried in his knapsack, or he would meditate, gesticulating as though he were talking to an unseen interlocutor ; above all he meditated with love on Him Whose work of redemption he was carrying on.

" Go on ahead," he would say to his friars, " and let us think about God." Imitating the example of Jesus, he spoke only of God or to God, and he wished this practice to be incorporated as a rule in the Constitutions of his Order.

That was St. Dominic's way of life—one which enabled him to identify himself in a sense with that Christ Who is revealed by the gospel as dwelling eternally in the intimacy of the Father and as being incessantly con-cerned for the salvation of the human race which He incorporates into Himself, member by member. With no less reason than the great Apostle could St. Dominic say : " I live, now no longer I, but Christ liveth in me." He was indeed well named Dominicus ; that is to say, " the Lord's man." Even as Sunday is pre-eminently the Lord's day amongst the days of the week, so also is Dominic pre-eminently " the Lord's man " amongst his fellow-men. Therefore all Christians owe a great respect to St. Dominic—something of the religious respect which we render to Christ Himself, since the great saint so closely resembles Him.

II. ST. DOMINIC OUR LAW-GIVER HAS A RIGHT TO OUR OBEDIENCE

Of the traits which characterize true Dominicans and distinguish them from their fellow-Christians, the first and foremost must be a true and deep veneration for St. Dominic.

Twelve years after the death of our Father, Pope Gregory IX, who had known him very well, severely censured the Friars Preachers for leaving his remains in such a humble tomb and for not rendering to their Father all the honours due to him : " I was acquainted with that apostolic man and I have no doubt that he is associated in Heaven with the glory of the holy apostles." The Holy Father repeated the same thing on the occasion of the canonization. " I no more doubt his sanctity than I doubt the sanctity of St. Peter and St. Paul."

The early friars may have allowed themselves to be guided in this matter by the humility of their founder, but there was no negligence in the manner they sought to carry out the directions he had laid down for them. And that was, after all, a much higher way of honouring him. They continued, so to speak, to make profession of obedience into his hands.

Following them, we say : " I make profession and I promise obedience to God, to the Virgin Mary and to our Blessed Father St. Dominic. . . ." That is how we still speak, those of us who utter the religious vows in the Order of Friars Preachers. After naming St. Dominic we mention the visible superior who is his actual representative. Others will succeed the priest who holds our hands within his whilst we pronounce our vows. But transcending those temporary superiors is he who remains permanently in office. Successive superiors will give us directions, according to the Rule and the Constitutions : but this Rule was enunciated by St. Dominic, these

Constitutions were formulated by him. Although there have certainly been some developments and even adaptations, the groundwork remains the same.

The Council of the Lateran had just prohibited the foundation of new religious orders when St. Dominic arrived from Languedoc to submit his plans to the Pope. The Sovereign Pontiff was promptly won over, and he invited our Father to choose one of the already existing rules. The former Canon of Osma chose that of St. Augustine, which was broad enough to admit of the inclusion of the Constitutions he was contemplating.

How carefully he drew them up ! They were so clearly formulated that there was never any serious discussion amongst his sons as to the true ideas of the founder. Other Orders have separated into several branches, each one interpreting in its different way the idea of their common Father. Our Order, in all the 700 years of its existence, has never known such schisms. After periods of fervour there have been periods of tepidity. But, like a soul that revives after a retreat, the Order has always regained its first fervour, permeating itself afresh with the religious ideals of its lawgiver and submitting itself to that great superior whom God has given it for ever.

The Rule of the Third Order itself is, at least in spirit, the work of St. Dominic. For the Rule, as promulgated in 1923 with the approbation of Pius XI, is but an adaptation to the needs of our times of the text which the Master General, Muño de Zamora, had published in 1285 under the approbation of Honorius IV : and Muño de Zamora merely codified usages which went back to St. Dominic himself.

In the Third Order, therefore, as in the First Order, it is always with St. Dominic that we are principally concerned. A particularly relevant illustration may be cited from Raymund of Capua's biography of St. Catherine of Siena, and similar revelations occur in the lives of Blessed Colomba and Blessed Stephana. As a young girl Catherine beheld in a dream several saintly patriarchs and founders of different Orders, and amongst them, Dominic. Together and separately these saints invited her to increase her merits by choosing one of their communities in which she might better serve the Lord. Directing her eyes and steps towards Blessed Dominic, she saw him coming to meet her, holding in his hand the habit of the Sisters of Penance, who were fairly numerous in Siena. He drew near and consoled her by saying : " Sweet daughter, be of good cheer ! Fear no obstacle, for most certainly thou wilt wear this habit which thou desirest."

What she subsequently did, we ourselves have also done, when we made " profession that henceforth we will live according to the Rule and manner of the Brothers and Sisters of the said Order of Penance of Blessed Dominic until death." Though it does not merit the name of vow, this is a very weighty undertaking and one which, in the words of Raymund of Capua quoted above, increases our merits and enables us to give a more acceptable service to God.

Why ? Because we have placed ourselves under the authority of St. Dominic to live after his Rule, and by so doing have enhanced the value of our life in the sight of God by the merit of obedience, yes, of religious obedience.

St. Thomas has expounded the great principles of the virtue of obedience in one of the articles of his *Summa*. He points out how natural objects are subject to the great cosmic forces which rule them, and from which they derive their vigour and fertility. The earth, for instance, revolves round the sun and, in proportion to the inclination of its axis, receives the heat which brings forth verdure, flowers and fruit. Men must likewise be subject to the authorities upon whom they depend, conform to their spirit and execute their will. It is through this submission that they are enabled to accomplish what God requires of them. A sage of ancient Greece once said : " I seem to hear a celestial harmony given forth by the stars in the silence of the night as they obediently follow their appointed courses." Sweeter still is the spiritual harmony of a human society in which each member strives to live in due subordination to the authority from which he depends. That is indeed divine order in all its beauty.

The Dominican Rule enables our souls to adapt themselves as perfectly as possible to that divine order which is everywhere required. In the midst of the general order created by Providence, it draws us together into a specially sacred order. *Ordo sacer Praedicatorum.* " Sacred," because obedience is hallowed by religion and the obedience it entails is religious obedience. We are directly obeying God, and, under the divine government, Dominic is the administrator of this sacred Order, through the medium of our visible superiors, who only reiterate and apply his precepts and counsels.

We know that among the various Orders approved by the Church, the Order of St. Dominic was from the first characterized by a breadth of spirit which others have since had to imitate. If religious obedience therein is at once both strict and delicate, this is not from any spirit of servile fear, but from a spirit of love. A well-known passage in the *Dialogue* of St. Catherine testifies to our Blessed Father's prudence in the formulation of his Constitutions. God Himself is the speaker and, to the saint's great joy, expresses Himself in the following terms : " That is how thy father Dominic has organized his ship. He has given it a royal discipline : he did not wish to force his subjects under pain of mortal sin. It is I myself, the true Light, that thus enlightened him. My Providence made provision for the weakness of the less perfect. Dominic thus associates himself with My Truth in not desiring the death of a sinner but rather that he should be converted and live. Therefore his religious spirit is broad, joyous and fragrant : it is a garden of delights."

Let us take heed not to convert what the saint calls
" a garden of delights " into a wilderness, by neglecting
to follow the Rule or by disfiguring it to suit our personal
fancies. Fidelity to the Dominican Constitutions through
the virtue of obedience with the sentiment of religion and
under the inspiration of love, that is the right way to
honour the great saint who founded our Order and who
still presides over its destinies.

III. ST. DOMINIC OUR FATHER CLAIMS OUR FILIAL
PIETY

On the day of our profession we undertook to obey St.
Dominic. But he might with truth have replied in terms
resembling those used by Our Lord to His apostles :
" You have not chosen me, it is I who have chosen you—
I who not only am your superior from henceforth, but
who have always been your father, your true father."

Superiors of various kinds we may have in abundance.
But, as St. Paul wrote to the Corinthians : " If you have
ten thousand instructors in Christ, yet not many fathers.
For in Christ Jesus, by the gospel, I have begotten you."
In the Dominican life, which is our personal form of the
Christian life, we have been begotten by St. Dominic our
Blessed Father. Our vocation was the outcome of his
secret intervention.

Jordan of Saxony had been studying in Paris for ten
years when St. Dominic arrived in that city. The young
man sought him out and received an impression which
was never effaced. Not till much later did he receive
the habit—actually at the hands of Blessed Reginald.
Only once more, and then for a very short time, did he
see St. Dominic. Nevertheless, he used always to speak
of him with emotion as " the father of his soul."

St. Dominic is no longer on earth. Yet by virtue of a
mysterious fatherhood he continues to communicate to
others the form of life which he originated. Let me illustrate this by a passage taken from the life of Blessed
James of Bevagna. He was still quite young when St.

Dominic appeared to him and said : " My son, carry out the design you have conceived in your mind, for I have chosen you—by the Lord's command—and I will be with you always."

So it is also with each one of us. Before we were yet fully conscious of the aspiration which was dawning in our hearts and was directing us towards the Order of Preachers, St. Dominic was there to enliven it.

A little child takes a long time to recognize its father. At last, however, the moment comes when it fixes its eyes upon the manly figure towards which its mother has persistently directed its attention, and says : " Daddy ! " On the day when we made our Dominican profession we, too, recognized our Father—St. Dominic.

He is more truly our father than was ever our parent according to the flesh. St. Dominic is as far superior to our earthly father as the soul is superior to the body.

As a matter of fact, even as far as this bodily life is concerned, we do not depend very much upon parents. They know nothing about the child that will be born to them. And with what astonishment—pleasant or painful —do they watch the development of that young life which differs from them far more than it resembles them ! Our life has so many links apart from our parents that even their death may not materially affect it. Quite strictly speaking we have one father, one only father— our Father Who is in Heaven. Apart from Him we could not survive for a minute. The whole of our existence depends upon His.

This omnipresent paternal Being Who bears us all and maintains us indefatigably and generously in His bosom—outside Whom there is but nothingness—this divine Father associates with Himself certain chosen and predestined men to serve as intermediaries between Him and different religious families. And thus it comes to pass that in the vast city of the children of God there are groups of souls bound by special relationships and ruled by the Patriarch to whom God has entrusted their training. On the single stock are grafted a number of principal branches which bear little twigs, and one branch will differ from another branch in the quality of its flowers and fruit.

We are the twigs that emanate from Our Lord through the main branch which is St. Dominic, and our life is one variety of the Christian way of life which is so complex that no single individual can realize in himself its full splendour. We are the children of the Patriarch Dominic, whom God predestined to the magnificent *rôle* of building up a family for Him in the great Christian city.

Yes, if all grace given to men is Christian, for us all grace is likewise Dominican. It moulds us in accordance with the spirit of that sacred Order which St. Dominic conceived with the help of the Spirit of Jesus. It comes to us from St. Dominic at the same time as from Jesus—each of them bending down towards us with continual attention and love, with the same spirit of fatherliness.

We receive this grace abundantly in the bosom of the Catholic Church and in that Dominican atmosphere which pervades the Convents and Fraternities of our Order, just as the child receives life and training from his kinsfolk in that social centre which is his family and his fatherland.

Woe betide the unfortunate child who leaves his home before he has been trained, who is deprived of the care of the father whom God gave him to maintain and develop his life ! Woe betide the flower and the immature fruit when severed from the branch through which the sap came to them from the vigorous stock ! You may appear to be drawing nigh to Christ, you may contend that you will do better by leaving St. Dominic. As the flower fades, as the green fruit shrivels once it has fallen to the foot of the tree, so does it fare with the soul that breaks away from the Dominican branch to which its vocation had grafted it.

Happy, thrice happy are those who remain united to that vital source of life which has nourished so many

saints. " Daddy ! It's fine here inside with you ! "
exclaimed a little child as he nestled under his father's
cloak during a thunderstorm which had surprised them
in the open country. Amid the difficulties and storms of
life we can likewise appreciate this shelter for our souls,
this sense of security, provided for us by the Order of
St. Dominic, this fulness of spiritual life, this sweetness
of the garden of delights which St. Catherine of Siena
speaks of and which at times almost makes us feel that
we have discovered the earthly paradise. But in our
darkest moments as well as in our happy days let us
rest assured that it is good for us to be there.

It is there that we shall find celestial bliss when our
time of trial is at an end. " Sons of St. Dominic, where
will our place be in the splendour of the saints ? In
God, of course, in Christ Who will be our All in All ;
in Mary who will be our Mother above as she has been
our Mother here below ; and also, I have no hesitation
in saying, in St. Dominic—in the very heart of the glorious
Patriarch. The gifts of God are indeed without repent-
ance. The laws enacted by Him follow their course
with a harmony and a fidelity guaranteed by His infinite
wisdom. Our glory above will be the crowning of that
grace in which we have been predestined and conceived.
Predestined in St. Dominic, we shall be glorified in St.
Dominic. The Dominican family willed and organized
from all eternity by God for a special end in the bosom
of Christ's vast family, after it has played its providential
part in this world will meet again on high in the integrity
of its original predestination, that is to say, in St. Dominic,
animated by his patriarchal grace, transformed in the
reflection of his glory, sheltered still in that heart which
God appointed to be its source and from which it derived
its life in this world, it will enjoy eternal rest, and in
him and with him sing praises for evermore." [1]

So thought also Brother Everard—a former archdeacon

[1] The Very Rev. Fr. Vayssiere. Letter to the Province of Toulouse on
the occasion of the seventh centenary of the canonization of St. Dominic,
1935.

of Langres. He had just been admitted into the Order by Blessed Jordan when the latter had to start off for Lombardy. The disciple, who was anxious to see St. Dominic, resolved to accompany his superior. But on the way Brother Everard fell ill, and it was obvious that his hours were numbered. " Death need be concealed from no one except from him to whom its name is bitter," said the dying man. " As for me, the prospect of being stripped of this wretched fleshly covering does not frighten me because I hope to go to Heaven. My one desire was to see the face of our holy Father Dominic ; but now God is calling me to Himself : I am going where the Father and his sons will meet together in the presence of the Eternal."

Until the time comes for us to realize that great hope, let us foster in our hearts a real filial piety towards our Father. To the submissive attitude which we have mentioned and which must be observed towards him, as to all in authority, there must be added a deep sentiment of love, of veneration and of reverence. Filial piety entails all that. Reverence is great respect, mingled with a sort of fear. We must be reverentially afraid lest we prove unworthy of our Blessed Father, and deserve the rebuke incurred by those religious in Bologna who were not following him in spirit and to whom St. Dominic appeared when they were singing : *Ora pro nobis, beate Pater Dominice !* " Do not call me Father," he said sternly, " I do not recognize you as my children."

Veneration is a great respect tinged with affection. That sentiment was very strong in the souls of Blessed Everard, whom we have mentioned above, of Blessed Jordan and of those sons of St. Dominic whose depositions for the canonization we have cited above.

Besides veneration and reverence, we must give to him who is our Father in God some measure of the charity due to God Himself—the Father Who is in Heaven.

Let us then revere our Blessed Father, St. Dominic, let us regard him with deep veneration, and let us love him with fervent affection.

THE SPIRIT OF ST. DOMINIC

I. WHAT IS THE SPIRIT OF A RELIGIOUS ORDER?

THERE are some religious congregations that have little to distinguish them beyond the name of the place that gave them birth, or some particular devotion which they practise more specially and from which they derive their name. The Order of St. Dominic, on the other hand, is one of those which, upon their appearance, constituted a new species in the Church. It is an Order which is definitely distinguished from others. Whilst the elements that enter into its composition are not all of them original, their organization at least is the outcome of an original conception.

This organization finds its full scope in the First Order, that of the Friars Preachers. Its aim, though complex, is clearly defined, and the means are perfectly regulated with a view to that end.

Like every other religious Order, it strives to realize in each one of its members the perfection of charity. Only, in its case, charity takes the form of contemplation. The love of God prompts the Dominican soul to fix upon Him the eyes of the intelligence. The Friar Preacher does not apply himself to contemplation with the sole object of procuring food for his preaching. Contemplation is for him a true end, to be sought for its own sake, the highest of all ends, the beginning here below of life eternal. But although contemplation is not just a means to the apostolate, although the life of union with God marks the summit of Dominican life, nevertheless, it is the source of the apostolate. Our contemplation must overflow and find its outlet in apostolic action.

We shall, accordingly, impart to others the fruits of our contemplation. This communication will take many forms, of which the most important are the teaching of sacred science, the preaching of Christian doctrine and spiritual direction.

We see, then, that whilst for us contemplation and the apostolate are two ends, they are not parallel and casually connected, still less are they subordinated the one to the other, as though the contemplation were made for the apostolate, but they are ends, the second of which arises from the superabundance of the first so surely that Dominican contemplation naturally overflows into the apostolate. Everything must be subservient to that twofold end. Poverty, chastity, obedience, the great fundamental means, not to speak of the various observances of monastic and canonical life, all take a colouring of their own in view of the goal for which they must be adapted, relaxed or extended as the case may require.

Great as is their use, vows and observances are more or less negative means. They separate us from the world and deliver us from its snares and anxieties. But the Friar Preacher, thus set free and protected, has to apply himself to the great positive means through which he must strive to reach his goal. Those means are choral prayer and, above all, religious study. By them we attain immediately to the contemplation and the apostolate to which we are vowed.

Such is, briefly stated, Dominican life in its perfection.

Just as there is in every man a spirit which is the substantial form of the human composite and which determines its organization, so also there is a Dominican spirit which has formed this composite whole, which maintains good relations between its various elements and animates all our life. Let us try to define it. By so doing we shall render good service to our Ter-

tiaries, who must permeate their entire conduct with
that spirit if they wish to be faithful to the Order to which
they belong.   They will not readily find in their Rule
the majority of the elements we have mentioned as ends
and means in the life of the Friars Preachers.   Indeed,
the various prescripts of this Rule, literally taken, do
not differ materially from those of other Third Orders,
or from those of certain pious associations.   This is not
to be wondered at.   It is by the spirit which animates
their observances that they must be distinguishable from
the other groups, and must fit themselves into St.
Dominic's great Order.

The Church understands this and recognizes a real
incompatibility between different Third Orders, as well
as between the religious profession in one Order and the
Tertiary state in another.   A Franciscan religious may
not be Dominican Tertiary, nor can one person belong,
at the same time, to the Third Orders of St. Dominic
and St. Francis without a very special dispensation.

The spirit of these divers groups is not identical, albeit
the spirit of all is Christian.   In Our Lord the Christian
spirit was manifested in its fulness.   The different religious
Orders emphasize different features of their divine model.
Each one sounds its own note.   From the combination
of these notes the Church obtains a noble harmony which
attempts to reproduce the perfect beauty of Jesus Christ
—a beauty that could be represented entirely by none
of them singly.

Let nobody be so fatuous, so narrow minded as to
despise the part assigned to others.   (Does the eye despise
the ear?   Does the mouth jeer at the wounded foot which
has been cut by the stones on the highway?)   At the
same time, let everyone remain faithful to his own *rôle*,
and to enable him to play it aright let him be permeated
with its spirit.

The Dominican spirit is made up of principles, maxims,
motives, tendencies, sentiments and tastes, in accordance
with which we must rule ourselves in the Order of St.

Dominic, under all circumstances and in all branches of the Order.

Manifold and varied are the occupations of the different congregations of our Third Order regular. And widely dissimilar are the family conditions and the civil avocations of our secular Tertiaries. But " because every spirit possesses the prerogatives of spiritual nature, which are simplicity and liberty (that is to say, the possibility of realizing itself in degrees infinitely varied), whoever shares in a spirit can aspire to the plenitude and total perfection of that spirit,• no matter to what kind of life he may be called. On the other hand, it is quite possible, alas, to accomplish all the external activities required by our Order without living by its spirit, or again we may be tempted to think that this spirit is confined to certain forms to the exclusion of others which are, however, no less Dominican." [1]

It is for the novice whom the Order of St. Dominic has taken to its bosom to assimilate the spirit of the family which has adopted him.

II. WHERE IS THE TRUE SPIRIT OF OUR ORDER TO BE FOUND ?

God Himself can best reveal to us the spirit that should inspire our conduct. Therefore nothing is so potent to obtain it for our souls as humble, trustful and persevering prayer. The Three Persons Who said : " Let Us make man to Our image," also took counsel together to produce this particular spirit which was to become incarnate in each one of the members of our Order equally and impartially. Only in the mind of God does the Dominican ideal exist in its absolute purity. The Father expresses it in the Son and They both love it in the Spirit of Love. The joy of apprehending it and of delighting in it will be vouchsafed to us when we attain to the Heavenly Vision.

Here below we see it manifested in those who have

---

[1] Fr. Couturier in *l'Année Dominicaine* of July, 1934, p. 206.

most fully realized in themselves the ideal God has conceived. And first of all in St. Dominic, our Father.

On March 19th, 1924, the Sovereign Pontiff, Pius XI, wrote to the Superiors of Regular Orders as follows : " Above all we exhort religious to take as their model their own founder, their fatherly lawgiver, if they wish to have a sure and certain share in the graces which flow from their vocation. Actually when those eminent men created their institutions, what did they do but obey divine inspirations ? Therefore the character which each one strove to impress upon his society must be retained by all its members if it is to remain faithful to its original ideal. As good sons let them devote themselves heart and soul to honour their father and lawgiver, to observe his precepts and to imbibe his spirit."

So we too must be steeped in St. Dominic's spirit— as it came to be gradually understood by our Blessed Father himself and as he finally evolved it. Not until the closing years of his life did St. Dominic, formulating his idea at last, arrive at a clear-cut conception of his Order. Until then it had been but an intuition which God had placed in him : persistent and powerful though it was, it remained mysteriously hidden in the depths of the soul of Jane of Aza's son, of the student of Palencia, of the Canon of Osma, and of the King of Spain's ambassador. The conclusion, to which he was led by perfect self-surrender to divine influence, coincided with the idea God had had for him from the beginning.

Like the Father Who expresses Himself in His Eternal Word, Dominic had a son who formulated his thoughts with a precision and a forcefulness which can never be surpassed. I have called St. Thomas Aquinas the word of our Father. We have none of St. Dominic's writings. The witnesses to his life at the process for his canonization mention the notes with which he covered his books, the theses he wrote against heretics, precious letters

addressed to his friars to direct them in his precepts.
. . . Alas ! they have all of them been lost. However,
we have the works of St. Thomas to console us.

The ardent zeal which inspired the Count of Aquino's
son, already received into a Benedictine Abbey, to persist
in his efforts to enter the Dominican Order which realized
his ideal, enabled him afterwards triumphantly to vindi-
cate that ideal when it was attacked by William of St.
Amour and other masters of the University, and to live
up to it until his death. No one was ever better qualified
to express what our spirit ought to be. Take his *Summa
Theologica* and study the moral part, which is later and
still more able and finished than the dogmatic part.
Everything in it helps to define the character of the Order
which St. Dominic conceived, and which is placed by St.
Thomas at the head of the hierarchy of religious Orders.[1]

By his theological teaching he has sealed the Dominican
spirit with his own permanent seal. The spirituality of
the Preachers has been profoundly influenced by " dear
St. Thomas, the Master, the shining light," as Bl. Henry
Suso called him. From henceforth the Dominican spirit
and the Thomist spirit are one and the same—for the
humblest Tertiary as for the Master in Theology. Read
the life of that fourteenth-century Sienese *mantellata*,
" one of the most amazingly simple souls who ever drew
nigh to God." " Ignorant though she is, St. Catherine
of Siena is steeped in the same spirit " (as St. Thomas).
" In artless speech which recalls the *Romaunt of the Rose*,
she utters pious thoughts which are redolent of the sweet
fragrance of the purest Thomism." [2]

After St. Dominic and St. Thomas, she is the greatest
figure in our Order. Born into the world at a time when
St. Dominic's family, like the rest of Christendom, was
experiencing a phase of great religious relaxation, she

[1] IIa IIae, q. 188, a. 6.
[2] FF. Rousselot and Huby, S.J., in *Christus*, 1133.

exercised a powerful influence over a group of Preachers who became the promoters of a reform movement amongst their brethren. After her death in 1380 at the age of thirty-three, her confessor and spiritual son, Raymund of Capua, having been elected Master General, laboured to restore the ancient discipline. Following Raymund of Capua and his collaborators we always call St. Catherine of Siena our mother.

Since we have compared our founder and our great doctor to the Eternal Father and the Word, we may well say that in the Dominican trinity she takes the part of the Holy Spirit. It would have been possible so to abuse Thomist intellectualism as to have been satisfied with a beautiful system, logically constructed, of mere philosophical and theological abstractions. The humble, noble-hearted woman whom the Holy Spirit overwhelms with His mystical favours helps us to preserve in the spirit of our Order the fervour of love which cleaves to reality, even to the reality of God. It is precisely this divine reality that must be born in us ; we must consecrate ourselves to it and we must bear witness to it before the world. St. Catherine gives us no encouragement to relegate to a secondary plane that pursuit of truth which St. Thomas, following St. Dominic, placed first. Like them, she is eminently intellectual and rational.

Many other saints, many other blessed and venerable persons, have defined and have lived the Dominican ideal between the thirteenth century and our own. We shall speak of many in the following pages. But it is more particularly to these three great souls that we must turn to discover the characteristics that should mark our life, the principles and sentiments that must guide our conduct, in short, all that constitutes what we call our spirit.

III. WHAT CONSTITUTES THE DOMINICAN SPIRIT ?

One word summarizes our spirit : it is the " motto " which appears at the top of the shield marked with the black and white cross. *Veritas !* We are the knighthood of truth.

Others have *Pax* or *Caritas* or *Gloria Dei.* None of these is outside the orbit of the Dominican soul, but she will reach them by the way of truth : it is in the light of truth that she looks at everything. Truth sets off and quickens the elements that she shares with other Christian forms of spirituality. A thirst for truth will be the ruling sentiment of our soul.

When we sing the praises of our Father, in a noble hymn every night after returning from our procession to the altar of Our Queen and Lady, Mary, we call St. Dominic "light of the Church, doctor of the Truth" : we say that he pours forth the water of wisdom and that his preaching diffuses grace. And if we add that he was a "rose of patience" and "ivory of chastity," these are but the accompaniments of his fundamental vocation to be a man dedicated to the truth. He espoused the faith as St. Francis espoused poverty.[1] Whereas St. Benedict wished that "nothing should take precedence of the divine praise," St. Dominic placed study in the forefront of his own life and of ours. St. Bruno forsook the schools to seek the wildest solitude and to shut himself up there : Dominic founded his priories and convents in the heart of the town and particularly in university centres to study and teach there. St. Bernard, like St. Augustine, wished his monks to spend much time in manual work : St. Dominic did not hesitate to suppress such labours entirely in order that spiritual work alone should be undertaken.

All ancient observances that he retained are subordinated and adapted to the pursuit of truth. Francis of Assisi, putting poverty above all else, reproved a young disciple who wished to study theology, on the ground that possession of the requisite books would entail unfaithfulness to holy poverty. Dominic, on the other hand, looks upon poverty as a release from temporal anxieties to

[1] Dante, *Paradiso*, XII, 61.

facilitate concentration upon study. Moreover, he authorizes his disciples to possess, as he did himself, the books which are the instruments of knowledge. Dominic, the former canon of Osma, attached though he was to choral prayer, nevertheless shortened the time set apart for the Divine Office to allow of more time for study.

Brother John of Navarre, who had known our Father intimately, solemnly deposed, during the process for his canonization, that both by word of mouth and by letter he often urged upon the friars continual study of theology and of the sacred Scriptures. St. Catherine of Siena in her *Dialogue* rejoices to hear the Eternal Father praise that love of science which characterizes the " barque " of Dominic. " Our Order is the first," said Humbert of Romans, " to have thus linked study to the religious life, *prius habuit studium cum religione conjunctum.*" [1]

It is not the pleasure of cultivating our mind that underlies our intellectual efforts : it is love of Him Who is the Truth itself, it is the love of God. Dominic seeks God in the sacred books where He has revealed Himself. Always, as he trod the highways which lead to Rome, he turned in search of God to the infallible Master of sacred doctrine.

" What is God ? " was the oft-repeated question of the little child in whom the Dominican vocation was beginning to awake, and who was to work until the end of his life to compile the *Summa* of what man can know on that divine subject. " Our spirit," said St. Thomas, " must strive unceasingly to know God more and more." [2]

St. Catherine of Siena bids us gaze upon God with a wide-open eye, the pupil of which is faith. Even simple Tertiaries should be relatively better instructed and more intellectual than other Christians, and assuredly no

---

[1] Humbert, *Opera*, t. II, p. 29.
[2] *De Trin.* II, 1, ad 7.

Dominican soul worthy of the name will ever prefer sentimental dreams to the certainties of the faith.

Study ought to upraise us towards God and lead us on to contemplate His perfections, His government and His activity within us. This contemplation will be the highest expression of that appreciation of truth which characterizes the Dominican soul. It must be attempted even by those who cannot make long and profound meditation. To help them St. Dominic instituted the Rosary, which places the contemplation of the Christian mysteries within the reach of everyone. As Pére Lemonnyer notes with pleasure in his book upon the Friars Preachers, it was by Masters of Theology that this splendid devotion was restored and propagated in the fifteenth century.[1]

Although St. Dominic placed study above every other means, he did not wish liturgical prayer to be sacrificed to it. For he rightly recognized the divine Office as the chief method authoritatively established by the Church for raising the soul to God. Moreover, he was irresistibly attracted to it by his appetite for truth. The Office of the Choir, with High Mass as its centre, seemed to him a perfect harmony of rites and forms well calculated to foster those contemplative intuitions which study begets and which it is easy afterwards to prolong in private prayer. This theme we shall deal with more fully presently.

We shall also explain how this cherished truth, once known and lovingly contemplated, must influence our whole conduct. We must set ourselves with fervent zeal to live the truth, to spread the truth and to defend the truth.

Entirely taken up with God and with giving Him the first place in the realm of action as in the realm of prayer, and knowing himself only in God, in accordance with St.

[1] *Les Frères Prêcheurs*, p. 103.

Catherine's advice, a Dominican is wholly intent upon
following the grace which God gives him through Jesus
Christ Our Lord and Our Lady and Virgin Mary, in order
to actualize his Creator's idea. The intellectual virtue of
prudence, of which St. Dominic was such a shining
example both in his own life and in the organization of
his Order, and to which St. Thomas consecrated a long
Treatise in his *Summa* (thus differing from other moralists
who only give a few pages to the subject), and which
St. Catherine, a worthy sister of St. Thomas, so strongly
urges on us under the name of " *santa virtù della dis-
crezione* "—prudence, I repeat, that is to say the just
appreciation of how to regulate our conduct, plays a
leading part in the life of a Dominican soul. St. Paul's
words, " doing the truth in charity," might well serve
as its motto.

Treading in the footprints of St. Dominic, who was
ever ready to preach and defend the truth, affiliated to
the Order of Preachers, whom the Pope, in approving
them, styled " Champions of the faith and lights of the
world," every Dominican, even those of the Third Order,
will be eager to enlighten those who are deprived of the
truth and also to avenge the truth when it is attacked.

Moreover, no one can be admitted to the Third Order
until it is satisfactorily established that he is an orthodox
Catholic and is zealous to promote and defend the truth
of the faith to the best of his ability. Where these dispositions are lacking, there cannot be a Dominican
vocation. And it is by developing them that we shall
prove ourselves to be true sons of St. Dominic (II. 8).

Following the example of Our Lord on the night before
His crucifixion, St. Dominic, as he lay dying, prayed
for his children ; and he promised that he would continue to pray for them on high. Our Patriarch's petition might almost be summed up in Our Lord's supreme
prayer : " *Sanctifica eos in veritate :* Sanctify them in the
Truth ! "

CHAPTER III

THE SUBLIME SOURCES OF OUR LIFE

SECTION I. THE BLESSED VIRGIN. PATRON OF THE FRIARS PREACHERS.

  1. Mary's Intervention in Favour of our Order.

  2. The Devotion of our Order to Mary.

SECTION II. JESUS OUR SAVIOUR AND LIFE-GIVING HEAD.

  1. Our Saviour in His Historical Reality.

  2. Our Saviour in His Mystical Reality.

  3. Our Saviour in His Eucharistic Reality.

SECTION III. THE MOST HOLY TRINITY.

FIRST SECTION

THE BLESSED VIRGIN. PATRON OF THE FRIARS PREACHERS

" Every best gift, and every perfect gift, is from above, coming down from the Father of lights, with Whom there is no change, nor shadow of alteration. For of His own Will hath He begotten us by the word of truth." There is to be found the highest source of our Dominican life. What St. James says about Christians in general is particularly applicable to the Dominican Order. An Order whose whole vocation in the Church is to spread the light of the truth and which, after blossoming in St. Thomas, has remained grouped round him for seven centuries to receive the light of his doctrine and to shed it about the world—such an Order must unquestionably have descended from the Father of lights, Whose splendour knows neither night nor eclipse. It has been begotten and it is preserved in His word of truth. Our life, in so far as it is truly Dominican, is a perpetual outpouring of divine life.

But we know that because sin had opened an abyss between God and mankind, there was need of a bridge— St. Catherine of Siena was fond of that simile—to lead humanity back to the divinity, of an aqueduct through which man could have the life of God conveyed to him. Our Lord Jesus Christ, Who unites in His person God and man, is the one and only Mediator. Apart from Him there is no salvation. That is why St. Thomas, in composing the *Summa Theologica*, after demonstrating in the First Part how from God all things proceed, and in the Second how all must return to God, devoted his Third Part to Him Who made Himself our way.

Now, by the side of Jesus and inseparable from Him, we find His Virgin Mother. She regards herself only as the servant of the Lord. " *Ecce ancilla Domini,*" she says. In reality she is the Eternal Father's favourite daughter. The Son of God took her as His mother when He was about to assume human nature. And the new Adam sees in her the new Eve when He gives His life for the salvation of all mankind. She is there, beneath the tree of life, the mystical spouse of the Redeemer. " *Amissus uno funere, Sponsus, Parens et Filius* " sings one of the Church's hymns. He Who was crucified is her Father : He is her Son : He is also her Spouse. The divine blood flows and is spent—seed of all the Christians she will bear, as in the womb of a mother, until they are born to the life celestial. Between God and us poor sinners she tenderly shares the mediation of Jesus, Whose grace has filled her in the first instance. Since the moment when with full comprehension she consented to bring Him into the world as its Saviour, she has identified herself with all His designs for the good of mankind. Specially disposed, as a woman and a mother, to be the dispenser of mercy, she co-operates with Him for our salvation. Her assumption into Heaven and her glorious coronation, far from putting an end to her activity and prayers, give to her intercessions marvellous powers which she could not wield here below. Nothing that is told us of her motherly intervention on behalf of our Order surprises us. And it is by responding with filial devotion, like that displayed by our saints, that we shall live our Dominican lives to perfection.

I. MARY'S INTERVENTION IN FAVOUR OF OUR ORDER

At the beginning of those truly delightful *Lives of the Brethren,* which are our *Fioretti,* compiled at the request of Blessed Humbert de Romans, St. Dominic's fourth successor, Gerard de Frachet tells how Our Lady herself obtained from her Son the Order of Preachers.

These things elude historians, who only note obvious

phenomena and the course of external events, and know nothing of the hidden causes which regulate their mutual relations. The theologian, by the light of faith, can conjure up the hidden workings of an invisible world intervening in our history. To holy souls also a vision of these mysteries is sometimes vouchsafed by God.

Humbert of Romans and Gerard de Frachet, brothers and contemporaries of St. Thomas, were themselves excellent theologians. Moreover, they had received the confidences of holy souls. And those two facts account for the opening passage of the *Lives of the Brethren.* " If we carefully examine the sacred Scriptures," says the author, " we shall clearly perceive that Our Lady, the Blessed Virgin Mary, is our gracious mediatrix with her Son and the very pious helper of the human race.

" Apprehensive lest sinners, rejected from before the face of God, should perish, she tempers by her patronage the severity of the divine justice and by her earnest supplication confers many useful things upon the world. Amongst these various graces not the least outstanding was the foundation of so great and so famous an Order. Her prayers obtained it from God for the salvation of men, as we know from the revelations that have been vouchsafed in several instances."

Shortly after the foundation of the Preachers, a holy monk deposed that when in ecstasy he had seen the Mother of Mercy praying to her Son. She was entreating Him to wait until the human race did penance. The Saviour refused several times to grant her request, but, as she still persisted, He eventually said to her : " Mother, what more can I do or ought I to do for men ? I sent them the patriarchs and the prophets, and they made little effort to amend their ways : I came to them, I sent them the apostles and they slew them as they had slain Me. I have sent them martyrs, doctors and confessors in plenty and they would not obey their voice. Nevertheless, because I will refuse you nothing, I will send them my Preachers to enlighten and to cleanse them." A

similar vision had been described to Humbert of Romans
by an aged and holy Cistercian, who concluded by saying :
" The creation of your Order is due to the prayers of
the glorious Virgin."

St. Dominic, when in Rome for the foundation of our
Order, saw himself presented by Our Lady to her justly
offended Son : " This " she said, " is my faithful
servant : he will preach the word of salvation to the
world."

" Legends ! " it will be said. Perhaps ; but I maintain
that legends often symbolically express profound realities,
as do these particular visions, if Dominic and the two
monks were actually favoured by God with them. Concerned as she is with the needs of the world and especially
with the overthrow of heresy (*cunctas haereses sola intere-
misti in universo mundo*), why should the Blessed Virgin
not have intervened at a critical time when Christianity
was in great peril, and have raised up this Order to save
the faith ?

With what motherly care the Blessed Virgin fosters the
budding Order ! She never ceased upholding Dominic
in his work—as we sing in the preface of our Blessed
Father's Mass, " *Ipse enim Genitricis Filii tui semper ope
suffultus.*" Always aided by the Mother of God, he over-
came heresies by his preaching, equipped champions of
the faith for the salvation of the nations, and won innumerable souls for Christ.

Mary provided these knights of the truth with their
armour. She has invested them with the buckler which
will effectually protect them, and has girded them with
the sword which they carry at their side as the principal
weapon for their conquests. I refer to the scapular and
the Rosary. We have incontestable evidence of the great
favour conferred upon the Order in the person of
Blessed Reginald, seeing that Jordan of Saxony, who
relates the incident, heard it from St. Dominic himself.
Reginald, the hope of the budding Order, was at the
point of death before he had even been admitted. Dominic

gave himself to prayer. He then saw the Virgin appear before the sick man and, after having healed him by anointing, " present him with the complete habit of the Order." From that time our scapular replaced the rochet of the Canons Regular, and our habit became what it still is. *Ordinis vestiaria*—the investor of our Order is the epithet which we apply to the Blessed Virgin in memory of that great event.

Was there also an apparition of the Virgin Mary to St. Dominic in which she bade him : " Go and preach my Rosary " ? Yes, if one may trust an ancient and venerable tradition. In his encyclicals Leo XIII repeatedly insisted that St. Dominic received from the Mother of God the mission of spreading throughout the world that most salutary devotion which is called the Rosary. Two facts, at any rate, are quite fully established. One is that the Blessed Virgin appeared at Lourdes with a Rosary in her hand to recommend this form of devotion to the world. " On the other hand, this devotion," said Leo XIII, as had said many other Popes before him, " is the rightful property of the Dominican family. To the Friars Preachers is entrusted the commission to teach it to the Catholic world. St. Dominic's successor alone has the right to establish Rosary confraternities." If we connect these two facts, it must be admitted that they can find no more fitting illustration than the well-known and often reproduced picture, which represents the Holy Virgin giving the Rosary to St. Dominic.

Those are great general benefits which give evidence of the patronage Our Lady exercises over our Order. But how many particular favours are recorded in our ancient chronicles—favours which, after all, are only a few that have become known amid many more that have remained secret.

She awakens Dominican vocations. " Come into my Order," she said to Tancred, a knight of Frederick II's court. Another, who is believed to have been Humbert de Romans, asked her to direct him to the Order she preferred : he was led to that of the Preachers.

At every stage of life the religious can rely upon her help. A young friar, whom we recognize as the future Albert the Great, was tempted to return to the world. She restrained him. St. Thomas Aquinas continually invoked her assistance. He told Brother Reginald in confidence that Our Lady had appeared to him to assure him that his life and his doctrine had been blessed by God. While Peter of Verona was arguing with a heretic he found himself assailed by doubt. In great alarm he had recourse to Our Lady. " Peter," she replied, " I have prayed for you that your faith may not fail." The Breviary mentions another of her sayings which consoled St. Hyacinth amid his immense apostolic labours. " Rejoice, Hyacinth, my son, for your prayers are well pleasing to my Son, and through my intercession all that you ask Him will be granted." Gerard de Frachet tells the story of a religious who had lost heart on the eve of starting for a mission amongst the Cumans. He was encouraged by a pious solitary who told him that in vision he had seen a number of religious of various orders quietly crossing a bridge over a river, whilst certain others below were slowly swimming, dragging after them, with great effort, skiffs laden with passengers. These others were the Preachers. At times they almost sank. But the Blessed Virgin stooped down to them, supported them and led them to the shore, where they and those whom they had assisted rejoiced with great joy.

St. Dominic in the first instance and other Friars since his time have, on many occasions, seen the Blessed Virgin pass by night through the dormitory and bless the sleeping brothers one after another.

Rapt in spirit before God, our holy Father once again beheld Jesus in Heaven, with His mother, clad in a cloak of sapphire blue, seated beside Him. Round about them stood a great company of religious. Distressed at recognizing amongst them none of his own sons, he burst into tears. But Jesus consoled him, saying : " I have entrusted thy Order to My mother." Then Mary spread out her cloak and showed her faithful servant the innumerable host of the Preachers sheltered beneath its folds.

Assuredly, all other religious, all ordinary Christians, once they have become members of Christ, are the children of the one who gave birth to their Head. After having, by God's grace, collaborated in the Incarnation of Him Who is the Head, she continues her work by co-operating with the same grace in the sanctification of all His members—without exception. In Heaven, whither she has been assumed, she is endowed with a gift which enables her to look out upon the whole world with maternal eyes, and her heart is large enough to be interested in one and all.

Truly indeed can it be said of the love of this Mother : " Each one has his share in it, and all have it fully." But if none are excluded from her tender care, we have been specially assured of being enfolded by it. That is the great lesson to be derived, for our particular edification, from the incidents which have been mentioned above and which form the most affecting part of our Dominican gospel.

The Feast of the Patronage of the Holy Virgin, which our Order celebrates on December 22nd, recalls many signal favours, and the Collect for that festival runs as follows : " O God Who, for the salvation of souls, didst place the Order of Preachers under the protection of the most blessed Virgin Mary, and wast pleased to pour out upon it her constant benefits : grant unto thy suppliants that we may be led unto the joy of Heaven through the aid of that same protectress whose memory we revere to-day."

After the vision which revealed to St. Dominic the heavenly destiny of his Order, our holy founder " came back to himself," says Theodoric of Apolda, " and with the bell gave the signal for Matins. The brothers immediately rose up. As soon as Matins were over he summoned the brothers to Chapter and delivered a great and beautiful sermon to exhort them to love of the Virgin Mother of God."

"What love and what praise do we not owe to this most excellent Virgin, the very worthy Mother of Jesus Christ and our benign Mother? To her we have been entrusted by the divine Majesty, under her wings we are protected, by her hands we are blessed : she sheds upon us the dew of her graces, she dilates our hearts, she preserves us, she saves us by her intervention."

II. THE DEVOTION OF OUR ORDER TO MARY

Rodriguez de Cerrat, a chronicler of the first century of our Order, asserts that St. Dominic entrusted the care of his Order to the Blessed Virgin and chose her as Patron. Such manifestations as those we have just related can only have served to confirm him yet more in his ideal and in his confidence.

When our Blessed Father succeeded, after great efforts, in assembling at St. Sixtus the nuns dispersed throughout Rome and, in order to effect the reform of which they were in need, had persuaded them to adopt Dominican discipline, he transferred to their new home the image of Our Lady which they had venerated on the other side of the Tiber. Known as the Miraculous Virgin of St. Luke, it had been carried round the city during an epidemic, and had put an end to the scourge. Accordingly, one night, accompanied by two Cardinals, he went to fetch the Madonna. As the populace was hostile to the removal, they were protected by armed guards who carried flaming links in their hands. "Impressive indeed must have been this nocturnal torchlight procession, especially when it was crossing the Tiber : Dominic in his white habit and black cloak, bearing the sacred image, the two red-robed Cardinals beside him, all three barefooted, and clearly visible in the gleams from the torches which were reflected in the dark river below : St. Dominic, the apostle of the *Ave Maria*, carrying into Rome on his shoulder the Virgin of the Apostles, Our Lady of the Rosary." [1]

"Jordan of Saxony, who succeeded St. Dominic, recognizing," says Gerard de Frachet, "the interest taken by Our Lady the Blessed Virgin Mary in the progress and preservation of the Order, was determined to rule only with her assistance."

History has preserved for us some touching traits of his devotion to Mary. "He was wont to spend the night in prayer before her altar," says the same chronicler, "repeating the *Ave Maria* often and very slowly. Brother Berthold was anxious to know his method of prayer. In reply to his disciple's inquiry, the Master told him, among other things, that he was in the habit of honouring the Virgin by reciting five psalms, each one of which began with a different letter of her name. "That is just an example, my son," he added. Would that he had given a few more examples, simpler ones ! We should then have known exactly what the Rosary was at that period.

It was Jordan of Saxony who instituted the solemn procession to the altar of Our Lady which we make every evening as we sing the *Salve Regina*. We all know how the diabolical assaults upon the Friars in Paris and Bologna were ended through this prayer, proffered by all to her who had crushed the serpent's head. The diabolical machinations were succeeded by glorious manifestations of the Blessed Virgin who thus consecrated the practice that had been established in her honour.

"How many devout tears have been shed during these praises of the Mother of Christ ! " writes Jordan of Saxony himself. "What sweetness has filled the souls of those who have sung them and of those who have heard them ! What hearts are too hard for her to soften or inflame with love ? Have we not reason to think

---

[1] Petitot, *The Life of St. Dominic.*

that the Mother of the Redeemer takes pleasure in these
chants, is gratified by this praise? A man of God, a great
religious and one worthy of credence, has told me that
often, when the brethren were singing *Eia ergo, advocata
nostra*, he had seen the Mother of the Saviour prostrate
before her Son and praying for the preservation of the
Order. We mention these things in the hope that the
pious zeal of the Friars in singing the praises of the Blessed
Virgin may increase more and more."

Saturday was entirely consecrated to her, and the whole
of the Office was reserved for her that day. Humbert
de Romans gives many reasons for this. A beautiful
sequence that was formerly sung that day in church
summarizes them perfectly :

> *Jublemus in hac die*
> *Quam Reginae Coeli piae*
> *Dicavit Ecclesia.*

" The Sabbath was the day Our Lord rested, and the
Virgin is the tabernacle in which He reposed.

" That day the work of natural creation was ended :
in Mary is accomplished the work of the renewal of
nature through grace.

" Saturday must be passed on the way from Friday—
day of penance—to Sunday—day of joy. So also one
cannot go from the troubles of this lower life to the
celestial joys except through the Mediatrix.

" Let us remember that great Saturday when the
little flock of Christ's disciples had lost both faith and
hope, and these virtues took refuge in the heart of Mary.

" Finally it is a fact that Saturday is the day on which
she specially responds to our prayers, and works the
greater part of her miracles." [1]

If Saturday was Our Lady's great day, every day the
Friars exercised great devotion towards her, which the

---

[1] Humbert de Romans, *Opera*, Vol. II, pp. 72–74.

early chroniclers like to describe and commend. As soon as they had risen for Matins, they began by standing to recite in the dormitory the Matins of her Office. Then they hastened to her altar for private prayer before the great Office. Matins over, they returned to it, awaiting the break of day. At night, after Compline —which ended with the Compline of Our Lady, just as Matins had been preceded by her Matins—all assembled once more at the altar of their Queen.

Sometimes they would range themselves in three rows and would pray to her, slowly reciting *Aves* accompanied by genuflections. Their day began and ended at her feet.

In their cells they had her image, with that of Our Lord on the Cross, to remind themselves of her and foster their devotion to her. When St. Thomas Aquinas was writing his books he often inscribed the words *Ave Maria* in the margin. This we may see for ourselves on the priceless manuscript of the *Summa against the Gentiles*, which is in the great doctor's own handwriting. " Our Preachers," remarks Humbert de Romans, " never cease praising her, blessing her and preaching her when they preach her Son." [1] Continual allusions to their devotion to Mary are to be met with in the Breviary lessons for the feasts of our saints and blessed. To several of them, to St. Hyacinth and Blessed Aimo, for example, was accorded the favour, so ardently desired by the great theologian Cajetan, of dying on the day of her Assumption.

The holy Virgin was their liege-lady. These Knights of a new Order had entered the Order of St. Dominic with the design of winning the good graces of this incomparable lady. " In the Order of the Preachers alone," writes Bernard Gui, " a vow of obedience is taken to the Blessed Virgin Mary." In this Profession we find, raised to the highest spiritual and religious plane, the homage paid by the Knight to his Lady. All that

[1] Humbert de Romans, *Opera*, Vol. II, p. 71.

enthusiasm, that fighting spirit, that devotion to noble causes which a knight could derive from his fealty to a noble dame, the Friar Preacher found in the consecration he had made of himself to Our Lady, the Virgin Mary. The earthly love which he had forbidden himself was profitably replaced by that higher fervour which moved him without either disturbing or weakening. No longer would the man of doctrine bending over his books all day run the risk of letting his heart dry up, or the apostle tend to be too rough, too rigid or too violent : their deep-seated fervent devotion to Our Lady released in their hearts a spring of tenderness which never ceased to flow. And about their spiritual life there gathered a genial atmosphere in which their natural dispositions grew gentler, simpler and more open-hearted.

The women saints of our Order have rivalled the men in their devotion to the Heavenly Mother. It was with *Ave Marias* that Catherine of Siena began her religious practices at the age of five : when she was seven the little girl asked the Mother of Jesus if she might have Our Saviour as her Spouse. Afterwards Mary herself appeared with her Son and asked Him to take Catherine as His spouse, offering Him, at the same time, the maiden's hand. In the lives of St. Rose, of St. Catherine de' Ricci, of Blessed Benvenuta of Bojani, of Blessed Catherine of Racconigi and of many others, similar incidents are related. One and all, they regard Mary as the sweet and tender Mother whom they cannot venerate and love enough, and to whom they offer their whole-hearted submission.

Venerable Elizabeth of the Child Jesus, whose spiritual influence was great in the seventeenth century, upon being named Prioress of the Daughters of St. Thomas in Paris, declared that the holy Virgin should be the real Prioress of the Convent. In token of her homage, she placed in the hands of her Sovereign Mistress two silver keys and a heart which contained the names of all her daughters. The place usually reserved for the Prioress,

in the Choir, Chapter Room, Refectory, etc., was occupied by a statue of Our Lady, because Mother Elizabeth
was determined to be only sub-Prioress under Mary, to
whom she subordinated all her own authority. According to *L'Année Dominicaine*, the innovation afterwards
became a permanent institution in that convent.

The outward expression of this submission matters
little, but the sentiment itself must prevail in the mind
of every superior of our Order. St. Dominic certainly
had it when he bore to St. Sixtus the image of the
Madonna. And Père Lacordaire was steeped in it
when, after being trained in the observances of the
Dominican life under the eyes of Our Lady della Quercia,
and after making his religious vows in her presence, he
asked Père Besson's permission to have a replica of the
image. " We shall make her our Patron," he said, " and
we shall take her everywhere with us until we can instal
her in our first French convent." That is why Our
Lady of the Oak is patron of the Priory of Nancy.

Who could count all the *Aves* which our Order has
addressed to Mary? It has linked them together in
series of 150 to equal the number of the psalms and thus
to form of them that Psalter of Mary which is our Rosary.
It has made *Aves* the accompaniment to those great
mysteries of our salvation in which the Virgin has played
so important a part beside her Son. It has everywhere
grouped the faithful into confraternities, in order to
ensure throughout the world the recitation of the Rosary,
in private or in public, in churches and at home. It has
organized a perpetual watch by day and night—relays
following each other in hourly succession to give uninter-
rupted praise to Mary and to invoke her through the
Rosary.

What were the characteristics of this devotion, the
many outward manifestations of which we have just
described? It was a religious *cultus* such as could be

merited by no creature other than that incomparable being of whom Cajetan said that " she comes near to the borders of the divine." Is she not actually the Mother of God, introduced into the scheme of the Incarnation, and placed, according to Leo XII, " above all that is most beautiful in the three orders of nature, of grace and of glory " ?

Profound reverence for the unique dignity of the Virgin Mother found expression in all those *Aves* accompanied by genuflections which the early Friars loved so deeply. At that time the *Ave* was just a manifestation of deep reverence and nothing more : the second part, the petition, was added later.

Besides this reverence, entire submission was also rendered to her who united so sublime a majesty to a sovereign authority over our souls. In calling her " Our Lady," our forefathers recognized that they were serfs of her dominion, knights in the service of their Lady. Were they not solemnly vowed to her on the day of their Profession, and did not the superiors of the Order govern in her name ?

> " I am completely under her subjection
> To be better subject to Our Lord,"

sang our Blessed Louis-Marie de Montfort, who practised and preached the service of Mary. What else do we do in the second part of the *Aves* of our Rosary but subject ourselves unceasingly to the sovereign lady of Heaven and earth, whose intercession is all powerful above to co-operate with Jesus for our salvation now and at the hour of our death ?

Mingled with this deep reverence and trustful submissiveness there was also, in the devotion of our saints, a strong instinct of filial piety and a sense of close intimacy. Filial piety there must needs be, since the Mother of Jesus is also the Mother of us all, who can only be saved by being members of Jesus. Blessed Louis-Marie de Montfort has written some powerful pages on this subject which reach almost to the heights of St. Paul and entitle him to be regarded as the doctor of the motherhood of grace. By virtue of the fact that she voluntarily conceived the Saviour, she has conceived and continues to bring forth all that humanity which the divine Head has incorporated into Himself.

An exquisite intimacy accompanied this filial piety. A very devoted and respected mother is not necessarily the friend of her children, but our Heavenly Mother was the bosom friend of her sons : they lived with her in a communion of thought, of love and of life, and they have taught us how to imitate them by contemplation of the mysteries of the Rosary.

Charity, our love of friendship with God, has no dearer object, after Him and ourselves, than the woman, blessed above women, who is closer than anyone else to the God to Whom our charity is primarily addressed, closer than anyone else to our life of grace which we love because of our charity. Thus, on every score, she calls for first place in our supernatural friendship. " *Santa mamma regina !* " Savonarola used to exclaim, but more often he would shorten it to " *Mamma mia !* "

And this is the deep underlying reason for all those *Ave Marias*, repeated for whole days at a time. Père Lacordaire realized it very clearly. " Love has only one word, and however often that word is uttered, it is never repeated."

It is by means of this unstinted devotion that we shall place ourselves, as our saints placed themselves in the past, in a state of soul in which we may benefit by the patronage of the Blessed Virgin Mary over our Order.

SECOND SECTION

JESUS OUR SAVIOUR AND LIFE-GIVING HEAD

OUR devotion to Our Lady must not, cannot, interfere with the devotion claimed by Our Lord. He alone is the foundation of our life. He alone is the Way, and no one comes to the Father but by Him : the Holy Virgin is Mediatrix only after Him and in Him : her mediation proceeds from that of Jesus, Who takes His Mother as His assistant in the work of our sanctification after having chosen her to bring Him into the world. That first choice entailed all that followed in the eternal designs. Mary collaborates with Him—our Head—to actualize in all its fulness the great mystical body which is composed of all the members who live by the grace of Christ. But she herself is the first to live by this grace and her influence only tends to make us cleave fast to the Head. If we go to her, attracted by her kindness—prompted also by Jesus Who says to us " Behold thy Mother "—it is actually to hear her repeat : " Whatsoever Jesus shall say to you, do ye."

We will now consider Our Saviour, first in His historic reality, then in His mystical reality, and finally in His eucharistic reality. Having regarded Him from these three points of view, we shall determine what our devotion to Him ought to be.

I. OUR SAVIOUR IN HIS HISTORICAL REALITY

What a true Dominican desires, in the first instance, is to know Jesus Christ as He manifested Himself to the world. He takes no pleasure in dreams : he does not fashion for himself a fancy Christ : legends do not interest him. He wants to discover the Christ of History, as He truly lived and spoke and acted.

And this accounts for the *cultus* of all really Dominican souls for the books of the Holy Gospel, carefully perused and pondered over. Our masters, headed by St. Thomas, have written commentaries upon them which help us to discover the treasures hidden in these pages and to fathom the secrets of the least of their words.

With the definite purpose of reconstructing Our Lord's life as it was in reality, by replacing it in its setting and giving it a background, and also to obtain a more vivid presentment of the object of their faith and thus increase their charity, sundry beatified members of our Order have been able to realize the desire (common to all) of making a pilgrimage to the Holy Places. To see those distant horizons with their fine unchanging lines upon which the eyes of Jesus so often rested, that lake which was repeatedly furrowed by His ship, those fields that He crossed whilst talking to His disciples, the well beside which He sat, those flowers, those trees, those birds which were the subject of His parables, to kiss in adoration that ground of Gethsemane over which His blood flowed, that rock on which His cross was erected, the stone of the tomb in which He was laid dead . . . ! We know that such a wish and its fulfilment are not confined to us. But it is interesting to note to what lengths the French Dominicans of our own time have been able to proceed in that direction.

Père Mathieu Lecomte, who went out to Palestine in 1882, was inspired with the idea of founding in Jerusalem a house to which the veterans of the Order might retire, and where they might spend the evening of their lives in recollection. A series of providential circumstances, however, and the express wish of the Sovereign Pontiff, Leo XIII, led the Fathers, assembled on the site of St. Stephen's martyrdom, to take up a line of work which the first founder had never contemplated. Under Père Lagrange, the Priory of St. Stephen soon developed into the famous biblical school in which every effort is made, by the study of both documents and monuments,

to arrive at a historical presentment of Our Saviour and
to make it known. The only book Père Lecomte had
brought was his Bible in one volume. The first money
available was devoted to the purchase of eight volumes
which comprise the works of St. Jerome. Did they not
intend to work in his spirit and to continue his labours ?
And little by little the library was furnished with all the
necessary books.

The biblical question was raised in antagonism to the
Church by Protestant and rationalist science.

Père Lagrange and his collaborators did for criticism
what St. Thomas had formerly accomplished for the
philosophy of Aristotle. They showed that far from
overthrowing any of our dogmas, it can, when used with
discernment, become an admirable means of justifying
them. And all unprejudiced persons recognize and
honour their disinterested search for truth.

Very soon " it began to be realized how much light
could be thrown upon the interpretation of the sacred
Scriptures as the result of a protracted contact with the
soil, with the ruins of towns and ancient monuments, with
the inhabitants—in short, with all the ancient East. Not
the least of the charms of Père Lagrange's *L'Evangile de
Jesus-Christ* lies in the impression it conveys of intimate
and long-standing communion with the land of Jesus." [1]

When in 1933 the *Revue Biblique* made public the result
of the excavations that had been made in the Antonia,
" the Holy Father made no secret of his satisfaction at
the recovery, in this year of the Jubilee of the Redemption, of those stones, venerable above all others, by reason
of their close association with the Passion." [2]

We can justly claim that our Order has always aimed
at historical accuracy in the contemplation of Our Lord.
In the scenes proposed for our meditation during the
recitation of the Rosary, there is nothing that is not
strictly authentic. And when our Blessed Alvarez of

[1] Fr. M.-L. Dumeste in *La Vie Dominicaine*, 1935, p. 124. (St. Maximin.)
[2] *Ibid.*, p. 218.

Cordoba, after his return from the Holy Land, constructed one of the earliest Ways of the Cross, at the beginning of the fifteenth century, he was equally careful in his selection of the various stations. Eight in number, they consisted of the Agony, the arrest of Jesus, His scourging, the crowning with thorns, the scene of the *Ecce Homo*, the carrying of the Cross, the crucifixion, and the descent from the Cross with the committal of the body of Jesus to His Mother.

How gratifying then to our eagerness for the truth are these recent researches and their outcome ! If we cannot all of us study the great works at first hand, let us remember that every serious modern commentary upon Holy Scripture is under obligation to them.

Knowledge of the history of Jesus, however thorough, would be of little assistance to our spiritual life if we did not also bring to our reading and our meditation upon Holy Scripture all that the Christian faith and the study of St. Thomas teach us respecting the personality and the psychology of Our Saviour.

This Man, Who was the Son of God in person, had in His human soul, from the very first instant, the vision of the divine Essence. And because in the whole of the creative activity manifested throughout history there is nothing with which He Who is the Saviour of the world and the universal Judge is not concerned, for there is no creature which is not subject to the God-Man, we must necessarily conclude that to Him it is given by God to reveal in Himself, as in their first cause, all the beings which have been, which are and which shall be. I will not dwell upon this incontestable truth. Nor will I speak of the infused knowledge which the spirit of Jesus also received from God to enable Him to be cognisant of all the beings in His Kingdom generally and in every detail. It is a fact that the divine Master, Whose history we read in the little books of St. Matthew, St. Mark,

St. Luke and St. John, Whose steps we can trace in
Palestine from the house at Nazareth to the hill of the
Ascension, had His thought fixed lovingly upon each
one of us even then.

He was waiting for us, on His Mother's knees, in His
stable at Bethlehem where the shepherds and the Magi
came in turn to contemplate Him. He saw the shepherds
approach from the neighbouring fields, He could clearly
perceive in their distant land the Magi who would soon
be setting out on their journey. At a much later date
and from a remoter region we, too, started forth on our
way, Rosary in hand. "The pious Magi kings," said St.
Dominic to his sons, " on entering the house found the
Child with Mary His Mother. Now it is certain that
we, too, can find the God-Man with Mary His handmaid.
So come and let us adore Him and prostrate ourselves
in His presence." [1]

With what devotion St. Dominic used to read those
various sayings of Our Lord's which St. Matthew has
preserved ! He was never parted from that gospel. When
he was travelling he would take it from his wallet and
open it with reverence. He liked to meditate upon it in
his cell. Often he would kiss its sacred pages, which
always stirred his heart as though they were a letter
from his dearest friend.

When Fra Angelico depicted our Blessed Father either
seated with the gospel on his knees or else kneeling at the
foot of the Cross gazing up at Jesus Christ Who looks
down upon him, the painter does but bring home to us
a spiritual reality, namely, the meeting between Our
Lord's thought, still living upon the earth, and that of
St. Dominic.

" I talk to Jesus Christ about the words of the Holy
Gospel, as these words come to my mind, making such
interior acts and petitions as they suggest " . . . wrote
Mother Françoise des Seraphins, in the seventeenth
century. " My way of dealing with the Son of God is

---

[1] Theodoric of Apolda. Book on the Life and Death of St. Dominic.

to talk to Him as though He were visible, and I take for the subject of our conversations the words of His Holy Gospel, in which I find ample matter for prolonged prayer." [1]

If we glance through the great volumes of *L'Année Dominicaine*, we see on almost every page pious members of our Order living again the whole life of Our Lord during the course of the liturgical year. Intensely conscious of the love Jesus lavished upon them in accomplishing these mysteries, they seem as though they had witnessed them in person. In 1232, on the Eve of Christmas, Blessed Jordan of Saxony wrote to his spiritual daughter : " Dear Diana, be of good courage, comfort yourself in the Lord and in the Divine Child who is about to be born for you." And St. Louis Bertrand, upon his arrival, on the same day of the year, at a parish where he was to preach on the morrow, could not make up his mind to spend that night in bed. He went instead to the crib and remained there in contemplation, kneeling on the straw.

The recurrence of the season consecrated to the Redemption moved them still more deeply. Mother Catherine of the Passion, of the Daughters of St. Thomas in Paris, expressed in written words the sentiments which have actuated those of our holy men and women who have been marked with the stigmata : " I wish to see nothing but Jesus on the Cross. Jesus Christ bows His Head to give the kiss of love ; He is bound to the Cross to await my amendment of life ; His side has been pierced, to open for me the way to His heart." [2]

On several occasions Our Lord has performed on behalf of our saints miracles which testify to this truth. Time is powerless to interpose a barrier between the Christ Who is born, Who dies and Who rises again and His disciples of the thirteenth century—or of the twentieth. Blessed Benvenuta, one Christmas night, received the

---

[1] *Les Filles de Saint Thomas*, pp. 157, 160.
[2] *Ibid.*, p. 217.

Child Jesus into her arms. Blood from the side of Jesus fell upon Blessed James of Bevagna, who, overcome with the fear that he was a lost soul, lay moaning at the foot of the crucifix. As Blessed Gertrude of Herckenheim was still bewailing the Passion on Easter Day, Our Lord appeared to her and said : " Why weepest thou the day of my Resurrection and triumph ? To-day I did indeed leave the tomb ; and not I alone, for thou also art raised from the dead to live with Me for ever in glory." And we know how, on the day of His Ascension, Jesus came in response to little Imelda's ardent desire and in a miraculous communion carried away her soul.

II. OUR SAVIOUR IN HIS MYSTICAL REALITY

The touching incidents we have been recalling serve to show that, for our saints, Christ Jesus is not simply a personage of a bygone age Who disappeared after He had played a great part in history. He is still alive in His awful personality which dominates our human race and governs the whole world.

" The motto of our devotion to the sacred humanity," says Père Clerissac,[1] " might well be ' He has ascended into Heaven to fulfil all things.' Attraction, gravitation, the sum of all the forces which act upon this little planet in the solar system, are not more real than the divine energy which reaches us incessantly from the wounds of Our Saviour."

Far too few Christians are conscious of the great empire Our Lord exercises over us and of our entire dependence upon Him. We do not in the least realize how completely we live in Him, in *Christo Jesu*. It is the mystery of Jesus which St. Paul never ceased preaching to the world, and which was a life-long subject of meditation to St. Dominic our Father, who was no less wedded to the great apostle's epistles than to St. Matthew's gospel.

This life in Christ Jesus may be understood in two senses : the one, which may be called the feeble way,

---

[1] Clerissac, *L'esprit de St. Dominique*, p. 175.

modifies and minimizes St. Paul's teaching : the other
is the forceful way suggested by the passage from Père
Clerissac quoted above. Do not let us be afraid of over-
stepping the truth. The general tendency is to fall short
of it.

Yes, we fall short of the truth when we only see in Our
Lord a Master to listen to and a Model to imitate. As
Père Bernard has well said : " By His twofold greatness
Christ unites us to Himself. He is unique. He dominates
and gives life to all who are His. By the greatness of
His being, which is the being of the Son of God, He
assumes into Himself all those of His race. By the rich-
ness of His spiritual life He is in a position to communicate to everyone His grace in this world, together
with His glory in the next. So that He veritably is all
in all, and we are all created in Him. God, who had
already created everything in His eternal Word, the
pre-existent Christ, has re-created it in His incarnate
Word, Who was in the first instance the mortal Christ,
but Who is now and for evermore the immortal Christ.
In Him is now united all that is divine and all that is
human. He is, as it were, a great Sovereign Being and a
great Spiritual Reservoir. All fulness resides in Him,
and we share in this fulness. . . . Without Him we do
not exist, so truly is it He Who has renewed our destiny
and merited grace for us. But, on the other hand, He
is not complete without us, and we are depriving Him
of a part of Himself if we withdraw ourselves from His
influence, because we are His complements as St. Paul
says, and He it is Who fulfils Himself in every way in all.

" To hold this as a firm conviction and to have a deep
sense that Christ Jesus continues Himself in each one
of us—that is the forceful and unquestionably the only
right way of cleaving to Him. The Apostle teaches me
. . . that I form one body with my Saviour—on the
model of a living, natural, physical body. Imagine a
body made up of thinking members. Jesus is the Head,
but a head which is present to all the members of the

body by the very definite idea which it had and still has of each one of them, by the control, direct or indirect, it has over each one, and by the care it takes of them. A head which is in some way spread through the whole body, not only by virtue of the divine presence it instils there, but also by that human presence which has just been described. And in the great mystical body which makes up the fulness of Christ, I, a Christian, am myself a member who has no being, no life, or motion except in the body, by means of the First Cause Who gives it life and for the ends that He pursues." [1]

This doctrine, thus forcefully summarized by one of our contemporary theologians, has been upheld by all our theologians since the beginning of our Order. When the devil was tormenting the Friars in the days of Blessed Jordan, he exclaimed angrily one day through the lips of a possessed brother : " There go those creatures in their cowls, arguing over the question of knowing if Christ is the Head of the Church ! " Peter Lombard, in his *Sentences*, dealt briefly with the subject. But in commenting thereon Albert the Great treats the question with an emphasis which shows the importance he attaches to it. He says : " We receive the grace of Christ—not by imitation and resemblance, for if that were the case we might receive the grace of Peter and of Paul, but by the influence which Christ wields over us—an influence similar to that which the soul exercises over the body. . . ." " St. Thomas finally gives it " (this question) " its decisive form," writes Fr. Mersch, S.J. " His successors, the commentators, will not be able to add much. The Thomists in general, be it said, are particularly faithful in treating of the grace of the Head. The Scotists, following the Subtle Doctor, often say nothing about it. The writers of the Society of Jesus when they, later on, come upon the scene will be brief—at least those who

[1] Fr. Rogatien Bernard, L'*Année Dominicaine*, February, 1932, pp. 47–48

lived before the nineteenth century." [1] How can we
Dominicans and Thomists avoid a feeling of pride when
we read in the same learned work these lines : " The
authors who have made the most weighty statements "
—on the Mystical Body—" are St. Thomas, Cajetan,
Medina and Nazarius " ? All these four belong to us.

Now what the theologians have taught is borne out
in the history of all the souls in our Order. St. Catherine
of Siena's whole life is an illustration of this doctrine.
Jesus taking Catherine's heart and giving her His own
in its place, Jesus substituting His will for hers, are phenomena which are extraordinary no doubt, but which
merely manifest what was continually taking place in
Catherine herself and, to some extent, in what she used
to call " the whole mystical body of the Church." When
she had been present at the execution of young Nicholas
Tuldo, who, thanks to her efforts, had died as a Christian
should, it was the blood of Jesus which she saw streaming
from the severed head, and she piously preserved the
drops which had fallen on her white habit.

At this present time, when from all sides there is a
tendency to come back to this Christian realism, we, the
sons of an Order which was always faithful to it, must
take care not to be outstripped by others. Day by day,
with the help of our Rosary, and year by year as we follow
the liturgical round, whenever we recall the great facts
of the life of Jesus, let us soar above the level of the historians—even of those who pay tribute to Christ's
divinity. And let us see all those facts for what they
actually and truly are, namely a succession of mysteries
where everything has been foreseen and willed. All
that took place before Jesus drew His last breath has for
us its meritorious value.[2] And everything, even that

---

[1] Mersch, *Le Corps Mystique du Christ*, t. II, pp. 160, 161 and 162.

[2] " The Passion of Christ causes the remission of sins by the way of
redemption. The Passion which He endured from charity and obedience
is, as it were, a price. By it, actually, because He is our Head, He has
delivered us, His members, from our sins : even as man by the meritorious
work of his hands might make amends for some sin committed by his feet.

which followed His death, is for us an efficient cause of
life. We are buried with him, our resurrection proceeds
from His, in Him we are already in Heaven and through
Him we shall definitely reach that home of our souls.
In speaking thus I only sum up in a few words St.
Thomas's teaching in the Third Part of the *Summa*.

Let us cleave to Christ ever living, actually present at
the right hand of God where He prays for us, from whence
He acts in us with an efficacy of which the rays, formerly
unknown but recently captured for us by science, can
serve as a faint image. Would that we could live in such
a state of recollection as to be perfect receivers of the
waves which convey His thoughts, like our venerable
Esprite of Jesus, who constantly heard Jesus whisper :
" I am looking at you " ; that we could so wholeheartedly
and meekly obey all those intuitions which His heart
communicates to us as to realize individually His intention for us and thus contribute our part to the building
up of His Mystical Body !

In preference to the method which consists in seeking
perfection on our own initiative and on a personal plan,
by attempting to imitate Jesus virtue by virtue, let us
choose that other method which counts only upon His
plan and His grace, and where we are content to listen
for His calls and to obey all He demands of us. Oh,
but it is not such an easy thing to do ! It entails self-
examination, frequent and thorough. How am I getting
on ? What is my predominant interest ? Does Our Lord's
demand find me attentive, ready, obedient ? Have I not
met His holy suggestions by definite refusal, or at least
by inertia ? Then I rouse myself, I rectify my intention
and I adjust myself to the actual work of grace within
me. This kind of examination is to be undertaken not

For, just as a natural body is a whole consisting of many members, so the
whole Church, which is Christ's mystical body, forms but one single person
with its Head who is Christ " (IIIa, q. 49, a. 1).

once or twice a day, but a hundred times. We should
do well if we used it each time we raise ourselves from a
mechanical routine to a consciousness of the life that is
in us.[1]

III. OUR SAVIOUR IN HIS EUCHARISTIC REALITY

The action of Jesus, which we have mentioned above,
makes itself felt at special times, reaching us by means
of certain sacred signs, which Our Saviour uses to touch
our body and through it to mark our soul and sanctify
it. I am speaking of those sacraments whereby we are
visibly incorporated into our Head.

Faithful here also to our Dominican tradition, we
see in these sacraments more than mere signs which
recall the merits of Our Lord. They are the channels
through which His grace reaches us. They are the
instruments which He uses to shape us and conform us
to Himself. One of our Masters of recent times, Père
Gardeil, when he received Extreme Unction, expressed
his great satisfaction at thus completing his incorporation
into Christ.

Especially in the sacraments which are of frequent
and daily use it is most important not to forget the
presence of Our Lord. This presence is only virtual in
the sacrament of penance. Nevertheless, Jesus does make
His influence felt, not only in the priest who absolves
and gives counsel, but also in the penitent himself.

Let us then examine our sins in the spirit we described
above, before those eyes which were fixed upon Peter
the renegade in the court of the pretorium. In order
that our contrition may be perfect, let us unite ourselves
to that hatred which Jesus felt for all sin—seeing in it
an offence against God. Let us also unite ourselves to
His will to take upon Himself in expiation all the penalties
which these sins deserve. Inspired by sentiments such
as these, very many of our fathers, especially in early

---

[1] These thoughts are further developed in the author's work, *Par Jesus-
Christ Notre Seigneur* (Desclée de Brouwer), Book III, Ch. II.

days, were accustomed to resort daily to the sacrament of penance. Nowadays we are required by our Tertiary Rule to make our confession at least twice a month.

Every fortnight we look into ourselves in order to bring to light all those cravings for esteem, for pleasure, for comfort, for ease which thrive undetected in the dark recesses of the soul. We take cognisance of our positive failings, of our sins of omission, together with their causes. We have to form a sufficiently clear conception of them to be able to give an account of them to someone. The priest who listens to us is unlikely to make a mistake because he judges without prejudice. Moreover, he is fully qualified to assist us in detecting evil and in finding a remedy for it. What a wholesome practice ! It prevents us from slipping imperceptibly into grave sin, and above all makes it impossible for our consciences to be deadened by sin. We are obliged to rouse ourselves from our tepidity, to advance towards perfection. Periodically, at fairly frequent intervals, there comes this check to that inertia which would hinder our progress towards perfection. We are continually braced up to practise virtue.

This psychological effort, which all educationalists would recommend, is reinforced, let us not forget it, by the grace of Christ which automatically supervenes in the reception of the sacrament of penance. It flows into us all the more freely because we have placed ourselves in the presence of Our Saviour and have united ourselves to Him in order to know our faults, to repent of them, to make expiation, and to form useful resolutions. Everything will be pervaded by His inspiration.[1]

There is another sacrament which, thank God, we may approach much more often than could our fathers of

---

[1] I venture again to refer to a work I have published under the title of *Aux Sources de l'eau vive* (Desclée de Brouwer). It contains in fuller detail ideas upon the Sacraments of Penance and of the Eucharist which I have merely outlined here.

old. The Rule encourages us to receive the Holy
Eucharist every day. There Jesus Christ is really present.
He enters sensibly into contact with us by His actual
substance. It is no longer a case of the influence from
afar, spoken of above, like the light and the heat which
the sun sends us. " When I make my communion,"
said St. Rose of Lima, " it seems to me that a sun comes
down into my breast."

Hidden under the appearances of bread and wine,
Jesus makes Himself our food. All that nourishment
does for our bodies, St. Thomas tells us, the sacrament
of the Eucharist confers upon our spiritual life. It
preserves it, protecting it from mortal sin. It increases
it, and the growth can continue without limit until the
consummation of the eternal union with God. It
refreshes it by repairing the loss of strength brought
about daily by venial sin. Finally, it gives to our soul a
spiritual well-being with which the bodily satisfaction
obtained by a good meal cannot be compared. And all
this can be explained, without metaphor, by the fact
that the Eucharist stimulates in us the fervour of charity.
Jesus, by coming into contact with our heart, is like a
lighted brand which kindles a fire, and thus from day
to day our communions may mark the progress of our
spiritual ascent from the lowest stage, where it is a question of struggling against sin so as not to die, up to that
transforming unitive state in which even as Jesus lives
by the Father and for the Father Who sent Him, so also
he that feeds on Him lives no more but through Him
and for Him.

Upon what conditions do these marvellous results
depend ? Upon the degree of excellence in the preparation for approaching the Eucharist, according to some.
On the frequency with which it is approached, declare
others. The former stressed the disposition which permitted of worthy reception, the latter the automatic
efficacy of the Eucharist which gives increase of grace
at each communion ; and so there came to be two schools

of thought in the Church. Of these, the former seemed
to have been in the ascendant in the past—long before
the days of the Jansenists. From the ninth century
until the thirteenth, which saw the birth of our Order,
communions became rarer and rarer. Theologians
insisted upon the purity and the virtues required in
preparation. " One experiences a sort of stupefaction,"
says M. l'Abbé Vernet, " when one reads in the Rule of
St. Clare, confirmed by Innocent IV (1253), that the
Poor Clares have only seven communions a year." [1]

According to the same author, the Constitutions of
the Dominican Sisters allowed them to communicate
fifteen times. That is rather better. But now we find
St. Thomas in remarkable terms extolling daily communion. He teaches that it is salutary for all those in
whom it increases the fervour of charity without diminish-
ing reverence. " Love and fear," he says, " are equally
related to the reverence due to this sacrament, the love
which desires daily communion and fear which prompts
occasional abstention. But love and hope whereunto
the Scriptures constantly urge us are preferable to fear." [2]

When St. Catherine of Siena in the following century
asked to be allowed to communicate frequently, Blessed
Raymund, her confessor, consented, and in reply to
adverse criticisms he said that she was exactly following
the precept of St. Thomas, for she communicated on most
days, but occasionally refrained so as to approach the
sacrament afterwards with more reverence and devotion.

The appeal of the mystics who, in our Order, imitated
St. Catherine, and the authority of our theologians, ever
faithful to St. Thomas, did much to bring about a return
to frequent communion. " Tauler, alluding to the days
of the early Dominican Sisters, used to say that if bi-
monthly communion was sufficient for them, a worse
age and weaker souls called for more communions." [3]

---

[1] *Eucharistia* (Bloud & Gay), p. 253.
[2] IIIa, q. 80, a. 10.
[3] Vernet in *Eucharistia*, pp. 257–262.

The movement, as we know, did not reach its culmination until the beginning of the twentieth century, when Pius X opened the way for all to approach the Holy Table daily.

The second of the two schools of thought is, therefore, triumphant to-day. Why is it that the results are not more evident? Here again it is St. Thomas who provides us with the explanation. No one has ever succeeded better than he in solving this question in all its aspects.

Although the baptismal character and the state of grace are all that are requisite for a valid, non-sacrilegious communion and for ensuring that a certain measure of supernatural growth will accrue automatically, this growth is slight and actually inoperative if we communicate with distraction. Moreover, if the distraction is voluntary, we commit a fault, and that fault can have disastrous consequences for our soul which more than counteract the very small measure of spiritual growth mentioned above. Does not a sin of that kind increase in us those natural evil tendencies which may lead one day to the loss of grace? We are very certainly lacking in religious respect. The fear of God diminishes little by little in our souls. We are heading for an almost certain fall which will make us lose the supernatural capital which has been uselessly accumulated and has remained well nigh unproductive within us. We shall then find ourselves bereft of everything, and at the mercy of our evil tendencies. That is what may be the final result of years of tepid daily communions. We are like the gardener who grafts cuttings on a tree, and at the same time encourages growth from the original wild stock.

What must we do then? Must we abstain from communion until the day when we shall have acquired the necessary virtues? No: to be in a state of grace is all that is required. It is not requisite, as was too long taught, to be free from all deliberate venial sin. This purification will be the actual fruit of frequent communion, says Pius X. "It is impossible that through daily communion we should not gradually free ourselves from venial sins, and from our attachment to these faults." But, as St. Thomas tells us, that only holds good provided we communicate devoutly, that is to say, if, approaching the Holy Table with the attention of faith and the eagerness of love, we place ourselves respectfully at the disposal of Our Saviour to accomplish His Will. In proportion to the degree in which, at the moment of communicating, you are actuated by these sentiments, your communion will effect in you a true and actual reformation ; and so, little by little, it will produce the wonderful fruits that Our Lord and the Church expect of it.

If you fail to find any such results in yourself, if, for instance, you are not detaching yourself from some irregular affection, then beware. The reason is probably that you are communicating as a matter of routine and without due attention. Set to work at once to stir up devotion in your heart. That can be done in no better way than by meditating upon the goodness and the favours of God, as contrasted with your wretchedness and with the need you have of submitting yourself to Him. Practically, it is enough to follow the Mass carefully from the beginning, either by making use of the words of the Missal or else by uniting yourself in a general way with our adorable Head, Who on the altar renders homage to His Father and Who leads us to consecrate ourselves to God by Him and with Him and in Him.

As a means of breaking the routine and rousing the soul, it may be well sometimes to abstain from communion. Anything that stimulates holy desire and expands the heart prepares the way to a fruitful communion. "In order to have light," says St. Catherine of Siena, "each one brings his own candle, a large one or small, as the case may be. It is through holy desire," she goes on to add, "that our candle increases in size and receives more light." And Louis of Granada remarks that the larger the pot you carry to the sea the more water it can bring back. The ocean is inexhaustible : our receptivity, however, is limited and often, by our own fault, excessively limited.

It was with the object of honouring this ocean of grace, this source of light, Christ Jesus really present in the Eucharist, that several Congregations of our Sisters organized in their convents a watch of perpetual adoration. In 1538 Fr. Thomas Stella founded in our Church of Sta. Maria della Minerva the Confraternity of the Blessed Sacrament which has now spread over the whole world. But no subsequent tribute has ever surpassed that paid by St. Thomas through his compilation of the Office for Corpus Christi, which is universally acclaimed as a masterpiece, with what Pope Benedict XIII described as " its incomparable and almost divine hymns." When we are singing in choir, in our solemn processions or in the more intimate ceremony of Benediction, whenever during our solitary visit to the Host in the Tabernacle we meditate on the *Adoro Te*, may the happy recollection that we are making use of family goods help our devotion to Our Lord to deepen and develop ever more and more !

THIRD SECTION

THE MOST HOLY TRINITY

JESUS Himself is alone the Way. Now no one remains on a way ; we pass along it to reach the journey's end. The ultimate goal to which Jesus leads us is identical with the first principle from which He started out to seek us : it is the Most Holy Trinity. From the Most Holy Trinity to the Eucharist whereby Christ Jesus, really present upon the earth, communicates His life to men—such is the road whereby the divine love travels down to us. From the Eucharist to the Trinity is the ascending road up which the divine love draws us, communion by communion, until it brings us to participate in the Triune life in eternal beatitude.[1]

That being so, a true Christian should have in his heart a sense of home-sickness and a great hope. Like a child who has never seen the parents from whom he received his life, but who is confident of finding them some day, he will be constantly thinking of them and will carefully treasure anything that will help him to form some conception of that God in Three Persons Who is the first principle of his existence and the final end of his destiny.

Unfortunately, too many souls, even amongst the best disposed, are content to think with awe of the divine Law which is imposed upon us as a condition of our salvation, and take no pleasure in meditating upon the intimate life of God. They speak of Him as the Jews may have done before the coming of Our Lord, if not like the philosophers of the last few centuries. For them God was a formidable Being, isolated upon the

---

[1] R. Fr. Bernadot, *From Holy Communion to the Blessed Trinity* (Sands, 2s. 6d.).

throne of His eternity. But as for ourselves, we know
that the divine Nature reveals itself in Three Persons—
the Father, the Son and their Spirit of Love—and it is
inconceivable that this should have no influence upon
our conduct.

That greatly venerated prelate, the late Cardinal
Mercier, in an address delivered to his priests during a
retreat, reproved them for not making " this mystery of
the Trinity their favourite object of prayer, the basis of
their lives and the dominating topic of their teaching." [1]
May the priests of our Order never merit those reproofs,
and may none of our Tertiaries lack a taste for meditating
on such subjects ! If they do, they will be unworthy of
St. Thomas and of St. Catherine, who would not recognize
them as belonging to their family.

With the first disciples let us set ourselves to follow the
divine Master. Let us see how He lives, and let us listen
to Him. He gradually reveals the Father Who is in
Heaven. He reveals Himself as a Son of God, One quite
apart, the Only-Begotten to Whom the Father communicates everything. Finally, at the close of His life,
He speaks of another Comforter Whom He and the Father
will send to remind them of His teaching and to lead
them into the truth. "Go and teach all nations, baptiz-
ing them in the name of the Father and of the Son and
of the Holy Spirit."

St. Thomas will help us by an analogy with the life
of our spirit to form some kind of conception of that
Sovereign Spirit Who knows and loves Himself. This
knowledge and this love issue forth, according to him,
as persons similar and equal to the source from whence
they are derived. From all eternity God knows Himself
and expresses Himself completely in one single idea
which is His Word, His perfect Image, His Son. And
the Father and the Son, contemplating each other in

---

[1] Cardinal Mercier, *La Vie Intérieure*, p. 309.

their indivisible perfection, conceive for each other a love into which their whole substance passes. . . . Our great Doctor, as he was dictating his reflections on that magnificent subject, fell into ecstasy and did not notice that the candle he held was burning his fingers.

St. Catherine, that humble Tertiary who had not even learnt to read and write, never dictated anything clearer or more fervent than her aspirations to the Holy Trinity : " Oh, eternal Trinity, one God ! One essence in Three Persons ! Thou art a vine of three branches, if I may be allowed to speak thus. Thou hast made man in Thine own image and likeness in order that through the three powers he possesses in one soul he may bear the seal of thy Trinity and Unity. By these three faculties he not only resembles Thee but he unites himself with Thee. By his memory he is like and unites himself to the Father, to whom power is ascribed. By his intelligence he is like and unites himself to the Son to whom is ascribed Wisdom. By the will he is like and unites himself to the Holy Spirit to Whom clemency is ascribed and Who is the Love of the Father and of the Son."

It is in the secrecy of the Triune life that we have been foreknown and predestined. St. Paul says so at the beginning of his Epistle to the Ephesians. St. Catherine puts the same thing in other words. On the Feast of the Annunciation she expresses herself thus : " O Trinity incomprehensible, in the great eternal council Thy wisdom has seen all that was necessary for the salvation of man, Thy clemency has willed it and to-day thy power has realized it. And thus, in that council, Power, Wisdom and Clemency have concurred to save us. . . ." It is in the mystery of the Most Holy Trinity that we are called to live eternally, enjoying God's very beatitude by associating ourselves through our intelligence with the generation of the Word and through our love with the procession of the Holy Spirit. After her great ecstasy in October, 1378, during the course of which

Catherine had received so many lights and in five days had dictated the *Dialogue*, she exclaimed : " O, eternal Trinity, O, Godhead, divine nature ! O, Godhead, Who hast given such value to the blood of Thy Son, Thou art a fathomless ocean into which the deeper I dive the more I find, and the more I go on seeking Thee. The soul is never satiated with Thee : she fills herself with Thee in Thy abyss, but without ever appeasing her thirst, for she continues to desire Thee, O Eternal Trinity, she longs to see Thee in Thy light. As the hart pants after the spring of living water, so does my soul long to leave the dark prison of the body to see Thee in truth. O, Eternal Trinity, how much longer will Thy face remain hidden from my eyes ! " It is by participating here and now in the life of the Trinity, Who dwells in them for their justification, that the elect advance towards their glorification. St. Teresa, who was vividly con- scious of the indwelling of the Three Divine Persons, was never satisfied, she tells us, until it had been explained to her by a Dominican theologian that the Holy Trinity dwells verily in a soul which is in a state of grace.[1] Our Order has always had such theologians who, by their comments on St. Thomas's articles on the divine Missions, have lucidly expounded this doctrine to fervent souls.

May we all live by this doctrine after the example of our mother St. Catherine—live by it in our acts of private piety as well as in the exercises of our Liturgical Office !

The Most Holy Trinity dominates our whole Liturgical Office. Advent is specially consecrated to the Father, Who sends His Son to save us. From Christmas until Ascension Day we follow the Son through His various mysteries. Then comes Pentecost, with the sending of the Holy Spirit. Finally, as a culminating Feast, we arrive at Trinity Sunday. And even as the first part of

---

[1] St. Teresa, *Autobiography*, Ch. XVIII, *end.*

the year leads up to it, so also is the second part reckoned, in our Dominican liturgy, as the time after the Feast of the Holy Trinity.

It is related in the life of Venerable Bartholomew of the Martyrs that after Matins of the Holy Trinity he was too much absorbed in contemplating that great mystery to be able to find his cell. He groped his way to the dormitory like a blind man, repeating with unction the last anthem of Lauds : " *Ex quo omnia, per quem omnia, in quo omnia, ipsi gloria in saecula !* " From Him all things proceed, through Him all things come to be, in Him all things are contained. To Him be glory throughout the ages !

Two practices will be specially dear to us, and we shall make a point of observing them fervently, not only during the divine Office, but also, as a matter of devotion, in our private life. These practices are the sign of the Cross and the *Gloria Patri*. By making the sign of the Cross we profess that we belong to Christ, the only Mediator, and we imitate His redemptive attitude, but we do this in order to act with Him in the name of the Father and of the Son and of the Holy Spirit. What a splendid preliminary to any important undertaking ! We embark upon it boldly in the very name of those Three Who predestined us and Who—present within us—support our efforts.

Then, when we are ready to put the final seal upon our works, what nobler formula could be found than the " Glory be to the Father and to the Son and to the Holy Ghost ! " We are associating ourselves not only with those who are praising the Holy Trinity upon earth, but with the glory which the Holy Trinity found in Themselves before the beginning of things, and which They will still find when time shall be no more. It is in this glory that we hope to participate in Heaven.

St. Dominic loved to make the sign of the Cross. When travelling he might often be seen from afar in the act of crossing himself piously. Moreover, writes Theodoric of Apolda, " He used to recommend the Friars to humble themselves before the Holy Trinity while they solemnly recited : *Glory be to the Father and to the Son and to the Holy Ghost.* And that form of profound prostration which we retain in our liturgy was the first of his special devotions."

CHAPTER IV

OUR CANONICAL OFFICE

SECTION I. THE DOMINICAN LITURGY.

SECTION II. THE MASS AND THE OFFICE.

    1. The Holy Sacrifice.
    2. The Office as the Outcome of the Mass.
    3. The Excellence of Our Office.

SECTION III. THE SEQUENCE OF THE HOURS.

    1. The Night Office.
    2. Morning Lauds.
    3. The Little Day Hours.
    4. Vespers.
    5. Compline.

SECTION IV. PRAYER FOR OUR DEAD.

FIRST SECTION

THE DOMINICAN LITURGY

The Rule of the Third Order recommends, as a principal means to the attainment of personal sanctification and apostolic activity, " assiduous prayer—as far as possible liturgical prayer " (I. 3). And later, in the chapter on the recitation of the Office, it is stated that the Office of Our Lady must be said according to the Dominican rite (VI. 1).

Has the Order then a liturgical rite of its own ? Yes. One has only to compare our Office books with those of the Roman rite to see that they do not always tally. Moreover, nobody who assists at the holy sacrifice of the Mass could fail to notice that the Dominican Fathers do not celebrate quite like other priests.

Some people are astonished at this. A few, who have not our reason for regarding with sympathy all the customs of our Order, are even scandalized. Why not conform to the ordinary use and thus promote unity ?

Unity ? Our Order was amongst the first to feel the need of it. And it is just because it realized this at a very early stage that it is distinguished from others to-day. Moreover, Holy Mother Church has no wish to sacrifice the treasure she possesses in the various liturgies which still flourish, even in the West. Amongst these, the Dominican liturgy occupies a post of honour. " At the beginning of the Order," says Humbert de Romans, " there was much diversity in the Office." The Friars whom St. Dominic had dispersed so speedily, in 1217, through all the countries of Christendom had had to accommodate themselves to the liturgies of the countries in which they settled, and these varied very considerably.

The Order soon found this diversity very inconvenient. For the purposes of study or preaching or government, the religious frequently passed quickly from one house to another and from one country to another. It was no easy matter for them to be constantly adapting themselves to a fresh liturgy. The Friars who met for a general Chapter would certainly use in choir the same bodily gestures that St. Dominic had taught them, but they had different psalms, lessons, antiphons, and responses for the Office. At Mass there were even greater divergencies.

To obviate these difficulties, it was decided to bring about unification. Even the faithful who attended our churches would derive satisfaction, in the course of their travels, from finding everywhere amongst the Preachers the ceremonies they had come to know and to love. As a living symbol of Catholic fraternity, it could not fail to promote still closer intimacy amongst those who had become associated with the great Dominican family.

Unification proved no easy matter, and it took twenty-five years to accomplish it. According to Père Mandonnet, " the first attempt was certainly made before 1235 and was probably subsequent to 1230. This first arrangement of Dominican liturgy remained the foundation and basis of all later reforms, which latter do not seem to have brought about any essential modifications." [1]

However, the result did not please everyone. Is that to be wondered at ? . . . The Chapter of 1245 appointed four religious chosen from the four provinces of France, England, Lombardy and Germany to correct and revise the Office. They worked together at Angers, and three general Chapters from 1246 to 1248 approved of their labours. But as the outcome of many complaints in the Order, the Chapter of London in 1250 instructed the four revisers to meet together at Metz to review their work.

Humbert de Romans, Provincial of France, who had

[1] Mandonnet, *Les Frères Prêcheurs et le premier Siècle de leur Histoire.*

been involved in the revision of the liturgy which had been carried out in his province and in which he must have collaborated, was in 1254 elected General of the Order, and he induced the General Chapter to commit to him " all the ordering of the Ecclesiastical Office." At the Paris Chapter of 1256, Humbert issued to the Order his annual encyclical in which he announced the completion of the liturgical reform. A monumental volume, a masterpiece of Parisian book production in the middle of the thirteenth century, was composed to be the model to which all copies must conform. Deposited at first in the College of St. Jacques de Paris, the most important house of the Order, it is to-day in Rome amongst the general archives of the Friars Preachers.

Finally, in 1267 Clement VII gave his approval to our liturgy. Since then it has undergone no important modification. When Pius V in 1570 imposed on the entire Church the breviary and Roman missal, he made an exception for the liturgies which were more than two hundred years old. The Dominican liturgy was one of these.

It has been asserted that our liturgy was inspired by the Gallican, and more particularly by the Parisian, Office. This would not be surprising, considering that it was unified in France, and under the influence of the Frenchman, Humbert de Romans. But those of our customs which we find in the Gallican liturgy may yet have been derived by the latter from the ancient Roman liturgy. At any rate, it has been established conclusively by the investigation of Fathers Laporte and Rousseau that the Dominican liturgy is essentially Roman. The peculiarities that characterize it are, in many cases, practices formerly observed in the Roman basilicas, but no longer preserved in the Breviary and Missal of the Pontifical Curia, from whence we get the present form of the Roman rite.

The Friars Minor, when they also wished to unify their liturgy, adopted the Roman Curia's Breviary and Missal. Not satisfied, however, with adopting them, they adapted them to their own way of life and popularized them all over the world. The books, as thus revised by the Franciscans, were imposed by Pope Nicholas III upon the churches of Rome in 1277, before they were made universally obligatory under Pius V. In that way several essentially Roman customs disappeared from Rome, but have survived amongst us.

The rites of the Dominican High Mass in particular have " remained very close to the ancient basilican rites and have preserved their majestic simplicity." [1] The Introit is actually the song of entrance. The celebrant and the ministers do not begin to advance to the altar until the Introit has been taken up by the choir. The celebrant remains seated on the sedilia from the Collects until the chanting of the Gospel. It is at this point that, after the Epistle, the sub-deacon proceeds to prepare the chalice. At a low Mass this is done by the priest as soon as he reaches the altar, before beginning the Mass with the *Confiteor*. The priest offers the bread and wine together. After the Consecration he prays with his arms extended—almost in the form of a cross. Other differences can be noticed if the Mass be followed with the Missal.

The Office also has its peculiarities—for instance, the five psalms *Laudate* for the first vespers of the *Totum Duplex* Feasts, a response after the Chapter, and the several hymns and anthems, notably those of the Lenten Compline, " which the Order of Friars Preachers has been instrumental in preserving, together with other beautiful things," says a liturgical writer. [2] After Lauds of the Office of Tenebrae, we sing in choir some dramatic and stirring invocations to Christ. Touching versicles also are appended to our *Libera*. The two sides of the

---

[1] Fr. Lavocat in *Liturgia* (Bloud & Gay), p. 862.
[2] Fr. Molien of the Oratory in *Liturgia*, p. 591.

choir stand and sit alternately, as a reminder that our Order is at once active and contemplative. According to the direction of St. Dominic himself, all is to be done briefly, succinctly and energetically. There are frequent deep inclinations of the body, especially at the *Glorias*, to help us to prostrate our whole being before God as well as to bring home to us His sovereign excellence and our entire dependence upon Him.

Two little illustrations may fitly conclude this section. Blessed Catherine of Racconigi, suffering under the inability to read or write, was supernaturally endowed with ability to read the Dominican liturgical Office— but nothing more, " Our Lord thus testifying," says Jean de Réchac, " that as she was a daughter of the Order she must not use any prayers or Offices except those belonging to the Order."

Blessed John Dominici, who worked so hard to heal the great schism of the West, did not consider that he was offending against the unity of the Church by clinging to our particular rite. And when he was offered the office of a cardinal, he accepted it only on condition that he might continue to use the liturgy of the Order.

SECOND SECTION

THE MASS AND THE OFFICE

I. THE HOLY SACRIFICE

" TERTIARIES should make every possible effort to assist
daily at the most Holy Sacrifice of the Mass, and piously
and attentively unite with the priest who is celebrating."
So says the Rule (VII, 33). And later, when treating
of the monthly meeting of the Chapter or Fraternity, it
prescribes that the Tertiaries assembled on that occasion should also hear Mass together if the hour be suitable
(XVII. 65). These are weighty recommendations, the
brevity of which does not obscure their importance.

Sacrifice is the noblest of all religious acts. And the
Mass is the Holy Sacrifice of our Christian religion, the
extension and expansion through the ages and throughout
the world of the sacrifice which our Sovereign Priest
offered to His Father by His death upon the Cross.

Like the first children of Adam in the Bible story, like
the most primitive tribes of our own day, like every
religious soul, to whatever height of civilization it may
have attained, we seek a symbolical ceremony in which
to express our religion to God. We take what best
represents our existence—bread and a little wine. Is
not this the fruit of our toil and our daily food ? Yes, we
are always working to earn our bread, and with that
bread we sustain our life. Then we go to the temples
which we have erected to our Creator. Having withdrawn a little of the food from profane use, we consecrate
it to Him in a beautiful act of oblation. In golden vessels
the priest uplifts the bread and the wine to God. And
this means that our whole existence depends on God
alone, and that we gladly recognize it.

When pastoral tribes, animated by the same sentiments, offered a lamb from their flock, they went so far
as to immolate it, reduce it to ashes.   That holocaust
was the best way of expressing that we are nothing before
God.   The whole of our life is but a gift of His goodness.
Having abused that goodness by our faults, we do not
deserve that He should continue to let us live.   Yes,
God could demand from Abraham the sacrifice of his
own son and of himself ; but He was satisfied to receive
the symbolical holocaust.

But there came a day when a little child, whom His
mother held in her outspread hands as upon an altar,
came into the Temple at Jerusalem and offered Himself
to God His Father to be actually immolated in the
place of all those lesser sacrifices.   Years later John the
Baptist would say, pointing Him out to the crowd :
" Behold the Lamb of God, behold Him Who taketh away
the sins of the world."   Appointed Head of all humanity
as had been Adam of old, Jesus, in His desire to save
what the other had lost, offered Himself in the name of
us all and shed all His blood upon the altar of the Cross.
He enacted that great drama like a sacred liturgy.
" This is My hour. . . . What thou dost, do quickly.
. . . Ye seek Jesus of Nazareth.   I am He—let these go
their way. . . . Thou wouldst have no power against
Me—thou who condemnest Me to death—unless it were
given to thee from above."   He resigns Himself into the
hands of the executioners who are the unconscious
instruments of His designs, and Himself offers His soul
to God, uttering a loud cry which rings out above the
cries of the Paschal lambs that were being slain at that
same hour in the Jewish temple.
Oh, the cry of that outpoured blood which rises up to
Heaven !   How shall human tongue express its deep
meaning ?   " Father, behold Me, Me who am actually
the King of all these men—as indeed it is written on my

Cross. I recognise that Thou alone hast being and that sinful men have no right to exist ; and therefore taking upon Myself all sins—from the sin of Adam until the last of the sins of the world—I accept death as expiation for all." Such indeed was the act of religious love and satisfaction which, ascending above the crimes of the executioners and the sufferings of Jesus, was well pleasing to the Heavenly Father. And it is because He foresaw it from the creation of the world that He looked with favour upon this little earthly sphere, from which there would rise up to Him the sweet savour of such incense. All the other planets, all the suns were as nothing in comparison with this poor little earth of ours.

It was because they foreshadowed this sacrifice that God was willing to accept the sacrifices of the Old Law : and from the day of its consummation He would have no sacrifices other than those which recall it, perpetuate it and extend it.

Jesus Himself provided for this. " The Lord Jesus, the same night in which He was betrayed," says St. Paul, instituted the Eucharist. " With desire I have desired to eat this pasch with you before I suffer," He said at the commencement of the Last Supper, and at the very moment when Judas goes out to set the seal upon his perfidy Our Lord exclaims : " Now is the Son of man glorified, and God is glorified in Him." It is then that, taking bread into His holy and venerable hands, and lifting up His eyes to Heaven, He gives thanks and says : " This is My Body which is given for you." Afterwards He took the cup of wine and declared : " This is My Blood which shall be shed for many unto remission of sins." Let us ponder these words, which bring about what they say, and let us realize that Jesus is presenting Himself to His disciples in the attitude of His sacrifice on the Cross. Under the appearances of bread and wine His body is, as it were, bloodless on the one side and His Blood shed forth on the other. By a mysterious anticipation the great Sacrifice is already realized.

Now what the Last Supper anticipated, Holy Mass will perpetuate, this Mass which the apostles and their successors will celebrate in obedience to the order Christ gave to them that day : " Do this for a commemoration of me." . . . " As often as you shall eat this bread and drink the chalice, you shall show the death of the Lord until He come," wrote St. Paul to the Corinthians some fifteen years later. Even as Jesus, on the last evening of His life, brought His disciples into the presence of the redemptive sacrifice to be consummated on the morrow, so the eucharistic consecration has brought the Corinthians and the Christians of all times into the presence of that self-same sacrifice.

The Mass, like the Last Supper, raises us to the summit of Calvary. The Priest is the same, at the Last Supper, on the Cross, in our churches. He is Jesus in person. The figure we see at the altar is only His minister. Qualified by virtue of his holy orders to serve Christ, he lends Him his spirit, his voice, his hands. Everything takes place as at the Last Supper. *Gratias agamus Domino Deo nostro.* And the prayer of thanksgiving which gave the Eucharist its name is prolonged. Over the bread and the wine which we have brought to the altar, solemn words are pronounced. By whom ? By the man we pass in the street and whom we address as Father So and So ? . . . Yes, but in reality by Jesus Who speaks through his lips and Who makes of our bread and wine His own Body and Blood.

Our Lord, truly present upon our altar under these appearances of an immolated victim, continues thus the self-same act of love which was so eloquently manifested by His death upon the Cross. From the heights of eternity God views in a single comprehensive glance the humble sacrifice of the Mass which we are attending and the sacrifice in which His Son actually died, and He applies to our souls the merits that Jesus earned, once for all, for the whole of humanity.

But that is only provided we assist in spirit and not

merely in body at this Mass, that we are attentive and that we devoutly follow to the altar the priest who mounts up to it in our name. When he offers the bread and the wine, let us not forget that they represent our life ; our whole soul must pass into that offering, and then, when Jesus takes the place of our poor symbolic offering, our soul will be caught up by Him, with Him and in Him— the whole forming one single homage, magnified and splendid, truly worthy of God and accepted by Him.

Our saints were conversant with these mysteries. Blessed Marcolino, whose life had become one unbroken prayer, and who was continually absorbed in God, only came back to himself to hear the bell at the moment of the consecration. Then he would run forward and prostrate himself before the Holy Sacrament. Our Father St. Dominic was wont to shed copious tears from the consecration to the communion. The Friars who served his Mass often saw them streaming down the sides of the sacred vessels. " One tear did not wait for the next." No less manly than he, St. Thomas and St. Vincent Ferrer also wept when they celebrated Mass.

At a period when " priests and religious were not accustomed to say their Mass daily, St. Dominic, out of devotion, had already adopted the practice of daily celebration. He remained faithful to it even when he was travelling, and we know that he must have encouraged this holy custom in others, because in 1221 he obtained from the Pope permission for his Friars to celebrate upon a portable altar. The founder of the Preachers thus contributed very effectually towards the introduction into the Church of the use of daily Mass." [1]

If our health, or the duties of our station, makes it impossible for us to go to church each morning, our heart ought at least to go there in spirit when we hear the sound of the bell which announces that the divine

[1] Petitot, *Vie de St. Dominique*, p. 461.

mystery is taking place. But whenever we possibly can, even at the price of rising half an hour earlier, we ought not to miss attendance at the Holy Sacrifice which will give our whole day its religious setting. If the opportunity presents itself, let us emulate the eagerness of the early Friars to serve Mass. " Everyone sought the honour of serving the celebrant," said Gerard de Frachet. St. Thomas himself liked to make his thanksgiving by serving another Mass.

When we are present in a body at Mass on the day of our monthly meeting, it is very important for us all to take part in the holy liturgy. How can we stand there as simple spectators when we are all actors in the great drama ? The sacrifice is not merely that of the priest : it is also ours. *Orate, fratres, ut meum ac vestrum sacrificium.* . . . We are no longer catechumens. Our baptismal character qualifies us to unite ourselves to the sacred minister so as to be offered by him as well as offering ourselves. It is eminently desirable that in token of our participation we should take part in the preliminary *Confiteor* and in all the responses that occur during the Mass ; that we should recite with the priest the *Gloria*, the *Credo*, the *Sanctus* and the *Agnus Dei*. All together as members of the same Fraternity, in communion with the Blessed Virgin, St. Dominic and all our saints, particularly those commemorated on that day, *communicantes et memoriam venerantes*, let us suffer ourselves to be caught up by Our Saviour, in Him and with Him into the most sublime movement of religion and of the love of God which could ever be conceived.

Then, after our eucharistic communion has set its seal upon this holy liturgy, we shall go forth to our duties which will be, as it were, an extension of our Mass. With regard to this detail and that of our lives, we must ask ourselves : " Can I, who have participated in the Holy Sacrifice, allow myself *this* ? . . . No ! Then let it be excluded from my life. But ought not *that* to come in somewhere ? Yes, because it is a sacrifice which Christ

Jesus wishes to unite to His and to transform, even as the drop of water fallen into the wine has become wine, and the wine itself has become the blood of Jesus Himself."

Although we may not be called, as so many of our brethren were called in the past, to shed our blood for Christ, we can at least offer it up day after day, and drop by drop. Gerard de Frachet tells of a Friar who, when he was accompanying St. Peter of Verona on one of his preaching tours, asked him to teach him a prayer. " I will tell you the one that I like best and that appeals to me most," was the reply. " Whenever I elevate the Body of Christ, or see It elevated by another priest, I implore the Saviour never to allow me to die otherwise than for the faith. That has always been my prayer."

II. THE OFFICE AS THE OUTCOME OF THE MASS

The Mass is the centre of Catholic worship. There was once a time when it comprised in itself the whole of that worship. Nowadays it dominates and gathers round it the several parts of our Office.

It would be interesting to trace, in the early history of the Church, the movement towards concentrating the liturgy which is condensed in the Mass, and then to follow through the centuries the evolution of the various canonical hours, which are separate from the Mass, but which gravitate round it. A short summary of this history may serve to help our Tertiaries to understand our Office and to recite it well.

The early Christians of Jerusalem continued for some time to attend the Temple at the official hours of prayer in the morning, at the third hour, at mid-day, which was the sixth, and again in the evening at the ninth hour. Like all pious Israelites when away from the Holy City, like Daniel for instance during his exile at Babylon, they still climbed to their upper rooms to pray at the same hours. So we see St. Peter at prayer one

day at the sixth hour on the terrace of Simon the tanner
at Joppa. Surely new thoughts filled his mind. Was
not this the hour when Jesus was crucified, was not *None*
the hour of His death? Had not the Holy Spirit
descended at the ninth hour? Soon the *Didache* would
enjoin the recitation of the *Pater* three times a' day.

The Jews dispersed over the world used also to gather
together in the synagogues, especially on the Sabbath
day. One meeting took place in the morning and the
other in the evening. Of these, the morning assembly
was much the more important. There was no sacrifice,
no oblation ; sacrifice took place only in the one temple,
but psalms were sung, there were readings from Holy
Scripture with comments, and there were prayers.
Jesus had taken part in such gatherings at Nazareth.
St. Paul attended them in order to preach the gospel.
The stubborn opposition of the majority of the Jews,
however, soon obliged him to desist.

Then the Christians began to assemble in the house
of one of their number to assist at the celebration of their
liturgy. It was a liturgy similar to that of the Jews.
But the psalms selected were mainly those that referred
to the Saviour, and new hymns were added. To the
books of the Old Testament were gradually added new
writings of which the apostles of Jesus Christ were the
authors, and these were read no less religiously. The
comments were inspired by the spirit of the Saviour.
The *Pater* was the usual prayer.

But there was one rite which was special to the Christians, a rite which was to become the kernel of all their
liturgy. It consisted of reproducing the sacred gestures
Our Lord had made at the Last Supper : of taking
bread, of blessing it and breaking it while repeating the
actual words of Jesus. At Jerusalem, we read in the
early chapters of the Acts of the Apostles, this *breaking
of bread* took place in the evening at certain private houses.

For the adherents of Christianity throughout the world
this was the great ceremony of the Sabbath Day. Whereas

with the Jews the morning assembly had always been the
more important, amongst the Christians the vesperal
gathering, which was that of the eucharistic rite, was
naturally more frequented.   Soon, for various reasons,
it became the only one attended.

Did this entail the disappearance of the other service ?
No, because it was united to the Eucharistic Feast which,
in any case, required special preparation.   On the other
hand, the actual meal, which lent itself to the abuses St.
Paul had already denounced, was eliminated altogether.
The table was now nothing but an altar.   Those who
gathered round it sang psalms and prayed whilst they
waited for the oblation.   This is the origin of the first
part of the Mass, formerly called the Mass of the Catechumens which, although in our Dominican rite welded
to the rest by the initial presentation of the bread and
wine, still remains quite distinct from the Holy Sacrifice.
As a rule the meeting lasted on well into the night so
as to commemorate more adequately the Saviour's
resurrection, and the eucharistic rite consequently passed
from the Sabbath to the morrow, which was called the
Lord's Day.   These all-night vigils were continued for
a long time on certain anniversaries, but the faithful
very soon contented themselves usually with assembling
before dawn.

Thus the first part of the Mass is actually that Office
abbreviated and it is obligatory on every Christian each
Sunday morning.   If it is a mortal sin to miss the
Holy Sacrifice by arriving at Church after the Offertory,
it is no negligible sin, venial though it be, to arrive too
late to take part in the epistle and gospel and in the preparatory prayers.

We now pass on to see how the Office developed from
and round the Mass.   After the Roman persecutions
were over, when magnificent basilicas arose, fervent
souls banded themselves together to partake more regularly

in the Lord's vigil and to make the watch a nightly one. In the churches lay people of good will, " ascetics " and " virgins," assembled during the night, and clerics directed the prayers and psalms. From the fifth century onwards, provision was made for the recitation of the entire psalter during the course of the week. We may notice, incidentally, that at a later date the same provision would be made by members of the Holy Rosary Confraternity for the recitation (spread over the week) of the whole psalter of Our Lady, that is to say, the 150 *Hail Marys* in decades.

The first cock-crow was the signal for Matins, and at sunrise the divine praises of Lauds were intoned. At nightfall, when the evening star began to shine, there was another Office—Vespers or *Lucernaria*. The monks in their monasteries also assembled at Terce, Sext and None. Finally, it was in the monasteries that the Offices of Prime and Compline were first instituted. Prime, the prayer on rising and previous to the distribution of work ; Compline the recommendation of the soul to God before the repose of night. Thus did the Church realize the Psalmist's words : " Seven times a day I have given praise to Thee."

The second half of the seventh century saw the beginning of the practice of adding the Office of Our Lady to the ordinary daily Office.[1] It was framed on the same pattern, and both Offices in their different hours bear a striking resemblance to the first part of the Mass.

In Matins particularly may be detected all the elements of the ancient vigil of the eucharistic service of which the preliminary part of the Mass is an epitome. We find the psalm singing, the readings from the Old and New Testaments, the homily, the responses and finally the *Te Deum*—an act of thanksgiving, like the preface and the canon of the Mass. Only the consecration is missing. The prayer which concludes each Office also carries us

---

[1] Lavocat, *Le Petit Office de la Sainte Vièrge* in *l'Année Dominicaine*, May, 1933.

back to the eucharistic prayer, because it also is offered to the Father through Jesus Christ Our Lord in the unity of the Holy Spirit.

The Dominican religious, men and women, after they had risen for Matins, proceeded to say the Office of Our Lady, and they completed Compline at night in the same way, ending with the *Salve Regina*. On Sundays and feast days, and daily throughout Advent and Lent, the Tertiaries liked to come to the Priory churches to assist at this Office. But their own special Office consisted in the daily recitation of *Paters* and *Aves* at the canonical hours. Seeing that most of them were illiterate, it was the best they could do.

In order to prevent any loss of the precious time required for study, St. Dominic, according to Blessed Humbert de Romans, directed that the Matins of Our Lady should be said by the Friars when they were dressing. Study has become even more intense, more prolonged, and exterior activities make all the greater call on our time, because apostolic vocations are fewer in number ; Pius XI has, therefore, suppressed, even for us, the obligation of the daily recitation of the Office of Our Lady which had been discontinued by the secular clergy several centuries earlier.

We can console ourselves by the thought that the intellectual level has risen amongst our Tertiaries, and most of them recite the Office of Our Lady in preference to the original *Paters* and *Aves*. This is actually required by the Rule in many of the congregations of the Third Order. The consciousness that they are supplying the place of the Fathers in this function should act as an encouragement and as an incentive to perseverance. And thus, thanks to our Tertiaries, the Order remains faithful to the ancient practice of supplementing the Great Office by the Little Office of Our Lady, its august Patron. This remains exactly the same as when it was recited by the early Friars Preachers. One detail proves it. The *Ave Maria* at the beginning and end of each hour does not close with the *Sancta Maria*, etc., which was introduced at a later date and which appears in the Roman liturgy.

May our Tertiaries, as well as ourselves, be ever on the alert to keep the whole Office in close relation to the Mass. May they make of it a framework for the Holy Sacrifice. The various canonical hours divide the day. Matins, Lauds, Prime and Terce gradually prepare the soul for the Mass. Sext, None, Vespers and Compline should be, as it were, its extension. In religious houses all the Office is recited'round about the altar. If that is impossible for us, may we at least upraise our heart and thought to the Tabernacle, and the course of the hours helps us, when we communicate, to place ourselves at the disposal of the Incarnate Word, our Sovereign Priest, our Saving Victim, Who offers Himself for us in the Holy Sacrifice and Who communicates Himself to us in order to draw us wholly into His religion.

To reward St. Catherine of Siena for dwelling continually on thoughts of this kind, and to encourage her to steep herself in them more and more, Jesus used sometimes to appear to her in visible form to repeat the canonical hours with her. . . .

III. THE EXCELLENCE OF OUR OFFICE

We say " Our Office," and our use of the term is a recognition that it takes precedence of all our other functions. It is pre-eminently our Office, our duty.

Sometimes it is called " the holy Office " because, whereas all our other activities, however important, are more or less worldly (though they must be turned to the glory of God), this is essentially an act of divine praise.

It is even described as " the divine Office." And, in point of fact, our Office *is* divine. In it God is the object which occupies our spirit and heart. A divine occupation indeed ! God Himself does nothing greater than to contemplate and love Himself. The creation

and government of the world is as nothing to Him in
comparison with this act which constitutes from all
eternity His intimate life. So also, be it said, the execution of the noblest masterpiece of human art or the
greatest work for the civilization of the world is little to
us as compared with this magnificent exercise of our
faculties. We can aspire to nothing higher than to
attach ourselves to God by our thought and by our
love.

That can, of course, be done apart from the Office.
But nowhere can we do it better than in our Office.
Because at that time we are not left to our personal
efforts, to our poor human speech. It is the very Spirit
of God Who enters into our soul and uses it as an instrument well attuned by baptism for that divine worship ;
it is the very Spirit of God Who passes through our lips
to sound the divine praises.

The spirit of God found, in the midst of the ages, the
perfect instrument for divine praise in the humanity of
the Saviour Jesus. David, whom our saints loved so
much and who was so often associated with Our Lord
in the spiritual espousals and other favours granted to
our women saints, David was but the figure of Christ
when he expressed in his psalms the various sentiments
of his soul. Thus Our Lord appropriated them from His
childhood at Nazareth. He was pleased when He heard
them well rendered in the Temple. At the Last Supper
He sang the psalms of the *Hallel.* And the supreme
words He uttered on the Cross were those of the psalm
Deus, Deus meus, which His soul must have continued in
silence, and which expressed His state of crucified dereliction as perfectly as though David had actually seen Him
dying in that agony.

Incorporated in Jesus by the sacramental character
which enables us to take part in the worship He renders
to God, we derive from the eucharistic communion the
grace to do so more and more worthily. If we cannot
daily assemble in church like our conventual brothers

and sisters, let us at least in spirit repair to the altar on which the sacrifice of Calvary is renewed each morning, and in union with Him Who is the Head of our choir, and with the same intention as His, let us celebrate the divine praise.

Some of the psalms are applicable only to Him, and we repeat them as in Him, lending Him our voice, as the priest does in the eucharistic consecration. There are many more which apply only to us ; but He says them with us, He Who is the Head of us all, Who instils His Spirit into His members and Who identifies them with Himself.

A priest who was an honour to our Third Order, the spiritual son of Mother Agnes Langeac, M. Olier, composed some beautiful devotions for the Holy Office from which I extract the following passages : " Oh, my God, Whose pleasure and delight is in our Saviour Jesus Christ, Who Himself alone, by virtue of Thy Holy Spirit by Whom he has been filled, renders to Thee all the honour and all the praise ever rendered to Thee by the holy prophets, the patriarchs, the apostles and their disciples, by the angels in heaven and the saints on earth ; express in our soul and throughout the Church that which He alone perfectly renders to Thee in Heaven. May the Church, O my Saviour, Jesus, unfold that which Thou didst enclose within Thyself and may she express outside herself that divine religion which Thou hast for Thy Father in the secrecy of Thy heart, in heaven and upon our altars." [1]

The whole Church owes to God its tribute of praise, and stands in need of addressing its supplications to Him. But how few of the faithful take their part in accomplishing that great duty. Most of them, even if they think of it, have very little leisure for it. And therefore a certain number of persons, chosen from their midst, are set free

---

[1] Olier, *La Journée Chrétienne*, 1st part.

from ordinary human cares and are solemnly consecrated for this purpose. They represent the whole Church before God.

We are amongst them, we members of the Order of St. Dominic. Our nuns, like the Fathers, live under the canonical rule of St. Augustine. " Our enclosed nuns who," Fr. Lemonnyer tells us, " are really canonesses, are specially deputed by the Church to celebrate the divine Office in choir." [1] But the Tertiaries? The Tertiaries must as far as possible participate in the spirit of the Order. St. Catherine of Siena, as we know, delighted in the recitation of the canonical hours. For unlettered Tertiaries a fixed number of *Paters* formerly took the place of the ecclesiastical Office. We have seen that the Office of the Holy Virgin was more than that ; it was really a part of the great Office. The First and Second Orders were until recently obliged to say it, and now it is the Third Order which voluntarily undertakes it. St. Catherine of Siena liked to associate herself with the Friars of San Domenico ; she also liked to rise at night and begin her prayers when theirs were over and they were taking their rest.

Virum canonicum auget in apostolicum, says the Church, referring to our Blessed Father St. Dominic. He became an apostle whilst remaining a canon. That is the twofold spirit of his Order. And the apostolate to which the Friars Preachers consecrate themselves is an additional reason for taking part in the Church's great prayer. Once it has been realized how greatly prayer is required to ensure the real success of preaching, it can be understood why St. Dominic insisted, in spite of all difficulties, upon retaining the Choral Office as obligatory for the Preachers, and also why he charged the Sisters to collaborate in the Friars' apostolate by the use of the same Office. It was the apostolic intention of their prayers which earned for them the name of Sisters Preachers. Tertiaries, who are also entitled to the name, are called

[1] Appendix to G. Lorber, *Les Filles de la Croix*, p. 234.

upon to assist the work of preaching by contributing their Office of prayer.

And, therefore, even if we should happen to be isolated in the recitation of our Office, that Office renders a public service. The Order and the whole Church praise and pray through our lips. "Lord," we may say, like the priest at the altar, "Regard not my sins but the faith of Thy Church of which I am the interpreter."

Let us strive to discharge our Office worthily, attentively and devoutly, in accordance with the prayer we are advised to say as a preliminary, *digne, attente ac devote.*

"Worthily," that is to say, in an attitude of great respect before the presence of the Majesty of God. How carefully that attitude has been regulated by the Dominican ceremonial. Turn by turn we kneel, we stand, we sit, we rise, we bow, profoundly or not, at the name of the Holy Trinity, of Jesus, of Mary, of Dominic. We make the pauses in the middle of the verses. These rules must be observed in the recitation of the Office in choir. But it is also desirable to follow the example of Bl. Raymund and to conform to them in private.

"Attentively" : let us be as attentive as possible to the meaning of the words we are uttering. "Reflect in your hearts upon what your mouth is saying," St. Augustine enjoins in his Rule. "Above all things let us pay attention to God Whom we are addressing," says St. Thomas.[1] We must beware of resembling those sacristans spoken of by Blessed Jordan of Saxony, who are so accustomed to passing in front of the altar that they end by ceasing to notice it. Let us recollect ourselves at suitable places, particularly at the *Glorias* and at those versicles which specially appeal to us. Blessed Osanna of Mantua, whose letters show an exceptional familiarity with Holy

[1] IIa IIae, q. 83, a. 13.

Scripture, derived it mainly from the liturgical Office upon which she nourished her soul.

Whilst on this subject I might also add that it is quite permissible to use a vernacular translation which has been approved by legitimate authority.

" Worthily " : because even more important than an attentive mind is a fervent heart and a will intent upon giving homage to God. It is told in the *Lives of the Brethren* that one of them saw and heard the Holy Virgin call to order some brothers who were prefunctorily reciting Matins. " *Fortiter ! fortiter !* " she was saying. " Louder, with more vigour ! " Venerable Mother Antoinette de Ste-Croix (*d.* 1619), a nun of the Convent of St. Catherine which Fr. Michaelis founded at Toulouse, was so zealous, all her life, in singing the praises of God that little surprise was felt when, several years after her death, her tongue was found to be as fresh and incorrupt as if she had just died. God showed by this marvel how well pleased He was with the devotion of this sister.

If it is thus properly recited, our Office furnishes us with an ideal means of moral progress. This is obvious, once its great meritorious value is realized. Is it not an excellent exercise in the love of God and consequently a source of life for all the moral virtues which charity inspires ? It has also immense impetrative efficacy in obtaining for us, day after day, the actual graces which prompt our good efforts, sustain them and enable them to succeed. Finally, I would point out one special and very valuable aid which comes to us incidentally through the Office in conjunction with Holy Mass. With Jesus in the Mass, with Mary in the Office, with the saints whom we commemorate daily in the Office and in the Mass, we are moving in an exalted circle in which we are less inclined to sin, and find it more easy to practise virtue.

Charles Péguy is said to have dreamt of a grand poem which he did not live to work out. A man under great temptation was about to write a letter with felonious intent. But his calendar, which he consulted for the date, showed it to be the feast of a great saint, and he could not bring himself to dishonour it by such a wicked deed. The morrow was the festival of another saint— equally prohibitive. And so it went on. . . . Without ever departing from our Dominican calendar, we shall find entered, under every day of the year, the names of holy men and women who will help us by their example and words if we know something about their lives and are ready to listen to the lessons they teach. " What is that book that you always carry about with you ? " Blessed Francis de Capillas was asked by the mandarin who was to preside over his execution, and who wished to know from what source the confessor of the faith derived his strength. " Read us something from it." Francis opened it at random and came upon the martyrdom of St. Catherine of Alexandria, one of the patrons of our Order. He was himself shortly afterwards to write with his blood a new page of our breviary, and the first in the martyrology of China.

The spirituality, which our Office preaches to us daily, is presented under an aspect which is far from being unattractive. For those endowed with a sense of appre-ciation there is incomparable beauty in the religious poems selected, as well as in the series of praises and supplications which recall the sublime colloquies between God, Jesus or Mary and the great souls who are the glory of humanity.

The lyric beauty of the psalms has never been sur-passed. Even in the sometimes faulty Latin transla-tion they preserve their essential value and even their rhythm, because this depends mainly upon ideas, senti-ments and figures which reverberate in parallel passages and which re-echo almost like rhymes. Moreover, their choral recitation, as a general rule, accentuates and increases the charm of those parallels.

Although the hymns of the Office of the Blessed Virgin do not mark the various hours with the same precision as those of the Great Office, the successive parts of the Little Office correspond with the different periods of the day and night, and, when they are recited with care at their proper times, they bear out the saying of the Wise Man : " Like a golden fruit on a silver dish is a good word spoken in season."

THIRD SECTION

THE SEQUENCE OF THE HOURS

I. THE NIGHT OFFICE

NIGHT has fallen. It is the hour for rest after all the labours of the day. The faithful who have attended Compline in the priory churches or who have joined in it from afar by their evening prayer have been able to address the last psalm of the liturgy of the day to those who have been officially charged by the Church with canonical prayer : " *Ecce nunc benedicite Dominum :* it is for you to continue to bless the Lord. You who remain in the house of our God, during the night lift up your hands in the sanctuary and bless the Lord."

So the religious, both men and women, will be praying in the place of all those who take advantage of the night to rest in unconsciousness and in forgetfulness of God, not to mention those who make evil use of the night to offend Him.

Some of our houses rise punctually at midnight and carry out quite literally the Psalmist's words : *Media nocte surgebam ad confitendum nomini tuo :* " in the middle of the night I rose to praise Thy name, O Lord." Others betake themselves to the choir at two or three o'clock in the morning. Père Lacordaire preferred to fix the night Office for four o'clock, and to follow it at daybreak by Lauds—which was quite in keeping with ancient Christian tradition. In many convents, on the other hand, the times for Matins and Lauds are taken from the early hours of the night rest.

Tertiaries like to feel that they are associated with their brothers and sisters who are praying in this way at one or other of these night hours.

Darkness shrouds the earth. Man is naturally liable to be seized with secret fear. He feels more conscious of his weakness. He stands there alone, encompassed by mysterious powers which might silently crush him. Instinctively he takes refuge in the thought of the Creator Who holds in His hands all the forces of the world. The psalm *Venite exultemus* invites us to put our trust in the all powerful good God Who guides our life and at the same time sternly forbids any lack of faith in Him. If we gave way to distrust we should be punished like the Jews who were not allowed to enter the Promised Land : we should fail to accomplish our eternal destiny.

At that hour the soul is more readily uplifted to God, because the darkness and silence seem to efface the reality of those wretched showy and noisy things which crowd our horizon during the day. As we raise our eyes at night to the boundless heavens we are borne into the presence of Him Who alone exists. " The Heavens show forth the glory of God," says one of the psalms we are about to recite. They proclaim it during the day in a thousand singing voices : they repeat it in undertones at night—night, that time so dear to contemplative souls, when the divine secrets can best be whispered to the ears of the heart.

Another of the psalms of our Matins is the one which is pre-eminently the psalm of the night. David, who was a shepherd and had often kept watch over his sheep, exclaimed :

> " I will behold the heavens, the work of Thy fingers,
> The moon and the stars which Thou hast founded,
> O what is man that Thou art mindful of him,
> Or the son of man that Thou visitest him ? "

Our Saviour also appreciated the religious atmosphere of the night. In the evening He would climb to the hill-tops, as though desirous of drawing nearer to His Father. A symbolical Ascension indeed. Let us rise up to the spiritual summit of our soul and let us unite ourselves to the Christ, either in His prayer during his transfiguration on Mount Thabor, or in that other prayer during His abjection on the Mount of Olives. Let us share His intention of glorifying the Heavenly Father of infinite holiness even whilst crying for mercy upon the sinful world. *Domine, in unione illius divinae intentionis qua Ipse in terris laudes Deo persolvisti, has tibi horas persolvo.*

After the versicles, which serve as introduction to our Office, we bow deeply as we say *Gloria Patri et Filio et Spiritui Sancto.* Here, at the very beginning, the aim of our divine Office is set before our eyes. In order that it may remain ever in our view, the *Gloria* will recur periodically, especially at the end of every psalm. These will be the best moments for renewing our intention and, if necessary, for rousing our souls. It is stated in the life of Blessed Bartholomew of the Martyrs that whenever he repeated the *Gloria* his soul was so enraptured with fervour and joy that the expression of his face was completely transformed.

After the *Gloria* comes the Invitatory, which sets forth the immediate object of our adoration and of our praises— *Regem Virginis Filium.* . . . The King, the Virgin's Son, come and adore Him ! Even if we are alone in our room we still form part of an invisible choir made up of all our brothers and sisters, and we exhort one another to render homage to the Incarnate Word in Mary's womb.

The psalm *Venite exultemus* has been chosen to develop the Invitatory. But this Invitatory, which is repeated after each strophe like the chorus of a song, gives the psalm a new meaning which makes it specially applicable to our Office. Its *rôle* is to inspire us, in its first half, with a great desire to praise God worthily, and in its second part with apprehension lest we abuse divine grace by performing our sacred function with indifference. Dissipated hearts will not enter the place of divine repose of which our psalm speaks. They will not be gratified by that mystical union which is upon earth a foretaste of Heaven.

The Office hymn usually deals with the mystery that is being celebrated, and which the Invitatory has summed up in a short formula. Our hymn, in a series of antitheses, fixes the attention of our spirit and the affections of our heart upon the Incarnation of Almighty God in the womb of the humble Virgin Mary.

> " O happy Mother that thou art
> Close underneath thy beating heart,
> Lies Thy Creator-God Who plann'd
> The world He holds within His hand."

The three psalms which form the nucleus of our Matins are borrowed from the first nocturn of the Great Office of the Blessed Virgin. In the Roman rite those of the second and third are similarly used. Three by three, they are spread out over the week. If we are tempted to regret the absence from our Dominican Little Office of the psalm *Eructavit*, which is so specially applicable to the Blessed Virgin Mary, we may nevertheless rejoice that our Matins involve the daily repetition of these three psalms which are amongst the most beautiful in the Psalter.

The first sings of Almighty God, Who made man the King of creation. The second one also praises the Lord, but this time as having produced the sun which gives light to the material world, and as giving to men His holy Law which illuminates souls. The last psalm likewise has a twofold theme : it sets forth the qualities demanded of those convened to meet God in His holy temple, and it celebrates God's triumphal entry into that same temple. In Jerusalem it was a processional psalm. Two choirs sang alternate passages as they climbed the slopes of Moriah and then passed from the outside to the inside of the Temple, in the same manner that the Palm Sunday procession enters our churches to-day.[1]

[1] My remarks are but a summary of Fr. Hugueny's commentaries in his *Psaumes et cantiques de l'Office de la Sainte Vièrge.*

Besides this literal sense, our three psalms admit of a spiritual meaning. For the realities signified by the letter are also symbols of higher realities, which the Holy Spirit had in view when He inspired the sacred writer. He tells us so elsewhere in Holy Scripture, and through the voice of the Church.

Man, whom God had established as King of the world, suffered a fall. But a new Adam came in the person of Jesus Christ. As is said in the Epistle to the Hebrews, He humbled Himself and was made for a time a little lower than the angels. In the garden of Olivet, at the very hour at which we are praying, an angel will come to comfort Him. But once His Passion is ended, He is crowned with glory and honour, everything is in subjection under His feet for ever. It is through Him that, despite our fall, we become capable of directing the world. All things are ours, and all will work for our good if we are Christ's. Most heartily indeed ought we to take up the burden of that magnificent song : " O Lord, our Lord : how admirable is Thy Name in all the earth ! "

According to the Church's interpretation in the Christmas liturgy, it is Jesus Who is symbolized by the sun in the next psalm. He comes forth like a bridegroom out of His chamber, that Virgin womb in which He espoused our nature, and the whole of humanity has the benefit of the beams of His light and His strength.

The last psalm also has a mystical sense. It celebrates Our Lord's triumphal entry into Heaven indeed, but primarily His entry into our heart, where celestial glory is inaugurated by grace. The doors through which He enters are the intelligence and the will. Let them be flung open in faith, in trust and in love, before the King of Glory Who has vanquished the powers of evil ! Let us try to fulfil those conditions of purity which God attaches to His spiritual favours.

When the psalms are finished, we turn to the Blessed

Virgin. By the fact of becoming the Mother of the
Saviour she has become also Mother of grace, *Maria
mater gratiae.* She is, therefore, our Mother in the spiritual
life. In us, as members of Christ, she continues to collaborate in the development of the life which began in
her maternal womb on the day of the Annunciation.

The rest of the Office is simply a series of praises and
prayers to the divine Mother. It is simple, it is filial,
it touches our hearts and hers. The lessons are couched
in particularly affectionate and endearing terms, and as
children of Mary we take pleasure in the little tuneful
verses.

It is brought to an end by the *Te Deum,* which was
probably originally a form of thanksgiving accompanying
the consecration of the Eucharist, corresponding in some
sense to what we now call the Preface and the Canon of
the Mass. As we know, the Canon was not always invariable. This *Te Deum* takes us back to the early centuries
of the Church when the Christians terminated, by the
breaking of bread, the liturgical vigil which was the
foundation of our night Office. They were accused of
being a people who shunned the light. But we know,
as they knew, that a higher light shines for our souls
during those night hours which foster recollection.

Matins ought to be for us a kind of spiritual Mass—our
evening Mass—which foreshadows and prepares us for
our morning Mass.

II. MORNING LAUDS

It has become usual to unite Matins and Lauds to
form one single night Office, and the Rule of our Third
Order says that this Office may be recited either in the
evening or in the morning. The evening is more suitable
for Matins, morning seems more fitting for Lauds.
But it is permissible to separate them, and after having
said Matins before going to bed to defer Lauds until the
following morning. Pius X, who authorized this separation, has stipulated, in his reform of the breviary, that

in those circumstances Matins must be concluded by the prayer of Lauds.

In former times when, for one reason or another, Matins ended before daybreak, the custom prevailed of awaiting sunrise before beginning Lauds. This is a point in the Rule of St. Benedict (Chapter VIII) which found ample justification in the long winter nights. St. John Chrysostom, at a much earlier period, had already commended the ascetics and virgins who, though they were living in the world, used to meet in church for the holy vigil, at the first cock crow. " They praise God with the angels, yes, with the angels, whilst we, men of the world, are still resting or, if half awake, are thinking only of our own paltry plans. They do not retire to rest until daybreak, and no sooner does the sun rise than they return to their prayers and say their morning Lauds." [1]

The note for this Office is given by the opening words (at least in the Latin text) of one of its psalms : " *Deus, Deus meus, ad te de luce vigilo.*" O God, my God, to Thee do I watch at break of day. That is the sentence we shall want to say as an ejaculatory prayer when we awake from sleep. We shall linger over it with relish to prepare ourselves for repeating it with heartfelt fervour when it comes in the Office.

In the Great Office, since the revision of Pius X, the psalms of Lauds vary from day to day. In the Little Office of Our Lady we always recite the psalms which, before that reform, had become practically of daily use in the Great Office, but which now are only the psalms of Sunday Lauds. If there are advantages in thus varying the daily round, yet it would be difficult to find for each separate day a selection of psalms so well suited as our own to the offering of praise to God. A little consideration of them will convince us of this.

[1] St. John Chrysostom, *Homily XIV* on 1 Tim. iv.

Night is over. The pious soul awakes with the first streak of daylight.

She becomes aware of all the creatures about her as well as the Creator Who made them, Who is always renewing them. She feels herself revived through the action of Him Who never sleeps. All through the night God has watched over her and He has, in a sense, re-created her.

What this great work actually is has been fully apprehended by only one human soul. It was the soul of Jesus as he entered the world—*ingrediens mundum*, as St. Paul puts it. He said to His Father : " A body hast Thou given Me : lo ! I come to do Thy will." We must unite ourselves to those sentiments which were those of our Head. We must open our soul to the influence which will flow from His and we must join with Him in praising the God Who reigns above His creatures in sovereign beauty. *Dominus regnavit, decorem indutus est.*

The stability of the solid earth and the great tidal movements of the sea give us some idea of His immutability and, at the same time, of His incessant though never monotonous activity. But the Church which He has founded, and which no storm will ever overthrow, enables us to form a still better conception of His power and of His holiness.

The second psalm is a song of jubilation. The soul which has awakened quite alert and refreshed, happy in the consciousness of the presence of God, utters a cry of joy. She addresses the whole earth. *Jubilate Deo omnis terra.* The psalm consists first of three appeals to the world to rejoice, followed by three causes for that rejoicing, and then of three invitations to the world to give thanks, followed by three motives for that thanksgiving. It resembles the *Venite exultemus* at the beginning of Matins, and it plays a similar part.

We have now been brought by these two psalms into the presence of God, and have been invited to bless Him.

With the third we have the perfect expression of our

morning prayer. O God, God for Whom I was made, and Whom I may call mine. My God, how my soul seeks for Thee ! how she thirsts for Thee ! This ardent desire underlies all true prayer ; it leads us in the morning into the sanctuary to contemplate God, and to appeal to His mercy ; it enables us to continue our prayer in the midst of the activities of our daily life until the hour for rest returns at night.

Adhaesit anima mea post te. My soul cleaves to Thee. Thanks to Thee, it fears nothing.

The human soul does not stand alone. Now it calls upon all creatures to bless and praise the Lord with it. This it is which justifies the name given to this part of our Office. They really *are* Lauds. *Laudes* means *praises.* Dominican souls will do well to remember St. Rose of Lima and how, when she opened the door of her father's house to go to her hermitage in the garden, she was wont to exclaim : " Trees, plants, grasses and flowers, bless your Creator ! " Her fervour pleased the Lord, Who manifested His satisfaction by a remarkable miracle. The insensate creatures immediately began to move, and their motion expressed what they had no voices to say. The trees interlocked their boughs and the shrubs inclined their branches to the earth, as though to adore their Creator. Could we not try to recite the *Benedicite* with the fervour of St. Rose ?

Celestial bodies and creatures of the earth are called upon in turn to take part in the divine praises. We lend them a soul with which to praise the Lord, or rather we make ourselves the interpreters of those who have no soul with which to give thanks to that Creator Whom they help us to know better. But amongst the creatures there are some who are intelligent like ourselves, and others who are even better qualified than ourselves to render thanks. And we call upon these latter, the angels in Heaven, the priests on earth, the holy souls above and here below, to supplement us in the acts of thanksgiving which we address to the Lord.

No mention is made of flowers and fruit in the *Benedicite*. But now, in the little Chapter, we find the Blessed Virgin referred to as a vine, the flowers of which are always sweetly scented and produce such excellent fruit. Thus it forms a perfect completion of the *Laudate* and the *Benedicite*.

After the hymn to the heavenly Mediatrix, the *Benedictus* of St. Zachary repeats the same theme. That hymn, which the Blessed Virgin may have heard sung by the father of the Precursor, thanks the God of Israel for having fulfilled His great promises. He has sent from on high His great light, a light compared with which our rising sun counts for nought. The Messias comes to illuminate men seated until then in darkness and in the shadow of death. He leads their steps into the way of peace.

As in the hymn to the Holy Virgin, where she is spoken of as the dawn which opens the door to the sun, so also in the *Benedictus* and throughout Lauds, everything suggests the morning hour.

"And thou, O child, shalt be called the Prophet of the Most High : for thou shalt go before the face of the Lord to prepare His ways, to give to all a knowledge of the salvation which the sacred heart of our God gives us."

St. Dominic was another great precursor. Our Lord gave him the mission of preparing for His coming into the midst of the world. And it is with this thought in our minds that we commemorate him and, after him, his sons, the friar saints. Then we pray that there may always be numerous holy and zealous apostles in our Order, and that we may be the first to follow their teaching. It is also customary, between the mention of St. Dominic and of all our saints, to make a commemoration of the particular saint of our religious family whose feast day it is.

With Lauds ends that part of our Office which apper-
tains to the night, and which is more especially contemplative. The day has come with all the labours it
entails. Fortunate indeed are the Preachers whose
activities are only the overflow and the outcome of their
contemplation, and whose vocation is to reveal God to
souls in order to lead them to contemplate Him too.
Fortunate also are the Tertiaries if, faithful to the spirit
of the Order, they try to preserve at all times and in all
places the recollection and the desire of divine contemplation. Calling to mind their morning Lauds, let them
strive to make such good use of all creatures as to continue
in the midst of their various tasks the *Benedicite* which
their lips have uttered. Otherwise, instead of pæans
of joyful praise, there will go up the groans of a natural
creation violated by sinners, those groans of which the
soul of St. Paul was conscious.

In order to furnish models for our imitation, the
martyrology of the day is read at this stage in the Great
Office of the Preachers and a commemoration is made
of our own saints and blessed. Then follows the reading
of a passage from the gospel or from the Rule, which
must regulate our life as it did theirs. At Christmas a
Father even preaches a homily. This is the last legacy
of a practice which was observed on numerous feast days
in the early days of our Order.

All the saints mentioned in the martyrology led a
life which was perfectly Christian, one might even say
Dominican, and they closed it with a death precious
before God. We invoke them for help to imitate their
courage, their patience, their persevering labours ; and
then, upheld by them, we make an insistent appeal to
God for His succour, asking Him to direct from on high
the development of our activities during the coming
hours.

In these extensions of the Office which begin with
Pretiosa, the two ideas of imitation and invocations are
intermingled. In the Roman rite they are said, as by

the monks of old, after Prime. Amongst ourselves they follow Lauds.

I mention them, although they find no place in the Office of Our Lady, because our fathers used formerly after the readings and the public prayers to remain on in church in silent prayer, and our Tertiaries have now a great opportunity of entering into their spirit and of inspiring themselves with the *Pretiosa* devotions in their morning mental prayer.

III.   THE LITTLE DAY HOURS

" When the sun ariseth, man goeth forth to his work and to his labour until the evening," says one of the psalms. And Jesus Himself quoted the saying : " One must work while it is day." In olden times, the day was divided into twelve hours, which varied in length according to the season. " Are there not twelve hours in the day ? " Our Saviour also said. The sixth hour alone was invariable : it coincided with midday. The third hour corresponded approximately with nine o'clock in the morning, and the ninth with three in the afternoon.

It is to sanctify these twelve hours by interrupting our work and activities with short prayers that we are invited to come back to the Holy Office every three hours. Those hallowed moments are the first hour of the day (Prime), the third (Terce), the sixth (Sext), and the ninth (None). Three psalms are recited every time as though to sanctify each of the hours ushered in by that portion of the Office. All these psalms belong to the series known as " gradual," because they were the psalms of ascent, short and beautiful songs, which the pilgrims of Bible times used to sing as they climbed the roads which led up to Jerusalem.

Pilgrims on earth are we all, travelling towards the heavenly Jerusalem. Our fathers were very fond of those gradual psalms, and used to recite them even on the days when the Little Office of Our Lady was omitted. In our Dominican rite we have them all, and we start them at Prime ; the Roman rite, on the other hand, does not begin them until Terce, and consequently omits three of them.

Many persons are not free to recite their Office at intervals of exactly three hours. Some are even compelled to say these four parts at one stretch. But all those who can, should try to separate them, and thus enter more exactly into the spirit of the Church. Take advantage of spare moments to open your little book of prayers. Think of the people you meet at home, in the street, at stations, on cars, in the office, and at the workshop, how they fling themselves upon the paper which brings them the latest news. The facts related are generally monotonous enough, being for the most part repetitions of the same old things ! Whilst they are spending their time conning the chronicle of the passing hour, withdraw your thoughts to the contemplation of eternal things. Read these three little psalms which will help you to keep your eyes fixed upon your last end, and invoke the help of your Mother in Heaven at the beginning and at the end of each section.

We are in urgent and constant need of that help, and we require to be continually taking our bearings. Even if it were only a matter of doing one ordinary piece of work in comparative seclusion . . . but actually we have to face calls, anxieties, business affairs, annoyances and distractions of all sorts. Into the very midst of these noisy hours, so crowded with ambitions, with envy, frivolities, vexations and worries, we must manage to insert a little calmness and prayer. Our soul is no longer pure and free as it was at the hour of Lauds : it has been caught up in the toils of the day and finds itself carried away into a life of agitation, it feels shaken, dissipated, tired and tempted. Let us at least seize a few moments in which to bring it back into the presence of God, and to make an appeal for the grace we need. *Deus in adjutorium meum intende.* O God, incline to my aid.

From the time he rises in the morning the Christian has to come in contact with the world, and he finds no difficulty in agreeing with the words of the Psalmist : Everywhere on earth I am in exile amongst people who do not speak my language, and who have not my spirit : everywhere I have to suffer and struggle (Ps. cxix). But whilst I go my way here below I put my trust in God Almighty Who watches over me unceasingly, and Who will preserve my soul from all evil (Ps. cxx). And I rejoice at the thought of the heavenly Jerusalem where I shall find happiness at last when my pilgrimage is ended (Ps. cxxi). That is the gist of the psalms of Prime. The hour of Terce finds us already involved in the numerous difficulties which are renewed every day. The three psalms teach us what the attitude of our soul ought to be in the midst of trial : we must lift our eyes with faith to the Heavenly Father (Ps. cxxii), we must thank Him for delivering us from the evil that was overwhelming us (Ps. cxxiii), and we must dwell with trust upon the thought that His protection builds round us an impregnable rampart (Ps. cxxiv).

The Chapter and the response lead us on to consider the Blessed Virgin as she rests above in the Holy City where she wields such marvellous power, and uses it in praying for us who invoke her aid.

Midday is the hour when we return to our homes to gather round the table for the common meal. It is also the time for Sext. Psalm cxxv, one of the gems of the Psalter, recalls the return from exile. Psalm cxxvi begins " Unless the Lord built the house, they labour in vain who build it." And Psalm cxxvii : " Blessed are all they that fear the Lord : that walk in His ways. For thou shalt eat the labours of thy hands : blessed art thou and well shall it be with thee. Thy wife shall be as a fruitful vine on the sides of thy house. Thy children as olive plants round about thy table."

It is scarcely necessary to add that these psalms are also capable of a spiritual interpretation which will gladden, with hopes of a harvest of eternal joy, hearts dedicated to virginity and souls who suffer in solitude. In their obedience to the divine will they will find the fruit of their daily efforts, and they look forward to the Father's house where we shall gather round the Mother that God has given us.   The Chapter and the Response allude to this heavenly Mother and to her large spiritual family : " God maketh her to dwell in His tabernacle.   My abode," says Mary, " is in the full assembly of the saints."

Finally, we come to None.   It is the dull, heavy hour when the burden and the heat of the day are felt.   It is also the dangerous hour when souls are tempted by what the Fathers in the desert called the noon-day demon. And we are apt to be discontented with our lot, and with our duties. We dream of other things, perhaps of pleasures which are unworthy of us, or perhaps, subtle temptation, of noble deeds that are beyond our scope.

Saepe expugnaverunt me a juventute mea !   Ah, yes, those demons have attacked me from my youth onwards ! (Ps. cxxviii).   *De profundis*, from the depths of my wretchedness, I cry to Thee Lord. . . . If Thou dost mark faults, O Lord, who can stand ? (Ps. cxxix).   O Lord, my soul is not puffed up to indulge in vain fancies. Humbly and in a childlike spirit I submit myself to Thy will, like the weaned child upon his mother's breast (Ps. cxxx).

These few notes must suffice for the exquisite psalms of the little hours.   We can ponder over them profitably with the help of a good translation.   When we are short of time it would be better to omit one or two of these hours, if the moment for saying them is past, rather than to repeat all hurriedly at one stretch, irrespective of the time and without allowing our soul to feed upon them and to digest them.

At every hour of the day the one thing necessary is to maintain union with Our Lord.   It is stated at the end

of the Gospel according to St. Mark that the disciples
went out into the world and that the Lord continued to
work with them. Each one has his task here below.
May we each perform our own with Christ's help,
realizing by His grace what He expects us to do towards
the accomplishment of the great work of Christianity.
Let us be His witnesses everywhere, " in Jerusalem, in
Judea, in Samaria and to the utmost parts of the earth."

One morning at the hour of Prime our risen Lord
appeared on the shore of the lake, and said to His
disciples who had been toiling unsuccessfully for many
hours : " Cast the net on the right side of the ship."
And the net was filled. Thanks to the help of Jesus,
given in response to prayer, our work will be productive
and will bring forth eternal fruits. Jesus had worked
hard also all His life, during the thirty years of His
hidden life, the three years of His evangelical preaching,
and the three days of His Passion. At the hour of Terce
the divine Workman of Nazareth was always busy in the
shop or in the houses of His customers. At the hour of
Sext, weary after His apostolic labours, He seated Himself one day beside a well in Samaria, and discoursed
upon heavenly things, while the disciples went in search
of food. At the hour of None He concluded in agony His
life's work. Having seen that His task was finished,
He resigned His soul into His Father's hands.

Whatever be the nature of the duty that devolves on
us, let us set ourselves to do it so well that we shall be
able to end in like manner our day and our life.

IV. VESPERS

In the early Church the Sunday Office started on Saturday evening, to be protracted in a holy vigil until the
following morning, and the custom, though confined to
the eves of great festivals, especially Easter, survived for
a long time. Our Holy Saturday Office, with the blessing
of the fire and the lighting of the great candle to illuminate the assembly, shows traces of this ancient custom.

But very soon the all-night vigil was discontinued before ordinary Sundays, as also, with even greater reason, before the other days of the week, and the first cock crow gave the signal for the commencement of the night Office.

And that is why there came into being a separate Office for the evening, at the hour when the Evening Star begins to shine, and when the lamp (*lucerna*) had to be lighted. Vespers or *lucernaria* was the name of that Office. At a later date St. Benedict set back the hour of Vespers. He wished the meal which generally followed it to be taken by daylight. Consequently the monks needed another prayer before bed-time. Thus arose Compline, the last Office, and one which is steeped in contrition for the faults of the past day. The function of Vespers, on the other hand, was to give thanks to God for all the gifts that He had vouchsafed. It corresponded with Lauds, which offered praise to God for the blessings of the night. St. Benedict, who introduced the singing of the *Benedictus* into Matins, also added the *Magnificat* to the psalms of Vespers.

Eagerness for union with Our Lord must follow us at every hour of the Office. What shall be our response to it now ? One word from the gospel occurs to us naturally, the very word to suit the occasion, *advesperascit.* " *Mane nobiscum, Domine, quoniam advesperascit.*" The day is far spent, we are at the hour of Vespers, abide with us, Lord. It was to the risen Christ that the two disciples addressed these words, when they reached the door of their home on their return from Jerusalem to their village of Emmaus.

The working day is done, the day which stands for all our toilsome life. We make our petition to the Head Who has completed His work on the Cross, and has preceded us into eternal rest ; we ask Him to abide with us, or still better we set ourselves to abide with Him. We wish to be where He is rather than to remain where we are. He is risen, He has entered into His

Father's house to enjoy His glory, and to prepare a place for us. We stir up in our hearts the hope of joining Him there at the close of our labours. And already in thought and in wish we are with Him, and with all those saints whose felicity is recalled in our Dominican liturgy in the commemoration of the Confessors (third response of Lauds). May our soul imitate them, especially at the hour of Vespers.

The first psalm to be recited is the *Dixit Dominus,* which is so familiar to us, and which begins the Vespers of Sunday and of nearly all feasts. It is often quoted in the New Testament and by Our Lord Who applied it to Himself. Christ is the Son of David, but is superior to David, who calls Him " My Lord." (The Lord said unto my Lord.) For He is the Son of God. Who has begotten Him before the dawn of the first day of the world.

After He has become the Son of David through the Incarnation, God invites Him, even as man, to take His place at His right hand in Heaven : *Sede a dextris meis.* From thence He sways the whole earth, upholding the courage of those who remain faithful to Him whilst waiting to crush His enemies. He is, therefore, King, King of all creation, as will be triumphantly manifested at the Last Judgment, when the heads of those who have risen up against the Sovereign Head will be crushed.

But He is a Priest as well as a King, even as Melchisedech, King of Jerusalem, was also a priest of the Most High. Melchisedech had offered bread and wine in sacrifice. Under those same appearances Christ offered His sacrifice at the Last Supper and still offers it through the hands of His priest.

Thus the first psalm of Vespers, like the first psalm of Lauds, sets us in the presence of the Lord, seated for ever upon His celestial throne. It is for us now to address our praise to Him. *Laudate, pueri Dominum :* praise the Lord, ye children. From sunrise to sunset, at Vespers as in the Lauds of the morning, praised be the name of the Lord ! There are two motives for this praise : His greatness and His mercy.

Knowing that Jesus sang this psalm before the Last Supper, we shall find it all the easier to say it in union with Him. God bends down to the humble to uplift them into His glory. He did so for Jesus : *Humiliavit seipsum, propter quod Deus exaltavit illum.* He has done so also for Mary, as she sings in her Magnificat. He will do it for us.

Laetatus sum. At night, in a sort of anticipation of eternal rest, we repeat the psalm which we recited in the morning to dedicate our activities to God. What a joy it is to think that we shall go into the house of the Lord ! The city of the elect is being built up around Jesus and Mary.

Nisi Dominus. Here we have again a repetition of one of the morning psalms. " Without Me, ye can do nothing," said Our Lord. It is only with the help of God that one can succeed in living aright. But how fruitful is the life of those who faithfully follow the inspirations of grace !

Another psalm of praise comes as a conclusion : *Lauda, Jerusalem, Dominum.* In the hour of success let us never forget from Whom it comes. Let us give glory to the Lord. It is He Who establishes us in security and peace, it is He Who satisfies us with the fat of corn in communion. He displays His power in the physical order by so many astonishing phenomena which are produced by His orders. He manifests it in the moral order by the commandments which He has given to His people, together with grace to observe those injunctions.

After having, in the hymn, apostrophized and petitioned the new Eve who co-operates with the divine Adam in saving us, we borrow the words of her *Magnificat* to complete our Vesper praises. May we, above all, claim

at the same time the help of her soul. The words, for
the most part, are reminiscent of certain psalms or hymns
which the Holy Virgin, like ourselves, was accustomed to
sing. But what a new spirit was instilled into the canticle
by her who was already the Mother of Christ ! She sinks
herself more deeply than ever in her humility to proclaim
that the Almighty alone has done in her the great things
which will lead all generations, after her cousin Elizabeth, to call her blessed. God alone is great : *Magnificat
anima mea Dominum.*

"What He had done for me," says Mary, "He does
for all. If He sends the proud, who think themselves
rich, empty-handed away, He overwhelms with good
things the little ones who acknowledge their poverty."

At the close of our day, especially if we are conscious
of a little progress, of having done some good, let us
establish our hearts in this humility and give thanks to
God. "It is Thou, O Lord, Who hast accomplished this
good thing in us."

V. COMPLINE

Very often we recite Compline directly after Vespers,
reserving the hour before going to bed for saying
Matins.

We have seen how St. Benedict, having changed the
time for Vespers, felt constrained to institute Compline.
When the hour for the night rest was approaching, the
monks used to assemble in a great hall for a spiritual
reading. Very often this was selected from the Conferences of Cassian (*Collationes*). A small draught of
wine or suchlike, which was taken during the reading by
those who needed it, gave rise to what is called the
collation on fast-days, and a trace of the spiritual reading
survives in the short lesson of Compline in the great
Office.

Tu autem, Domine, miserere nostri. Those were the words
with which the reader concluded, when the Abbot gave
the signal for rising. The latter said : *Adjutorium nostrum*

in nomine Domini, and Compline followed at once, beginning with the *Pater* and the *Confiteor*.

Our Dominican communities still use the same formula at the close of the collation, which is accompanied by spiritual reading, and also at the beginning of Compline of the Great Office. Because Compline of the Little Office of Our Lady used to follow on without a break, it has neither the short lesson nor yet the preamble which are to be found in the Great Office. Nevertheless, I have thought it well to mention this piece of history. It is sure to be of interest to our Tertiaries, who like to attend our Compline when they can, and who have undertaken to recite that part of the Office which is no longer incumbent upon us, viz., the Compline of Our Lady.

They, too, should endeavour, by a course of spiritual reading, to provide themselves with food, which their soul needs no less than their body. St. Thomas himself delighted in the Conferences of Cassian mentioned above. Souls who have not his knowledge of the things of God have even greater need than he of spiritual books.

Although Compline of the Little Office has not even the *Confiteor*, Tertiaries must be in the disposition that the *Confiteor* implies and puts into words. The *Converte nos, Deus*, which ushers in this part of their Office, seems to take that state of mind for granted.

Alas ! God alone, on the evening of the days of Creation, was able to pronounce that all He did had been well done. It is seldom enough that we know the ecstasy felt by a good craftsman when he has put the finishing touches to a good piece of work, the joy experienced by the good Christian when he has consistently carried out God's will all day long. We never possess it perfectly. How many have been our sins of thought, word, and action ! How many our omissions ! We must recognize it and confess it to those whom our profession obliges us specially to honour, to our Father St. Dominic, to the Blessed Virgin Mary and especially to Almighty God.

Converte nos, Deus. . . . " Turn us toward Thee, O
God our Saviour.—And turn away Thine anger."

Like the day, our life will also have its evening, prelude
to the darkness of the tomb. We have just had occasion
to realize how rapidly one passes from the Lauds of
daybreak to the hour of Sext, which marks the zenith of
the light, and then to None, when it is already sensibly
declining. Very soon afterwards we are murmuring
Compline in the dark, as a preliminary to sleep. Similarly, from childhood to maturity, and then to decrepi-
tude and death, how short is our life ! Each one of us
can be sure that death is near, and with it the terrible
judgment which will suddenly decide our future life.
St. Lewis Bertrand always trembled at this thought.
Following his example, let us each night sorrow for our
sins, but also put our trust in God Who wishes to save us.
Deus salutaris noster. In short, let us set our souls in the
disposition in which we should wish to be found at our
last hour. Let us make of our daily Compline a preparation not only for this night's sleep, but also for our
eternal rest.

The Compline of Our Lady does not contain the
pathetic tones of the *Miserere mei Domine* which is such a
perfect expression of compunction, nor yet that noble
act of surrender to Providence, the psalm *Qui habitat*
which St. Basil selected for the evening prayer of his
monks, and which was the first nucleus of Compline.
In the Great Office it is sung on Sundays and feast days.
Compline of the Little Office in the Dominican rite is
made up of the last three gradual psalms. The first
one reminds the pilgrims to Jerusalem of David's vow
and prayer concerning the temple he wished to erect to
God, and also of the response vouchsafed by God, Who
blessed the vow and marvellously rewarded the prayer
by the promise of the Messias. This psalm lends itself
to many interpretations : it can be applied to the sanc-

tuary of our soul, to our stone temples enclosing the
eucharistic tabernacle, to the Catholic Church which is
built of living stones, and which will find its magnificent
consummation in Heaven. We shall also wish to apply
it to the Order of St. Dominic, our family chapel in the
great church of souls in which worship is going up to
God unceasingly. May the priests be clothed with
sanctity, and may the faithful abide in joy !

The second psalm is an expression of this joy of the
Dominican brotherhood, an inner ring of the great
Christian brotherhood of which the Jewish community
was but a faint image.

In the third our Tertiaries greet their cloistered brothers
and sisters of the Order, relying upon them to carry
on the divine praises in the middle of the night, when
they themselves are prevented from doing so by the duties
of their station, and by their need of sleep. They also
appeal to our saints in Heaven, who never sleep and never
interrupt those *alleluias* of which St. John speaks in the
Apocalypse.

Tertiaries would do well to familiarize themselves
with the choice collection of anthems, little chapters,
versicles and responses which constitute the incomparable
charm of the Complines of the Great Office, and more
particularly with those anthems and hymns which our
Order alone has preserved for Lent and Eastertide.
St. Thomas could never recite the *Media vita* without
tears. In the midst of our life we are in death. To
whom can we have recourse but to Thee, Lord, Who art
justly angry with us ?

In the early days, when our Fathers were wont to
protract Compline with private prayer, they derived
great inspiration from those holy words. But they also
liked to meditate upon the little hymn to Our Lady,
Virgo Singularis and the antiphon *Sub tuum presidium* with
the prayer that follows it, all three of which were formerly

appended to their Office, though they now remain the
monopoly of the Tertiaries. The final beautiful canticle
of Simeon belongs to both Offices and suggests many
edifying thoughts.

Nunc dimittis servum tuum, Domine, sighed the aged Saint.
He could die in peace now that, in the midst of the
darkness that covered the earth, he had seen with his
own eyes the One Who is the true light. Short though
it be, this evening hymn is magnificent. After we have
been thinking of the day as an image of life, and of sleep
as suggestive of death, what can be more moving and
appropriate than these brief strophes at the hour of
Compline ?

The light that was kindled to illuminate the liturgical
assembly has been regarded from primitive times as a
symbol of Christ, " our light and our true day. Who
destroys for us the darkness here below, and Who gives
us even now, in the faith, a portent of the radiant light
of eternity." I am quoting from the hymn in the Lenten
Compline of the Dominican rite. The Greeks used to
sing every night a song in honour of " the gladdening
light of the holy glory of the Immortal Faith, the heavenly
holy and blessed Jesus." The same theme inspires the
triumphal *Exultet* of the Paschal vigil. But it finds expression also every day and everywhere in the last verse of
the *Nunc Dimittis.*

Finally, the *Salve Regina* concludes Compline. In our
religious houses it is a rite of obligation. Our Tertiaries
will certainly wish to add it to their Office of Our Lady.
The custom of singing this anthem goes back, as has been
already said, to the very early days of the Order. A
truly diabolical persecution was raging against the
Friars, especially at Bologna and in Paris. Blessed Jordan
of Saxony, St. Dominic's successor, gave orders for the
singing of the *Salve* every night after Compline. The
persecution immediately ceased, but its very cessation

served to establish the practice, which became general. The faithful, especially the Tertiaries, crowded into the churches of the Preachers to see the Friars leave the choir and come into the nave, singing the *Salve Regina*. The chant is a melancholy one, plaintive yet unaffected. A solemn procession of souls who pass mourning through this vale of tears, but who are upheld and comforted by a celestial hope. Is not the Queen of Heaven also a Mother of mercy? She looks down from above upon her exiled sons, and she makes herself their advocate with God. One day she will show them her Son. And the thought of that vision which will constitute their eternal bliss already gives them a sense of exquisite sweetness.

Upon arriving at the Lady Altar, the Friars kneel to sing *Eia ergo, advocata nostra*. Then one of them comes out to sprinkle the rest with holy water, one by one, in memory of the time when the Holy Virgin was seen by St. Dominic to go the round of the cells, sprinkling each brother as he lay asleep. *O clemens, o pia, o dulcis Virgo Maria.* When they utter that beloved name, the Friars bow deeply, as though a great gust of wind were bending them all at the same moment.

Those Tertiaries who cannot have the advantage and the joy of taking part in this conventual ceremony may like to think of it at night, as they recite the *Salve*, or as they take a little holy water with which to bless themselves before going to bed.

FOURTH SECTION

PRAYER FOR OUR DEAD

Dear Brother and Sister Tertiaries, you have come into an Order which is devoted to the dead. You will eventually profit by it, and in the meantime the Rule requires you to do your part to maintain this devotion. That is why I am going to describe the ceremonies which precede, accompany and follow the death of a Friar in an ordinary priory.

An old thirteenth-century processional contains a *prosa* with a beautiful musical setting, specially composed for brothers dangerously ill. In it the patient is invited to contemplate his departure with serenity, even with joy.

" Sweet brother, if thou art passing, let not thy heart be troubled." And the prose goes on to say that one can only congratulate oneself at the prospect of escaping from a shipwreck, and of being borne on a raft safely into port. All our brethren, who are gathered round St. Dominic on high, will rejoice and will welcome the new arrival into their company. The angels will carry him ; they will console him in the hour of his solemn passing. The good God will wipe away all his tears and amid the holy souls will admit him into Paradise where blooms eternal spring.

Fra Angelico has depicted it all in one of his most charming paintings. The guardian angels appear to the awestruck newcomers, embrace them like brothers, and draw them away to join a happy ring on a flowery meadow. St. Dominic glides over the lawn and rises up majestically to introduce one of his Friars into the light divine.

" Think no more of science, nor of having abandoned study, for soon thou shalt know all things, thou shall behold them in their first Cause.

" Perchance thou hadst hoped to do great things for God ; but against His Providence one must not hold out.

" Jesus Who knows far better what is fitting for the elect, will, of His clemency, do with thee what is most expedient for thee."

It is to be regretted that we can no longer in these days appreciate these beautiful sentiments, these moving invocations, and find strength in them in the hour of death. Nevertheless, that hour is a formidable one, formidable for the body struggling in its supreme agony, formidable also for the soul because there are other destinies possible after death. No one is absolutely secure of attaining to Heaven. At the very least we have the prospect of Purgatory and its terrible purifying. A Mass for the dying was introduced into our Missal in 1921. Its tenor is quite different. Here we find cries of supplication addressed to the divine mercy on behalf of a poor being whose limbs are suffering and whose soul is troubled. " Lord Jesus Christ Who hast procured for mankind the remedies of salvation and the gifts of eternal life, look with favour upon Thy servant whose body is sick and revive the soul Thou hast created, so that by the intercession of Blessed Joseph, Spouse of Thy Holy Mother, he may be presented without spot of sin at the hour of death by the hands of the Angels to Thee, his Creator. . . ." The sick man upon his pallet enters into his agony. At once in the cloister and throughout the priory the signal is given with the Holy Week clapper, and Friars come from all directions reciting the *Credo*, that act of faith in eternal life and in all those mysteries which give us access to it. The first comers begin to recite the litanies of the saints, and the rest join in as they arrive. Our canonized saints are invoked specifically one after another for the deliverance of the soul of our brother, who is also theirs, from the supreme anguish. Then, if death is delayed, the presiding priest may also repeat in the name of the dying man the noble pro- testations of faith, hope and contrition contained in our processional, and the beautiful prayers to Christ dying upon the Cross and to Our Lady commiserating His suffering. The priest may then read the Passion to enable the sufferer to unite his sacrifice to that of Christ. When the last moment has come, he exclaims : *Proficiscere anima christiana* . . . and recommends the soul to God.

Our rubrics do not mention the practice, a very cherished and venerable one among us, of singing the *Salve Regina* at the bedside of the dying Friar. The custom is, however, alluded to in our Breviary on the feast day of Blessed Sadoc and his companions. These brothers of the Priory of Sandomir by their martyrdom gave it its initial consecration. They were butchered by the Tartars as they were concluding Compline by the singing of the *Salve*. The *Salve Regina* which is, as it were, the cradle-song which lulls us to rest every night, is also sung for our brothers at the approach of their last sleep, that apparent sleep which is actually the great awakening. More fervently than ever do we implore the Mother of Mercy, in this final Compline at the end of our exile, to show us Jesus, the blessed fruit of her womb.

At last the soul has left the body. The priest says : " *Subvenite*. Come to his help, saints of God, come to meet him, angels of the Lord : take his soul and offer it in the presence of the Most High. . . . "

The dead Friar is clothed in his habit, to which is added his stole if he is a priest. The Office for the recommendation of the soul is completed. Then the Friars start the psalter at the beginning and recite it beside the departed until the time comes for him to be carried into the church. In the meantime the passing bell tolls the knell. A procession of the whole community precedes the body, which is carried into the middle of the choir. There it is placed with the head towards the altar. Some of the Friars continue the recitation of the psalms, which is interrupted only for the canonical hours.

As soon as possible—*quantocius*, say the Constitutions—messages are sent to inform all who owe suffrages for the departed Friar, because the dead man is entitled to a great deal more than the long funeral Office which is celebrated solemnly over his remains in the church, the beautiful prayers peculiar to our Order recited at his tomb, and the *Libera*, which will be sung for him after dinner for eight days. All priest-friars of his house owe him three masses, and others of his province must say one mass.[1] And in addition there are the prayers of the lay brothers and the psalms which are recited by clerics who are not yet priests : the whole psalter for a member of the house, the seven penitential psalms for any other member of the province.[2]

In the same spirit of mutual assistance the Rule of the Third Order enjoins that within eight days of the notification of the decease of a member of the Chapter or Fraternity, each brother and sister shall recite the third part of the Rosary, shall hear one Mass, and shall offer one communion (XIII. 46). Is that all ? By no means. The deceased, to whatever branch of the family he or she may belong, is now one of our dead for whom the Order will never cease to pray and to offer Masses and Offices.

Every year each priory makes itself responsible for twenty Masses ; each priest offers thirty Masses ; and each cleric recites thirty times the seven penitential

---

[1] In this connection let us not forget that " all the Masses which are celebrated for deceased Brothers and Sisters are privileged always and everywhere " (*Analecta S.O.P.*, January, 1923). In some Provinces, as in England, all the priest-friars say three Masses for each member of their Province who dies.

[2] As with the Masses, so with these other suffrages, in England and other Provinces.

psalms. Our sisters of the Second Order, and those of
the Third, also provide a large contribution of Masses
and suffrages on behalf of the dead of the whole Dominican
family. As for the secular Tertiaries, they must each of
them have three Masses a year offered (XIII. 48).

Every week of the year, with four exceptions, a conventual Mass followed by a procession is celebrated for our
dead in all our priories. The complete Office of the Dead
is also recited weekly, and the Superior is required to fix
it for a convenient hour, when it can be attended by all
the Friars, even by those who are normally exempt from
the choral Office. Those who are absent must fulfil
their obligation individually.

Finally, every night after sunset, the priory bell rings
for a considerable time as a summons to prayer for the
departed. Tertiaries must never let a day pass without
reciting a *Pater* and an *Ave*, followed by *Requiem* (XIII. 4).

At the approach of November, with its festival for the
dead, we in the First Order of St. Dominic are obliged
to think specially of our brothers and sisters, and also
of those associates admitted to a share in the suffrages of
the Order. Every priest must celebrate three Masses
for them, and each cleric must recite the psalter between
the Feast of St. Dionysius and Advent.

I have just mentioned associates. Our benefactors
likewise benefit by these suffrages, as can be seen from
the prayers of the Office and of the Mass. Moreover,
every day before dinner and supper, mindful that their
generosity has provided the meal we are about to take,
we recite the *De profundis*.

Our fathers and mothers, for whom a special prayer
is said at the Mass and in the Office, also have a share
in these spiritual favours. They seem to be considered
as belonging, in a sense, to our Order once they are
in the next world. Like St. Dominic's mother, who is
liturgically treated as being so definitely one of the
Blessed of the Order that we say : *Ora pro nobis, beata
Joanna*, our own parents have been to a certain extent

identified with the deceased members of the Dominican family.

Furthermore, all those who are buried in our ceme-teries, a privilege formerly greatly valued, benefit by our prayers and particularly by that *De profundis* which, in obedience to the Constitutions, is recited on the way through the cloister of the dead.

Each one of these four groups of the departed has its own anniversary in all our religious houses. A Mass for them is then celebrated, together with its Office which is binding upon all Friars who have to say the Breviary. The anniversary of our parents falls on the third day after the Purification ; that of our benefactors and friends is the day after the octave of St. Augustine ; for our brothers and sisters it is November 10th, and for those who rest in our cemeteries it is July 12th.

And this round continues, day by day, and year after year. It is not only because death is always taking fresh victims that we never cease repeating these prayers and these Masses. As long as we have no certainty that our dead ones have left Purgatory, we go on offering suffrages for them. Every morning in the choir the lector reads the names of those who died at this date, and have been inscribed in the martyrology. Then, after he has made a general mention of all our unknown saints (*alibi aliorum plurimorum*), we celebrate their death, so precious in the eyes of God. Next follows another commemoration, that of all the rest of our dead, begin-ning with a list of those Masters General of the Order whose anniversary it happens to be, and we pray God that they may eventually enter into eternal rest with the saints in Heaven.

The *De profundis* is said for all who have not been beatified by the Church, even for Humbert de Romans, who died in 1263, and to whom the title of Blessed is usually accorded. Yes, it is a privilege to be allowed to

die in the Dominican family, even as a simple Tertiary.
" Die among the Friars Preachers " was part of a proverb
current formerly in pious circles, and not without reason.
It expressed the dream of souls who believed firmly
in eternal bliss, and in the conditions requisite for its
attainment.

CHAPTER V

DOMINICAN PRAYER

SECTION   I.   THE TRADITION OF OUR ORDER.

SECTION   II.   THE BASES OF OUR PRAYER.

1. A Doctrinal Foundation.
2. Liturgical Inspirations.

SECTION III.   THE VARIOUS FORMS OF DOMINICAN PRAYER.

1. Private Prayer.
2. Holy Meditation.
3. Religious Meditation.
4. Contemplative Meditation.
5. Mystical Contemplation.
6. Ejaculatory Prayers.
7. The Holy Rosary, a Method of Prayer.

SECTION IV.   TOWARDS PERFECT CONTEMPLATION.

FIRST SECTION

THE TRADITION OF OUR ORDER

FROM the early days of our Order it has been the custom to supplement the choral recitation of the psalms in common by " private devotions " and " holy meditations," in which each one freely lifts up his soul to God.

Our Blessed Father set the example, and an ancient chronicle which Theodoric of Apolda appends to his life of St. Dominic describes his mode of prayer, as observed by brothers who concealed themselves at night in a dark corner of the church to watch him, or who, as his travelling companions, were able to see and hear him on the roads and in the houses of their hosts.

His way of praying was very human. God has formed us of soul and body. St. Dominic did not believe, as certain individuals since his time seem to have thought, that prayer can be perfect only if the soul is completely abstracted from the body. His soul, on the contrary, used his bodily members as vehicles to carry it more devoutly to God. An upward glance, reading, certain attitudes and gestures may serve as useful means for stirring the soul and touching the heart. His father, St. Augustine, had already said so.[1] The soul, in return, reacts upon the body, and the exuberance of its sentiments overflows and is translated into words and gestures. Moreover, the body as well as the soul owes homage to God, and the body must co-operate with the soul in making penitential satisfaction for sins in which it has also had its share. These reasons, which were those by which St. Dominic was actuated, have since his time been fully developed and expounded by St. Thomas.[2] I would

[1] *Letter to Proba*, Ch. IX.
[2] IIa IIae, a. 80, a. 12.

add here that St. Dominic's Castilian temperament was
probably partly responsible for the extraordinary vehe-
mence he brought to his prayer.   Only at night, however,
and when he thought he was alone, did he give vent to
this exuberance, of which we will give a few instances.

It was a common practice with him to stand before
the altar with his head and shoulders deeply bowed in
the presence of his King, Our Lord.   In that attitude
he would meditate upon his own servile state and upon
the excellence of Jesus, whilst his body was paying its
own tribute of respect.   But he frequently prayed lying
outstretched at full length on the ground, exclaiming
repeatedly : " Lord, be merciful to me, a sinner," or a
passage from a psalm, such as : " I am not worthy to
lift up my eyes to heaven. . . . My soul is humbled to
the dust."   Prostrations of this kind and deep reverences,
in which the elbows are lowered to the level of the knees,
still figure largely in the Dominican liturgy.

Occasionally, with his eyes fixed upon the crucifix,
St. Dominic would genuflect perhaps as many as a
hundred times.   He is known to have spent the whole
of the interval between Compline and midnight in doing
nothing but alternately kneeling down and rising up.
He was pleading for mercy upon himself and upon
sinners.   Now and again a cry would escape him.   Then
he would stand still, as though astonished, and would
appear overcome with admiration and radiant with
joy.   And his genuflections would be an expression of
the emotions of his soul.

Or again he would stand facing the altar with his hands
spread out before his breast like an open book in which
he had been reading.   He was, in all probability, meditating in his prayer upon the oracles of the Holy
Scriptures.

Sometimes he used to join his hands together and
press them tightly against his eyes ; at other times he
held them up apart, at shoulder height, as at Mass.   In
moments of crisis he was wont to spread out his arms

to form a cross, like the Saviour at Calvary. Very often he would stand erect, with his arms above his head and his finger tips meeting, looking like an arrow that was being shot from a bow into the sky. If, after praying in this attitude, he had to administer a rebuke or deliver a sermon, his words were as the words of a prophet.

We saw just now that St. Dominic was accustomed to mingle meditation with prayer. Sometimes meditation predominated ; but it was of so holy a character that it still deserved to be called a prayer. And that is why the old chronicler goes on to say : " Our holy Father had another method of prayer, beautiful, fervent and full of grace. After the canonical hours and the grace which usually follows the meals, the Father, ever abstemious in the matter of food, but sated with the spirit of devotion which he had imbibed from the divine words sung in choir or at table, would quickly retire to a solitary spot, his cell or elsewhere, in order to read or to pray alone with God. He would sit down quietly and open a book, arming himself with the sign of the cross. He then began to read, and his soul was sweetly moved as though he could hear his Saviour speaking to him. . . . He rose from reading to meditation and from meditation to contemplation. . . .

" He also pursued this course of action during his journeys, when he was crossing some lonely tract. . . . Ahead of the others or, more often, behind them, he prayed as he walked, and the fire was kindled in his meditation. That is how he acquired that intimate acquaintance with Holy Scripture which roused admiration and gave the power to his preaching."

The Friars themselves prayed and meditated after the manner of their Blessed Father, not only when they were on the road and were told by St. Dominic to go forward and to think about Our Lord, but regularly in the Priory after Matins and more especially after Compline before they retired to rest.

They were at liberty to choose in church the spot that suited them best. One would pray with downcast eyes under the shadow of a pillar : another before a sacred image upon which he gazed. Some stood up : others prostrated themselves or made many genuflec-tions. A certain number visited the various altars. Sighs broke the silence. . . . The regular daily duties put an end to these prayers in the morning ; in the even-ing, after a time, the Blessed Father would tell them all to go and rest. He would then remain alone to continue his prayer.

" These private prayers and holy meditations are devotional practices," Humbert de Romans was after-wards to declare. " They are doubly so. First, because they are not imposed by the Rule, but proceed from the good will of each individual. And secondly because they generally kindle the fervour of holy affections. . . . We must apply ourselves with zeal to our private prayers, since they are a manifest indication of sanctity, and it would be difficult to find anyone who, after being addicted to them, eventually lost his soul or failed to make progress in religion." [1]

Yes, that was indeed a source of deep devotion. And that is why the Friars practised it with diligence and why others have been glad to follow their example. Already at the time of Blessed Humbert, the practice of private prayer after Compline had become semi-official. He gives as one of the chief reasons for attending Compline " the fruit which is reaped from the secret prayers that, in accordance with our custom, are appended to it." He even fixes the length of the interval the sacristan is to allow before giving the signal for retiring : it was to be about the time required for the recitation of the seven penitential psalms and the litanies.[2] It was in 1505,

---

[1] Humbert, *Opera*, t. II, pp. 86, 91.
[2] *Ibid.*, p. 248.

more than two centuries later, that the general Chapters
set about regulating the practice of mental prayer, as
the result of a movement that was making itself felt at
the time, particularly in the Low Countries and in
Spain. A new community exercise was prescribed
which was to be made silently in choir for half an hour
twice a day. The evening half hour was always the
favourite, and until 1868 it had to follow immediately
the singing of Compline. No one might be regularly
exempted. If, for some reason or another, a Friar failed
to attend, he was bound to make up for it in private,
under pain of forfeiting his share for that day in the merits
and good works of the Order. Only travellers and the
sick were excused. In recent times the exemption has
been extended to those who are hindered by a legitimate
impediment, and the form of excommunication mentioned above has been entirely eliminated. In other
respects the Rule, which has prevailed for several centuries, remains much the same and is still in force. It
may be noted, however, that half the time of the evening
meditation may be spent in the recitation of the Rosary
in common.

The Constitutions of the various communities of
Dominican Sisters are more or less similar to our own.
As for the Tertiaries living in the world, the Rule simply
directs them to practise mental prayer as far as they
can (VII. 33).

Even amongst the religious of both sexes, notwithstanding the regulations given above, Dominican
prayer has always retained a great freedom of procedure.
Each individual spends this sacred half hour in his or
her own way, which may even vary from one day to
another. There has never been any one method officially recommended. But there are a few general principles which may help us to achieve the particular
objective we have in view, and also certain counsels
about mistakes to be avoided and measures to be taken
to ensure the profitable use of that silent time. St.

Thomas, who formulated Dominican thought and shed so much light upon it, is still the authority to whom one must refer. We cannot do better than consult him directly.

Our half hour can be spent in at least four exercises which have his approval and for which he has prescribed definite rules. They are four distinct exercises calculated to bring into play the various functions of our supernatural organism, and they tend to different ends, although they are not unrelated and indeed grow out of one another. In order of progression they stand as follows : private prayer, religious meditation, contemplative meditation and mystical contemplation.

Private prayer is a lifting up of the soul to God, to ask for His help, by means of a little discourse which we improvise, more or less, ourselves.

Religious meditation, a thing distinct from moral meditation with which we shall also deal, introduces into these private prayers prolonged reflections upon God and upon ourselves to convince us of our essential need of having recourse to God, to induce us to place ourselves under His authority and thereby to give a greater religious value to our petitions for divine assistance.

This meditation, the immediate aim of which was to bring us into religious subjection to God, will forthwith lead us on to desire simply to behold Him with love, asking nothing else, though we know well that all the rest will be added to us : our meditation will then become contemplative.

Mystical graces may perhaps prolong and intensify this contemplation to which our meditation was aspiring, and which it could attain to only in very brief acts.

We shall have occasion presently to speak of ejaculatory prayer that instils the spirit of devotion into every department of our life.

Finally, we shall see how the holy Rosary, bestowed upon us by the Virgin Mary, sums up in itself all these forms of prayer, and consequently suits all souls irrespective of their state or condition.

But whatever forms our prayer may assume, it will only be truly Dominican if it is sustained on the one hand by solid doctrine, and on the other hand by the liturgy of the Church.   This fact must be clearly understood at the very outset.

SECOND SECTION

THE BASES OF OUR PRAYER

I. A DOCTRINAL FOUNDATION

A DETERMINED effort of the will is required to enable us to reserve the right time for our daily prayers in spite of the difficulties we meet with in our surroundings and in ourselves, in the cares which preoccupy us, the distractions that assail us, our slothfulness and our carelessness. It also calls for a strong effort on our part to keep the attention fixed for any considerable time upon supernatural objects : sometimes it entails a real spiritual combat which has been aptly compared to Jacob's wrestling with the angel.

But goodwill alone is not enough. In vain would it seek to achieve success by resorting to clever methods in which we pass through divers preludes and from point to point, applying to each one in turn our five senses and all our powers. All these divisions, all this ingenuity, all these recipes would yield nothing of value unless our spirit had already been stocked with a store of doctrine capable of nourishing prayer.

Failing that, even our ejaculatory prayers would remain more or less empty words, and our spiritual bouquets would be dried up flowers, discovered in the morning between the pages of a book of meditation, artificially varied from day to day and without any influence upon our lives. . . . Whereas they ought to be the living, spontaneous and personal expression of a deep-seated sentiment, evoked by a great thought which is very dear to us, which may remain the same for a long time, perhaps for ever, and which illuminates and stimulates our whole life. A Dominican soul, more

than any other, should be supplied with these grand
ideas. No sooner had our Father, St. Dominic, called
together his first sons than he led them to the feet of a
master in theology.[1] And we know what a high place in
his constitutions he accords to study, placing it from the
outset in the forefront of the means of our religious life.
Necessary as it is for the apostolate, it is even more
essential for contemplation. Our apostolate, in any case,
consists primarily in communicating to our neighbour
the subject-matter of our own contemplation. We
impart to him what we have contemplated, in order
that he may contemplate it too. *Contemplata aliis tradere
contemplanda.*

Veritas! We have to discern the great divine truths
and try to fathom them. God Whom I love, and must
ever love more and more, Him would I fain know in
His beauty that I may love Him still better. What is
God? inquired the little child, who was one day to
become the greatest and most perfect of St. Dominic's
sons. And he laboured all his life to formulate the answer
to that question. No one has ever surpassed him. It
is to his works that we all resort, directly or indirectly,
to derive a true knowledge of the beloved object of our
contemplation.

Many of us will remember the picture of the Crucifixion
at San Marco in Florence. Behind the kneeling figure
of St. Francis of Assisi bathed in tears, Fra Angelico
has represented, amongst other saints, St. Dominic
standing erect, his face painfully contracted under the
influence of concentrated thought. Not content with
gazing sorrowfully at the bleeding wounds of the Crucified, he is probing as far as he can into the mystery of the
Son of God, Who became Incarnate out of mercy, to
expiate our sins upon the Cross, and to reconcile us to
His Father. These reflections arouse in him a deep
emotion which is betrayed by the poignant expression

[1] Alexander of Stavensby, who afterwards became Bishop of Lichfield
in Staffordshire, England.

of his countenance. We may regard this as a model for
our Dominican contemplation.

Excellence of prayer is not to be attained by stirring up
a great many different ideas. Only a very limited number
are necessary. But those few ought to be well chosen
and so perfectly assimilated after prolonged rumination
that they present themselves to the mind in a very simple
and natural way.

What is it that we are expected to do ? We must, in
any case, place ourselves in the presence of God and make
contact with Him, whether it be to speak to Him and
pray to Him, or whether it be definitely to unite ourselves
in love to Him. All those fruitful ideas which, as we saw,
are so necessary for us, can serve to lead us back to the
threefold divine Presence. God is present in three ways :
by His presence of immensity in all things, by His
intimate presence in our soul in a state of grace, by our
unity in Our Lord Jesus Christ.

We will begin by considering His presence by immensity. God has been compared to a spiritual sphere, the
centre of which is everywhere and whose circumference
is nowhere.

God is everywhere by His power, like a King whose
absolute power extends to the extremities of his Kingdom.
God is everywhere by His presence, like the King in his
presence chamber, where he sees with his eyes all that is
going on. God is everywhere by His very essence, like
the King upon the throne where he is seated.

These are but feeble similes. God is more intimately
present to all things than the King is to his very throne,
for in the case of God it is not a question of simple juxta-
position. God is spirit, and as such He is entirely present
to all that He makes, even as our soul is present to the
whole of the body it animates. And since it is He Who
creates and continually conserves all being, that is to
say, the substance of all things, therefore God in His

entirety is also present in all things as intimately as it is possible to be.

He is there in all the fulness of His perfections which are all revealed in greater or less degree by some reflection of them. So much so, indeed, that a well instructed and meditative soul finds that everything can provide an occasion for contemplating the various attributes of God, His wisdom, His justice, His infinite power.

Though present everywhere by His immensity, God permits only a few beings to enjoy His intimate presence. It is the privilege of souls in a state of grace, and it is one which gradually develops from the state of soul of the little child brought back from the baptismal font after having received into his soul, as yet spiritually unawakened, the capacity to return to God, up to the state of soul of the saint who, having reached the summit of that marvellous destiny, sees God as He sees Himself and loves Him as He loves Himself.

Through the activity of grace we can participate in the very life of the Holy Trinity. " It is My Father Who has revealed it to thee, O Simon Peter, who hast just confessed thy faith." Yes, God the Father extends even to our intelligence the knowledge He has of Himself in His eternal Word, and afterwards we participate by charity in the love of the Father for His Son, and of the Son for His Father, that love which is the Holy Spirit in person.

O, holy and adorable Trinity, Father, Son and Holy Spirit, You make Your Heaven in me, and I have but to discover You there with clear vision to be able to enter into Your beatitude, and find my heaven in myself! Draw me daily more intimately in to You. Vouchsafe that I may live of Your life ever more and more.

A third divine presence is that presence in unity with which only one man—Our Lord Jesus Christ—has ever been favoured. In Him human nature is united in person to the divine nature. God unites Himself with everything by His creative power : the just on earth and the blessed in Heaven are re-united to God and in some sense embrace Him ; but Jesus and Jesus alone is One with the Father, He is God in person.

If the Son of God made Himself incarnate, it was in order that He might incorporate us all in Him as our Head, and it is in that way that His divine presence touches us all, just as we now are. Let us briefly recapitulate the substance of what has already been said on this subject.

The same Jesus, Who has left in history the record of thirty-three years lived in Palestine, was thinking of me even at that time, was preaching for me, died for me. I must read His gospel and meditate upon it, as though it were a letter written to me which had only just reached its destination.

Jesus, Who quitted the earth to dwell in a region suited to the glorious body which the apostles saw and touched during the great Forty Days, that very Jesus still continues to be interested in me and in all His other members here below. I live under His eyes : I may even say that the pulsation of His Sacred Heart is always sending spiritual life into my soul. And His Mother, who was united to Him in the mystery of His earthly life, continues in the heavenly life to collaborate with Him for my salvation. The Rosary stands for this doctrine. The Holy Eucharist recalls and prolongs amongst us the life of Jesus upon earth, besides giving us the sure means of uniting ourselves to His life in Heaven. It is close to the tabernacle and in our communions that we can best rejoice in that third—that truly singular and unique—divine presence.

Surely in this triple divine presence are summed up all the dogmas which generate Christian life.

Consider one who, by study and reflection, has become familiar with these truths. Thanks to his fervent faith, and still more to the gifts of the Holy Spirit, when he places himself simply in the presence of God, there is often in the dim apprehension he has of the divine Being the quintessence of all these truths at once. And his heart unites itself to God in all His mysterious reality, prolonging the contact and, as far as possible, renewing it.

However simplified such a prayer may be, yet it is the fruit of the rich doctrinal nourishment that we have assimilated. In us, as in the Trinity Which transforms us after Its own image, love proceeds from the word— *Verbum spirans amorem.*

II. THE LITURGICAL INSPIRATIONS OF PRAYER

Whilst it is eminently desirable that we should supplement by mental prayer the public worship that we render to God in our attendance at Mass, and the other Offices which constitute the Church's liturgy, it is a great mistake to treat the two as though they were opposed, or as if the one excluded the other. The two forms of prayer ought to be auxiliary and interpenetrative. A priest who vocally recites his Breviarys without fixing his mind upon God and upon the thought, which the words express, is satisfying the letter of the ecclesiastical injunction. He is lending his mouth to the Church which prays through him, but his own supernatural life is deriving no benefit, because he is not combining mental prayer with his vocal prayer. Such a loss, if daily repeated, becomes in the long run quite incalculable. Perhaps he is hurrying through his Breviary in order to apply himself to some form of mental prayer of his own selection, fancying quite erroneously that in this alone can he find a source of spiritual life. But a mental prayer which is completely divorced from the liturgy is in danger of losing much of its vital value. The subjects and the formularies set forth for us by the Church so lavishly and with the guarantee of orthodoxy are generally preferable to those that we find for ourselves. Of course, an excellent subject of meditation may naturally present itself as the result of some theological study upon which we have been engaged that day, or after reading a book which kindles our piety, or if providential events provoke particular reflections. But as a rule we shall be left to the mercy of our own caprices, or of a manual which undertakes to regulate the course of our daily meditations. And all the time Holy Church, our Mother, is displaying before our eyes the great Christian truths in perfect order, and is tracing for us through the seasons the sure itinerary of our spiritual renewal.

Moreover, our spirituality ought to be homogeneous. To introduce diverging elements would be disastrous to its vitality. Now although there are certain days, in the course of the year, which are not marked with any very definite liturgical stamp and therefore admit of a certain freedom in the matter of prayer, yet during the greater part of the year the liturgical character of each day is very clearly marked. Therefore, if we wish to be faithful to the inspiration of the Church, to participate in her Offices with our spirit and with our heart, and to celebrate worthily the divine mysteries, our first duty will be to stir up within us the thoughts and the affections which correspond to the readings, the prayers and the acts in which we shall be engaged. Our interior state will then find a congenial atmosphere in these liturgical days. The ceremonies, the colours of the vestments, the decorations, the singing—everything will tend towards its development. If, on the other hand, we fill our souls with a different current of reflections and sentiments we shall be divided against ourselves. Such dualism would be detrimental to our life of prayer, as well as to our liturgical life. Both would be impoverished unless the one were subordinated to the other. Instances are not unknown of good priests, wedded to their chosen form of mental prayer, who have relapsed, as far as the liturgy was concerned, into routine and formalism. Lest we incur this danger, let us attune our life of prayer to that of the Church. The liturgy has been pronounced by Pius X to be " the primary and indispensable source of the true Christian spirit."

The Church has not only given us subjects for our prayer ; she has supplied us with excellent formularies. Most people lament their inability to speak to God as they would talk with those they love on earth. They do not know how to improvise the right sort of conversation to carry on with that unseen and silent interlocutor. To meet their requirements, since the half hour of meditation first made its way into the life of devout souls, innumerable books have been written containing formularies and pious colloquies which they only have to adapt to themselves.

But there existed in the past and there still exist two official books of meditation in the Church of God. These are the Breviary and the Missal. Nothing can surpass these. The more important of the two, the Missal, has been translated into every language and placed within the reach of all Christian souls. It contains the most perfect utterances which the Holy Spirit has ever inspired. The Church has selected them with the utmost care, and her harmonious arrangement of them should awaken in us some of the salutary emotions which they have inspired in so many of the saints in all ages. They can suggest to our souls the behaviour and the loving sentiments that God is pleased to find in His servants and sons. It is " the only method authentically instituted by the Church for assimilating our souls to Jesus."

In our daily practice it is expedient that our prayers should precede, accompany and continue our liturgical worship, whether this latter includes the canonical hours from Matins to Compline, methodically distributed throughout the day, or whether it is confined to the Mass which is its essential part.

We ought first to prepare ourselves, by reading or meditation, to grasp the importance of the acts in which we shall take part, to enter into the spirit of the feast or of the season, and to penetrate the meaning of the words as well as of the liturgical ceremonies. Now is the right moment for reading such commentaries as may sometimes be necessary to show us how the different parts of the Mass throw light upon one another, and to give us the key which will enable us to apply to our soul the teaching of the collect.

During the Office, during Mass, we shall taste, we shall contemplate, our soul will take upward flights to God, at such times and in such manner as will be suggested by the formularies and the ritual gestures. Have we not here a great sacramental through which the Church calls forth in us the dispositions she has received from the Holy Spirit? St. Augustine has told us of the fervent prayers which the liturgy elicited from him : " How many tears have I shed, O God, under the powerful movement of Thy hymns and canticles—the melodious voice of Thy Church. Those sounds rang in my ears and through them the truth was spread in my heart and they aroused feelings of fervent piety, and the tears flowed from my eyes, tears of happiness to me." [1]

Formerly, after each psalm there was a pause of a few instants to allow of private meditation or secret prayer. The *Gloria Patri* and the anthems have taken the place of those silences. When the priest chanted *Oremus*, it was also a call to silent prayer. *Flectamus genua*, said the deacon, and the kneeling congregation prayed mentally. Then the priest pronounced aloud a short formulary which summed up and concluded the prayers of all. The *Paternoster*, murmured in silence with bowed head at the close of the hours, is a relic of those ancient practices.

Let no one imagine that mental prayer during the liturgical Office has become impossible to-day. The elaborate reasonings of certain set meditations are indeed out of the question, but not those eager and instinctive intuitions, those upward glances full of faith, those acts of love and of worship which constitute our best prayers.

[1] St. Augustine, *Confessions*, B, IX Ch. VI.

Everyone has ample opportunity for these when the Office is chanted by a double choir. During a sung Mass, the music and the silences encourage the out-pourings of the soul. Who has not thrilled to the impressive and reiterated appeals of the *Kyrie*, to the triumphal shouts of the *Gloria* and the *Sanctus*, when taking part in a community Mass ? And if the Office is said individually, if we are assisting at a Low Mass, what is to prevent our making use of the pauses to dwell on some thought or to breathe forth a devout aspiration ?

And then afterwards, after the Office whose several hours measure and hallow our day, and especially after the Mass, our souls will retain certain impressions which will influence our contemplation. The many texts which we have heard during the Office and during the Mass will resolve themselves into dominant ideas which will often recur under different forms, and will imprint themselves upon an attentive mind. One particular verse will come back to us again and again, and will then go forth in an ejaculatory prayer. We have already seen how, in the first century of the Order, the Friars delighted in prolonging, by long private prayers and by fervent colloquies with God, the liturgical Office which had kindled the fire of their charity.

Louis of Granada, in treating of this form of devotion, urges that it should always be preceded by some vocal prayers and he adds, truly enough, that these vocal prayers are more useful if they are in rhyme. One can modulate them according to one's fancy, and they exercise a sort of charm which enables the soul to find more relish in the things of God. And yet what are they, at their best, but faint echoes and feeble imitations of that noble liturgy whose beneficial effect upon our life of prayer cannot be emphasized too insistently ?

THIRD SECTION

THE VARIOUS FORMS OF OUR PRAYER

I. PRIVATE PRAYER

LITERALLY speaking, mental prayer is synonymous with private prayer. And, as a matter of fact, the mental devotions prescribed by the Dominican Constitutions and recommended by the Rule of the Third Order would seem to be identical with those private prayers which are extolled in the Lives of the Friars, and which are so strongly recommended by Humbert de Romans—prayers in the strictest sense of the word, petitions addressed to God and improvized with a good deal of freedom, even when based on some recognized formulary.

" The praise of God to which the choral Office is specially consecrated is unquestionably a great duty that we shall continue in eternity," said Blessed Humbert, " but petition is necessary here below, and that is what forms the chief subject-matter of our secret devotions.

" We certainly ask for graces during the course of the Office, but we do so mainly on behalf of the whole Catholic Church. In our secret prayers we think more particularly of our own needs.

" Our choral singing of the psalms leaves us little time for dwelling upon our personal concerns. Secret prayers help us to do this. Moreover, we find it more easy to open our hearts and to say what we wish in an intimate *tête-à-tête* than in the midst of an assembly.

" For the Office we need books, and very often light also. Nothing extraneous is required for secret prayer : it can be carried on at all times and in all places in accordance with the Master's injunction : *Oportet semper orare.*" [1]

---

[1] Humbert de Romans, *Opera*, Vol. II, pp. 91–93.

Prayer, St. Thomas tells us,[1] is an act of the practical reason whereby we organize our existence and put order into all that concerns us. This order cannot be made actual by the reason alone. Appeal has to be made to other faculties, to other beings. The aforesaid ordering takes the form of a command when it is addressed to those who are subject to us, but it is only a prayer when we address persons who are not in a position to receive commands from us. And that is particularly the case with regard to God, the supreme Master.

Notice the great difference that exists between prayer addressed to a man and prayer made to God. My prayer influences a man and disposes him to come to my assistance, whereas with God, Who is immutable, it is myself whom I dispose by my prayer to receive His benefits : and that is why God wishes us to pray to Him.

Prayer to God is an act of the virtue of religion, that highest of all the moral virtues which leads us to do our duty to our Creator, particularly in the matter of tendering Him our respect and our submission. Everything in us ought always to be in a state of reverence and of dependence in the presence of God. But when we pray, it is the mind, the noblest part of ourselves, which recognizes Him as Sovereign and expresses its need of Him.

Other virtues are involved in prayer, notably the great theological virtues from which the whole of our Christian life ultimately proceeds. It is through faith that we know God and His merciful power to which we appeal. Charity governs our desires, and in so doing introduces order into our petitions. Hope transforms these simple desires into a confident expectation of their being granted. The virtues of humility and penance then co-operate with the virtue of religion to deepen our sentiments of reverence and submission to God.

How can we best set about this prayer which we wish

_____
[1] IIa IIae, q. 80.

to improvise ? Well, we must begin by finding God in
order to speak to Him : we must approach Him and
address Him in terms suited to the object we have in
view. These titles will be suggested to us by the various
Christian virtues mentioned above, and we shall find
them enshrined in the formularies which Our Lord
Himself, or the Church assisted by His Spirit, has taught
us, in the invocations of the litanies, in the initial clauses
of the liturgical prayers, and in the opening words of the
Lord's Prayer : *Our Father Who art in Heaven.*

The preamble of a well formulated request aims at
enlisting the goodwill of the person to whom the petition
is addressed. The goodwill of God has already been
obtained. " He first loved us," says St. John. It is in
our own hearts that trust in His intervention has to be
aroused. This we do by considering His goodness and
His power. Father Thou art good—Father Whose
child I am. Thou art powerful, Thou Who art in Heaven
regulating all the movements of the material universe,
all spiritual forces . . . !

The first point of our private prayer, the lifting up of
our mind to God, exercises a decided influence over all
that follows. It is important for us to do it aright, and
to repeat it at frequent intervals in order to keep in
touch with God. That is what gives to litanies the chief
part of their efficacy.

Only then shall we put forward our petitions. They
should conform to the desires inculcated in us by charity.
In the perfect formulary of prayer which Our Lord
taught us, the good things we may ask for are enumerated
in their proper order. First, the glory which creatures
must give to God : " hallowed be Thy name." Secondly,
our blessed participation in that glory : " Thy Kingdom
come." After the goal, seen in its twofold aspect, comes
the way to reach it, viz., by the fulfilment of the divine
Will : we must abandon ourselves to the good pleasure
of Providence in whatever circumstances it may place
us, and under those conditions do from day to day what-

ever God enjoins in His commandments and counsels. We need food to sustain us on this way—food for our body and food for the soul : we ask God to give it to us daily. In this manner the soul sets out its requests for good things in the order of their value.

On the other hand, we may, if we like,' reduce our requests to a simple general appeal, invoking God's pity, but not specifying anything in particular. *Have mercy on us ! Have mercy on us !* we say in the litanies. Or we can repeat again and again : *Deus in adjutorium meum intende,* as in the prayers of *Pretiosa.* St. Catherine of Siena was wont to pray after that fashion.

It is possible to go yet further in this direction and, without making any petition at all, just to display our misery before the eyes of God. " *Lord, he whom thou lovest is sick,*" was the message sent to Our Lord by the sisters of Lazarus.

Into these more or less definitely formulated petitions which constitute the essential part of prayer, other kinds of acts may be inserted and embodied as integral parts, those thanksgivings and supplications which St. Paul recommends in the First Epistle to Timothy.

Thanksgiving is particularly appropriate, because nothing is better calculated to induce a patron to continue his favour than gratitude for past benefits. " I make this request of Thee, Lord, Who hast thought of me from all eternity, Who didst bring me out of nothingness and hast given Thy life to redeem me, of Thee Who this very day art giving me such and such a grace of which I am specially conscious. . . ."

If we can plead any claims that entitle us to a favourable hearing, we shall not fail to put them forward to obtain the intervention of God. Our greatest claim—actually our only real plea—is the redemption wrought by Our Saviour and all the series of mysteries which constitute its successive acts. " By Thy Nativity, deliver us, Jesus ! By Thy childhood . . . by Thy labours . . . by Thine agony and Passion . . . by Thy Cross and dereliction . . . deliver us, Jesus ! "

These thanksgivings for favours, these pleas which we
shall unite with our prayers, will dispose God to grant us
His gifts, or rather, as we must always remind ourselves,
will produce in us the disposition of the soul that will
make it possible for God to confer His favours upon us.

St. Thomas remarks that the greater number of our
liturgical prayers can be analysed under four headings,
and he points out those four headings in the Collect for
Trinity Sunday. " Almighty, everlasting God " (here
we have the upraising of the soul to God), " Who in the
confession of the true faith hast given Thy servants to
acknowledge the glory of the eternal Trinity, and in the
power of that majesty to adore the Unity " (this is the
thanksgiving) ; "grant, we beseech Thee, that by stead-
fastness in this faith we may evermore be defended from
all adversity " (petition), "through our Lord Jesus
Christ . . ." (adjuration). And thus in every feast-day
collect and especially in the beautiful Sunday collects
we have subjects for our prayer clearly marked out for us.

Private prayer, when combined in this manner with
choral prayer, has the great advantage of enabling us to
understand and to relish the most forceful passages, the
most edifying sentences of the Office we have celebrated
in common, and over which we have not been able to
linger—that *Pater*, for instance, or that *Ave* which was
said with a profound bow, yet brief, at the beginning
and end of the canonical hours, and that collect, full of
meaning, which had to be pronounced or listened to with
the appropriate ritual gesture.

And this is a very easy form of mental prayer which is
within the reach of the humblest of our Tertiaries. Louis
of Granada himself advised it, enforcing his recommendation with one of those picturesque similes which are so
characteristic of him. " Those who, from lack of devotion, do not know how to converse with God, will do well
to have recourse to the sacred sentences and to the
inspired words which will uplift and guide their spirit ;
and, like children enclosed in a little wheeled pen to

encourage them to walk, they will find in these formularies the spontaneity they do not find in themselves." [1]

II. HOLY MEDITATION

In treating of holy meditation and of private prayer, Humbert de Romans asserts that they may be combined, although they are indeed essentially different.[2] We have gathered as much from our recent survey of St. Dominic engaged in the one and in the other.

Their chief differences, as forms of mental devotion, are as follows : Holy meditation is more strictly *mental* than are private prayers. The latter are perhaps best expressed by the now obsolete word " orisons "—being religious petitions addressed to God. Holy meditation, on the other hand, is rather an elevation of the soul to God in order to contemplate Him.

Though fundamentally mental, the prayers of the early Friars often found expression in eager utterances which gushed from their souls and then were translated into bows, genuflections and prostrations. They were strongly influenced by the divine Office which they prolonged. Holy meditations, pursued without a book, are generally practised in silence and are assisted by quiet. They have an affinity with religious study.

Private prayers are more especially requests made to God in a spirit of the utmost respect and religious submissiveness by a soul who feels very insignificant and destitute in the presence of the Sovereign Master. Meditation may likewise be an exercise of the virtue of religion, also leading to prayer, but in quite a different way, for it causes the soul to reflect upon the perfections of God and upon our personal misery in order to induce us to have recourse to Him.

Meditations are sometimes inspired by the virtue of prudence which settles what we ought to do to lead our life aright. And it is to this purely moral meditation

---

[1] Louis of Granada, *The Memorial.*
[2] Humbert, *Opera*, Vol. II, p. 231.

that the mental devotions of too many pious souls in the
religious life and in the world are confined in these days.
Dominican souls, whilst not underrating this kind of
meditation, will prefer contemplative meditation in
which they exercise their virtue of faith, reflecting upon
the divine truth in order to arrive at contemplation in a
simple and peaceful vision of God. We have seen how
St. Dominic was wont to rise from meditation to contemplation.

We will now apply to St. Thomas for the principles
which must underlie these various forms of meditation.
Let us start by saying a few words about the lowest—
moral meditation. Religious meditation will come next
and then contemplative meditation.

Moral meditation itself is useful for the contemplative
life. If we consult the Treatise that St. Thomas devotes
to the latter, at the close of the Second Part of the *Summa*,
we shall see that, after a first article upon the principal
part played by divine love in the contemplation of God,
he asks himself whether the moral virtues are not also
necessary for this contemplation. Yes, he replies, they
are needed to place the soul in the right disposition.
It is they that impart the purity and the peace without
which the soul, troubled by its passions within and
by the disorders which assail it from without, is incapable of resting in the thought of God. At the same time,
therefore, that the moral virtues are perfecting the soul
on the plane of the active life, they are also preparing
it to devote itself to contemplation.

"Let spiritual directors take special note of this,"
says Cajetan in his Commentary, "and let them make
sure that their disciples are proficient in the active life
before suggesting to them the summits of contemplation.
One must conquer one's passions by habits of gentleness,
of patience . . . of liberality, humility, etc., before it is
possible, passions now subdued, to rise up to the con-

templative life. For lack of this preliminary mortification, many who, instead of walking have bounded along
the way of God, have found themselves, after a long period
devoted to striving after contemplation, destitute of all
virtues, impatient, passionate and proud at the least
provocation. Such persons have not achieved the active
life, nor the contemplative life, nor yet the mixed life :
they have built upon the sand. And would to God that
this defect were rare ! " [1]

A form of meditation which plays a natural part in
this ascetic preparation is moral meditation.

There is no question here of making theoretical considerations or of rising to lofty contemplation. We have
to bring into play our practical reason, and the supernatural virtue of prudence to examine carefully " the
thing to do, the reasons for doing it, and the way to do
it." These words, which are those of St. Thomas,[2] form
a good summary of this sort of meditation which finds
favour with so many spiritual authors to-day. Its
immediate outcome is a practical resolution, definite
and immediately realizable. It is with that end in view
that we meditate, trying to convince ourselves firmly
that a certain supernatural disposition is indispensable,
and that we want to attain it. To deepen that conviction
we consider the reasons which render that particular
virtue desirable, and which make it incumbent on us to
practise it.

To persuade ourselves of the need we have for it, we
carefully review our sentiments, our words and our
actions. Such a survey, if properly carried out, will
arouse in our hearts keen regret for the past, and a
steadfast determination to emerge from our present
state.

We all know these formularies—very excellent, no
doubt, in their way. During a retreat of a decisive
nature we do well to follow some such method, and it

[1] Cajetan in IIam IIae, a. 182, a. i, § VII.
[2] *De Veritate*, q. 14, a. 4.

may prove helpful for a short daily examination upon some special virtue or practice.

But here we find ourselves faced with the question : Does this kind of meditation deserve to be called a prayer ? Only in so far as it begins by adoring God or Jesus, the model and exponent of Christian perfection, and as it appeals to God through Jesus Christ Our Lord for aid to enable us to participate in that perfection. Those two points alone differentiate it from the efforts of stoic moralists, past and present. In itself this kind of meditation is not prayer. And it is a mistake to devote to it the greater part of the time allotted to mental prayer.

It will be far better to append the practical part of such a meditation to the religious meditation which we shall now consider.

III.   RELIGIOUS MEDITATION

There is a form of religious meditation in which our time for mental prayer may well be spent. St. Thomas specially recommends it, and he has formulated its principles.[1] It is actually the work of the virtue of religion. Unlike lengthy and endlessly reiterated moral meditations, it does not expose us to the danger of thinking too much about ourselves. For the virtue of religion has this characteristic which makes it superior to the other moral virtues, it is directed to God Himself. With it we cease to be concerned about ourselves, except to turn to God to honour Him and to do homage to Him. Religion places everything at His disposal, our exterior possessions and the members of our body, but, above all, our inner being, our reason and our will. As has already been said, it is our reason which pays homage to the Sovereign Master when we pray. And it is our will, the most personal part of us, which generously subjects itself to Him by the act of devotion. This latter is the supreme religious act which will carry in its train all the others, prayer itself, bodily worship, sacrifices—

[1] IIa IIae, q. 82, a. 3.

everything. Devotion can rule the whole life. Not satisfied with practising on certain days and at certain hours such and such a religious exercise, we shall turn all the acts of life, even the most humble, into homage. That is the ideal aspired to by those who are religious by their very profession. " Whether you eat or drink, whatever you do," said St. Paul, " do all for the glory of God."

How shall we stimulate this most important devotion ? The principal cause of devotion, replies St. Thomas, is God, Who bestows it upon whomsoever He will. Obviously it will call for prayer. But St. Thomas speaks of religious meditation first, as being necessary to enable us not only to do what lies in our own power to excite that devotion, but also to pray for it aright and to dispose ourselves to receive of it from God in response to our prayer.

In an earlier work, our great Doctor had already treated of this kind of meditation which, he says, occupies a place midway between the reading of Holy Scripture, whereby we hear the Word of God, and prayer, in which we speak to God. God speaks to us. But how many there are for whom His intervention is non-existent ! By meditation we try to apprehend it with the heart and with the mind. In this way, being established in the presence of God, we can petition Him better.[1] Obviously such a meditation should form part of our private prayers, to inspire them and to increase their fervour.

What precise form does this religious meditation take ? It consists in making reflections calculated to convince us personally of the necessity of having recourse to God, and of subjecting ourselves to Him. As our food does not nourish us until it has gone through a considerable process of mastication and digestion, so the great Christian truths will not be assimilated until they have been

[1] IV Sent., d. 15, q. 4, a. 1, qla. 2, ad 1.

subjected to a meditation which St. Thomas somewhere describes as intellectual rumination.

Our reflections will be upon God and upon ourselves. Those are the two points, and they are indeed inseparable, to which this meditation will ever lead us. Its model was furnished by Our Lord to St. Catherine when He said to her : " Daughter, knowest thou who thou art and Who I am ? If thou dost know these two things, happy shalt thou be. Thou art she who is not : I am He Who is."

The meditation will open with reflections upon the plenitude of being and of goodness that is God, and upon the blessings, general and particular, which He has bestowed upon us. None of those subtle considerations which may be admissible in a course of higher theology, but only thoughts capable of awaking devotion. In theory the thought of the perfections of the divine Being should best tend to do this. But our poor human spirit needs something tangible to start with, and that is why the humanity of Our Lord is the practical means of raising us to an effective knowledge of the divine Being. Come to Him as He is revealed in one or other of the gospel episodes, or under the form He assumes in some parable. See in Him the Father of the prodigal son, the good Shepherd, the Sower ; or, again, the incomparable Master Who receives His first disciples on the banks of the Jordan, and begins their education which will continue for three years ; consider Him as the great Spiritual Director Who talks with the Samaritan woman at Jacob's well, and gradually raises her soul from earthly cares to the noblest conceptions, the divine Physician receiving and healing body and soul, the perfect pattern of all virtues, so devout, so pure, humble, gentle, patient, merciful, so devoted to His neighbour.

After having thus meditated upon God, and still bearing Him in mind, we shall go on to consider our own helplessness ; how our very being was drawn out of nothingness, only too easily relapsing into it through sin, and of the great need we have of our Creator and Saviour in all and through all. Ah ! we are indeed incapable of being self-sufficient !

This meditation upon our misery, as displayed in the presence of the divine goodness, will lead us to abase ourselves before God in admiration and praise of His infinite perfections, and finally to ask Him to give us His saving gifts. Our petition will be for things that are really good, a very humble, very confident, very persevering form of prayer it will be, and far more efficacious than if it had not been prepared for by some such form of meditation as the above. With M. Olier we might well describe it as a spiritual communion.

All that remains for us to do is to correspond, to co-operate with the grace received. Under the sway of this grace we shall formulate a good resolution vastly superior to any resolution we might have taken at the close of a meditation prompted by the virtue of prudence alone.

What kind of resolution will it be ? Will it have as its object some particular practice ? It will be primarily of a general character, covering the whole life so as to make thereof a complete and entire homage to God, but will be applicable afterwards to the details of our daily life to give them the necessary moral value to render them presentable to the divine Master. This is the moment for prudence, motivated by the virtue of religion, to interpose a guiding hand, and for the collaboration of such other moral virtues as the case may demand.

The morning meditation of one employed in the works of the active life will be very insistent upon this point. He will make what he foresees to be the necessary resolutions, and will examine himself from time to time during the course of the day to ascertain how he is carrying them out.

Apart from its utility in thus penetrating the whole of our life of devotion, religious meditation when it precedes the exercises of worship properly so called, such as the Office sung in choir or individually recited, will help us to perform them *digne, attente ac devote.* If, as is frequently the case, it precedes the greatest of religious acts, the holy sacrifice of the Mass in which Christ Himself comes for us into our midst, to proclaim by His self-immolation the sovereignty of Him Who alone has being, it will rouse our soul which too readily sinks into the routine of habitual formularies and gestures, and will enable us better to apprehend the sacred mystery and more completely to associate ourselves with it.

IV.   CONTEMPLATIVE MEDITATION

We have already recommended two methods which the soul can use during the time of prayer—private prayers and religious meditation.   There are two others which have an even greater claim to be called mental prayer because they are loftier ascents of the soul to God.

These likewise have their source in charity.   We have seen how, in the case of those other methods, charity gives an impetus to the virtue of religion which makes us pray or meditate in order to serve God.   But here our charity asserts itself more directly and admonishes us that we are servants of whom God has made His friends. After that, it is satisfied with stimulating our faith to behold the divine Friend in order to love Him better. This is a simpler, and at the same time a higher, kind of prayer which deserves the name of "theological" prayer because of the virtues which underlie it.

If I have preferred to call it contemplative meditation, that is because these words have the advantage of showing clearly the transition between religious meditation and mystical contemplation.   Moreover, the term exactly summarizes the article in which St. Thomas expounds the principles of this exercise of the contemplative life.[1]

---

[1] IIa IIae, q. 180, a. 3.

In my prayer of petition, in religious meditation, I was pursuing a practical objective ; I was occupied in a work of the active life ; I was doing something. I tried to improvise a little discourse, or I formulated my requests to God, or else I reflected with a view to persuading myself to consecrate all my activity to God, and I made resolutions to that end. A very meritorious work indeed ! But when the time for inactivity comes—when it is the hour for sacred repose—*Vacate et videte*—" Rest," says the Lord, " and look at Me." The hour of prayer is an ideal moment for the contemplation of God. The true Dominican ought to apply himself to it whole-heartedly, as befits the member of an Order which is pre-eminently contemplative. Moreover, through this exercise of charity, the whole of his religious and moral life will be radically perfected.

After the apparition in which Our Lord told St. Catherine of Siena what she was and Who He is, there was another vision in which He gave her a second injunction : " Daughter, think of Me ; if thou wilt do so, I will think of thee unceasingly. . . ." " When she was talking to me privately about this revelation," wrote Blessed Raymund of Capua, " the saint told me that the Lord had then ordered her to retain no will of her own except the will that drew her to Him, and to exclude from her heart every other consideration, because any care for herself, even for her spiritual salvation, might hinder her from resting continually upon the thought of God. The Master had added : " And I will think of thee," as if to say, " Daughter, be not troubled about the salvation of thy body and soul—I who have knowledge and power will think of it and will provide for it ; only apply thyself to think of Me in thy meditations ; in that lies thy perfection and thy final goal." "

This is not the simple uplifting of the soul to God, which is the preliminary to every prayer, properly so called : it is the application of the mind to God—an application both reiterated and penetrating. I am not just placing myself in God's presence to persuade myself, by considering what He is and what I am, to be submissive to Him, as in religious meditation. I am no longer at all concerned with myself : I am concerned only with Him. My whole aim is to behold Him, to behold Him because I love Him, and to behold Him in order to love Him still more.

If I think of creatures, if I observe the marvels of the material universe, if my spirit seeks to roam in the world of ideas, if I admire the still higher splendours encountered in holy souls in Heaven and on earth, if I am conscious of what grace has been able to effect in my own soul, all these things have been for me mere steps to lead me up to the divine Cause Who manifests Himself in His works. The only object to which my thought ultimately ascends is God, as He has revealed Himself to us in Jesus Christ and through Jesus Christ.

It is Jesus Christ, therefore, that I am considering, our God made man. Jesus once alive on earth, now alive in Heaven and giving life in the Church composed of His members scattered over the globe. I also consider the Holy Trinity, the relations between the three Persons and the perfections of the one Nature, as they have been revealed to me by Jesus.

When we have become like to the angels in Heaven, this contemplation will be spontaneous and continuous in the eternal vision, face to face. Here below, conditions are very different. Our spirit has to do much searching, observing and reflecting : it must make distinctions and comparisons, and it must go through a more or less lengthy course of reasoning before it can attain to a brief and dim contemplation. These efforts, which will necessarily have been preceded and facilitated by preparatory study or special reading, not to speak of prayer, will all come under the category and heading of meditation. But by dint of meditation, one gradually succeeds in simplifying all these mental processes so that one can quickly rise to a contemplative glance. Once we have reached that stage let us not waste time over preliminary considerations which have been useful in the past, but which have served their turn. Let us rather endeavour to repeat that loving gaze, to protect it by means of a familiar colloquy in which our soul will freely express to God its sentiments, the affections that spring from its charity. Hence the description " affective " which is applied by many authors to this kind of prayer. Let us lift ourselves up to that supreme act, an act which was not mentioned in treating of the preceding devotions because it cannot be made the object of a desire, nor, consequently, of a petition. It consists simply in rejoicing that God is perfect and infinitely happy. Our divine friendship will make us find in that our purest bliss.

This form of devotion in the early stages deserves its name of meditation better than its qualifying adjective " contemplative " because the reflections require many efforts and much time. But it will soon prove a contemplation, rather than a meditation, when once a little recollection becomes all that is necessary to enable us to see God in some mystery with which our spirit has made itself familiar.

Those eager glances of faith which charity prompts, and which actually increase our charity, may be repeated many times during the course of the celebration of the divine mysteries which St. Thomas describes as the principal work of the contemplative life. The whole liturgical Office with the Mass as its centre constitutes, especially when it is chorally sung, the most favourable possible occasion for the devotion we have been dealing with, and it is not surprising that during the first centuries of the Order no need was experienced for the prescription of a separate fixed hour of prayer for all the community. The Friars then delighted in freely prolonging

their liturgical worship by private individual prayer.
Charity, quickened in them by the celebration of the
Office, inspired our ancient Fathers to adopt this practice.
We should be acting in full conformity with their spirit
if we were to choose, as a suitable moment for private
devotion, the time immediately following a Mass and
Communion in which we had devoutly participated,
and if we took as our guide St. Thomas's *Adoro Te.*

If our Blessed Father wished the choral Office to be
shortened in favour of study, if in those priories which
are entirely consecrated to the latter only one half hour
of mental prayer is obligatory, that is because study
such as must be practised by true Dominicans is immediately directed, under the impulse of charity, towards
the acquisition of a better knowledge of God. Therefore
it forms an excellent preparation for contemplative
meditation, and can even take its place, because it
readily leads up to those loving intuitions which form
the ultimate goal of both.

But it is more particularly in the evening, when the
close of day suggests the close of life, when the night's
rest recalls that of Heaven, that we seem naturally called
to this more or less simplified contemplative meditation which prepares, outlines and inaugurates our
eternal occupation. May sleep find us engaged in these
great thoughts of eternity ! Our Order, especially in
its contemplative branches, has always insisted very
particularly upon this evening meditation and upon
this way of performing it.

V.   MYSTICAL CONTEMPLATION

As Dominicans we are bound daily to recognize it to
be our primary duty to think of God with love, and to
apply ourselves heart and soul to the consideration of
one or other of the mysteries of Jesus, and all available
means must converge towards that end—theological
studies, liturgical offices, spiritual reading, and meditations properly so called.

But as we proceed with our efforts we are apt to be woefully astonished at the meagre results we achieve. How paltry and dim is the thought that faith strives to fix upon God, and how quickly our spirit is distracted and drawn down to inferior objects !

Actually we have no cause for astonishment. It is difficult even to rise from the tangible world to the world of ideas, and very few human beings can breathe the rarefied air of those heights long enough to dwell there. When we pass from philosophical knowledge to supernatural truths, it is only natural that the effort should be greater and the success very poor. But a dim light upon such subjects is worth more than knowing all the contents of the daily paper, and seeing all the busy world which throngs the streets.

Let us not be discouraged ; let us go on trying, in the hope that the Holy Spirit will reward us by bestowing upon us a loftier form of contemplation than any we can acquire for ourselves.

It is not presumption to entertain such hopes. What we can do through our friends, says a Greek philosopher whom St. Thomas quotes in this very connection, we do in a certain sense through ourselves. Now God actually dwells in our soul as a friend. *Tu in nobis es Domine*. . . . Thou art in us, Lord, Thou to Whom St. Paul addressed his petition on behalf of the faithful in Ephesus, asking Him to give them the spirit of wisdom and of revelation in the perfect knowledge of Himself and to illuminate the eyes of their heart.

Has a Christian, then, eyes in his heart for seeing God ? Yes, in addition to faith which St. Paul associates with hearing, *fides ex auditu* (the faith based on the word heard from the divine mouth to give us conviction of the reality of the invisible world, *argumentum non apparentium*), our hearts possess a certain possibility of vision, thanks to the intellectual gifts of the Holy Spirit which have been granted to us since our Baptism.

Only we cannot exert those capabilities at will, as we

can open our eyes upon the world of sense, or as we apply
our intelligence supernaturalized by the virtue of faith.
It rests with us to exercise our supernatural virtues as
well as our natural faculties. Grace co-operates with us,
undoubtedly, but the initiative must be ours. In the
case of the gifts of the Holy Spirit, especially those which
enable us to contemplate God, the initiative belongs to
the Holy Spirit Himself. His intervention depends upon
His good pleasure.

Nevertheless, seeing that He has deposited within us
spiritual organs which await this intervention, are we
not justified in assuming that He will use them when
the right time comes ? And will not that time have
arrived when we have done all we possibly can in our
human way ? After we have exerted ourselves to the
utmost to practise the moral virtues so as to be in a fit
state to apply ourselves to contemplation ; and after
we have proceeded to make sufficient efforts in contemplative meditation ; then the Holy Spirit will supervene to prolong our effort and to open the eyes of our
heart on God in a knowledge of Himself which will be
as an intimate and personal revelation.

If we cannot, properly speaking, merit this illumina-
tion, we can certainly merit the perfecting of the organs
that await it, and welcome it within us. For they develop
and become better and better fitted for their function in
proportion to our progress in the state of grace. And it
also lies in our power to add to our insufficient merit
the efficacy which prayer possesses to hasten within us
the advent of infused contemplation. St. Thomas advises
those who give themselves to contemplative meditation
to pray for the spirit of wisdom. He quotes the words of
Holy Scripture : I prayed and the spirit of wisdom came
into me.[1] St. Paul, as we have seen, made the same
petition for the Corinthians.

[1] IIa IIae, q. 180, a. 3, ad 4.

Let us pray humbly, trustfully and perseveringly, continuing untiringly the efforts that depend upon ourselves. Let us practise such self-denial as may enable our spirit to rule over all our passions and to develop unhindered. In the over-agitated life of our spirit itself, let us secure pauses in which we may recollect ourselves and fix a quiet glance upon God. And then do not let us form exaggerated ideas about infused contemplation. It begins in a small way, and the boundary is not easily determined between the intuition one arrives at through a well-ordered meditation and one which emanates from the Holy Spirit's initiative. However much it may grow, this infused contemplation does not lift us out of the shadows of faith ; it remains always dim as well as mysterious, and that is why it is called mystical contemplation.

Like active contemplation, it proceeds from the love of God. But in its working it is very different. Whereas formerly, in a resolution of love, one forced oneself to think about God, now in a movement of love God forces Himself upon our thought. Love is no longer the fruit of our effort, we do not stir it up in our heart by a deliberate act. We seem to receive it ready made ; one might almost say that it rises within us automatically, like a spring which wells up from the very depths in which the Holy Spirit dwells. This infused love is the principle of mystical contemplation, and constitutes its permanent basis in the different phases of its evolution. Whether we be at the initial stage of reaching anxiously after God Who conceals Himself, or whether we attain finally to the sensation of enjoying His presence, we have always, in the midst of this fervour of spontaneous love, at least the vivid consciousness that God is the great reality.

" In spiritual things," says St. Thomas in reference to the words *gustate et videte* which occur in a psalm, " one begins by tasting and afterwards one sees." Lights accordingly emanate, under the influence of the Holy

Spirit, from that loving relish which is at the base of mystical wisdom. At first, experience thus tasted comes to complete our speculative knowledge of the divine mystery. But certain positive lights may also be given us upon God, and the truths He has taught us. Especially shall we have a vivid intuition of His absolute transcendence. Ah, yes ! He does indeed surpass all that we can think of Him ; all the poor ideas we can conceive can never truly represent that living God Whose all-powerful attraction our heart feels, and Whom it seeks to embrace with all the force of its love.[1]

VI. EJACULATORY PRAYERS

Our divine Master said that we must always pray, and St. Paul has repeated : Pray without ceasing—*sine intermissione orate.*

It is certainly impossible that any prayer, strictly so called, should be absolutely continual. If a few privileged souls can lift up their thought and heart to God almost without relaxation, most people here below have cares which engage their attention and which do not leave them enough liberty of mind for this constant prayer.

Nevertheless, we ought always to keep ourselves in the fundamental disposition for prayer, in the state of soul from whence proceeds that spiritual uplifting which is called prayer. This fundamental disposition, this state of soul, consists in the love of God. Whatever our occupation may be, divine love must be the principle of our activity. It may well happen that we are not thinking every moment about God, but it is essential that the influence of charity should persist, at least virtually, through all our acts in such a way that they will follow the direction thus given them. This comes about provided we have not renounced the primary intention which prompted us to act for God alone. The man who goes to work to earn bread for his family,

---

[1] These pages are but a summary of the author's book : *La Contemplation mystique d'après St. Thomas d'Aquin.*

even if he is not thinking about them, is labouring for them and thereby gives evidence of his love. In the intervals for rest he thinks of them as a matter of course, and goes back to work with renewed energy. Similarly our love of God, if it is real, will break out from time to time in prayer properly so called. This prayer, whenever it is made, will render us more devoted to the service of God, and consequently our very work thus supernaturalized will be more or less a continuance of our prayer. In that sense it is right to say that he who works prays.

By reason of this effect which it produces as well as by reason of the love from which it is itself derived, prayer goes on continuously—after a fashion. Is this sufficient to satisfy the divine Master's injunction? Because they felt that something more frequent was necessary, the first Christian ascetics, the holy Fathers of the desert, made a great point of those ejaculatory prayers, which have been so praised by St. Augustine and St. Thomas,[1] and which it would be difficult to estimate too highly.

In the beautiful letter on religious perfection, addressed by the Most Reverend Fr. Ridolfi to the congregation of St. Louis in France (1630), he recommended that the two half hours of mental prayer should be supplemented by frequent ejaculatory prayers throughout the day and at night. And in support of this counsel he appealed to the authority of Blessed Humbert de Romans.

In what do these ejaculatory prayers consist? In just a few words or a few reflections which suddenly spring from the heart, and which go forth, hurled like a javelin (*jaculum*), to touch the heart of God.

These prayers are brief, very brief indeed, and therefore we need no leisure to enable us to proffer them. They are so short that they do not even interrupt our

[1] IIa IIae, q. 83, a. 14, with quotations from St. Augustine.

ordinary occupations. They can be inserted into the middle of a conversation, and the people to whom we are talking will never notice them.

If our spirit is naturally volatile and easily distracted, we cannot readily concentrate upon lengthy mental devotions, but these will be no strain upon us. An instant is all they need, and they cannot possibly bore us. A simple motion of the heart is sufficient, no effort whatever being required.

Do we really love God ? Everything depends upon that. If we do, these prayers will flow from their natural source. The mouth speaks out of the abundance of the heart. And at the very moment that our ejaculatory prayers are expressing this love, they are fanning its fervour, and are maintaining the good intentions of our Christian life.

Ejaculatory prayer may be composed of one word, and that one always the same. It will perhaps be the name of God, of Jesus, of Mary, words which will be tinged by the various sentiments of the soul, to express in turn our hope, our love, our devotion, our petition, our thanks, our contrition, etc. Blessed Catherine of Racconigi used often to murmur as she worked at her loom : *Jesu, spes mea.* And St. Catherine of Siena liked to repeat the words with which she always ended her letters : " Sweet Jesus, Jesus Love."

At other times it will be a phrase formulated by ourselves or borrowed from some pure source of Christian spirituality. The Holy Scriptures, especially the psalms, liturgical prayers, the saints, especially our own, will furnish us with abundant phrases which we can make our own. We have seen how St. Dominic diversified his ejaculatory prayers according to the different attitudes he assumed at his devotions.

One may say, for instance, when rising in the morning : " Lo, I come to do Thy will, O God ! " In the evening it will probably be : " Lord, into Thy hands I commend my spirit." In moments of religious recollection : " I

adore Thee here present, O hidden God. . . . Glory
be to the Father and to the Son and to the Holy Ghost."
In the midst of our work or in the difficulties of our daily
duties : " I am Thy servant, and the son of Thy handmaid." In the hours of gladness : " I thank Thee, my
God. . . . What shall I render to Thee for all the
benefits I have received from Thee ! "

When we feel weak and tempted, we may wish to say,
like St. Catherine of Siena : " O Lord, incline to my
aid, O Lord, make haste to help me." After a fault,
that other saying which was a familiar one to her :
" I have sinned, Lord, have mercy upon me." Or with
David : "Have mercy on me according to Thy great
mercy." " Eternal Father," a humble nun of our own
day used to say, " I offer Thee the wounds of Our Lord
Jesus Christ to heal those of our souls."

Is it necessary to give other instances ? Here are a
few exclamations of hope and love, inspired by the Holy
Spirit and charged with the fervour of innumerable
Christians who have re-echoed them : " Lord, Thou
knowest that I love Thee. . . . To be united to God is
happiness for me. . . . Lord Jesus, suffer me not ever
to be separated from Thee. . . . Thou wilt fill me with
joy at the sight of Thy countenance. . . . Come, Lord
Jesus, come ! "

Let us also invoke the Blessed Virgin : " Show thyself
to be our Mother." Let us whisper to her those caressing
words of the *Salve Regina* : *Mater misericordiae, vita,
dulcedo et spes nostra !* For those who are familiar with the
liturgical language, those terms have a sweeter savour
in their Latin brevity.

Everyone ought to follow the inspiration of his own
spirit and the bent of his soul. " I feel in the depths of
my soul," said Mother Frances of the Seraphim, " a
certain instinct which impels me very frequently to
rise up and reach after God, and that is my customary
state of mind." [1]

[1] *Les Filles de St. Thomas*, p. 165.

Seasons, places, the sights we see, the sounds we hear—everything can provide us with an occasion for uplifting our heart to God. The important point for us to grasp is that these ejaculatory prayers should express great virtues which are in us by divine grace, and that they should bind us to the sacred Persons upon Whom our salvation depends—the Holy Trinity Which communicates Its life to us, the Son of God Incarnate for us Who incorporates us into Himself to lead us to His Father, the Blessed Virgin who is our true mother in divine grace, and St. Dominic the father of our religious life.

After many years spent in extreme austerities, one of the most celebrated of the desert Fathers, St. Macarius the Elder, learnt by divine revelation that he was not yet as perfect as two married women who dwelt in a neighbouring town. Immediately he set out to seek them. He discovered two very humble individuals who, in the midst of their ordinary household duties, constantly turned to God in ejaculatory prayers. Then Macarius, who had already felt attracted to that form of devotion, set himself to practise it more and more. A favourite prayer which he often repeated in all sincerity was : " Lord, have pity upon me as Thou knowest and as Thou wilt " : *Domine sicut scis et vis, miserere mei.*

To quote the words of Louis of Granada [1] : " Those who are given to this practice have already travelled half the way when the moment arrives for prayer, and they find no difficulty in recollecting themselves. How is it that in their prayers some souls are immediately filled with fervour, whilst others find it so extraordinarily difficult to establish peace within themselves ? Often the reason is that the former maintain the warmth of devotion by means of short prayers, and the latter allow themselves to grow cold in forgetfulness of God. Like a baker, who is careful not to let his oven cool because of the difficulty he would have in raising it to the right

[1] On Prayer.

temperature when he wants to use it, even so should fervent souls keep alive within them the ardour of devotion if they wish to spare themselves the task of rekindling it every time they wish to apply themselves to prayer."

I would add in conclusion that our special half hour of mental prayer may quite well be spent in a series of ejaculatory prayers—rather more sustained than at other times. . . . Make a little selection to suit yourself, and try. Massoulie used to recommend this.[1] Do not be afraid of repeating over and over again, and for quite a long while, the thought that you find profitable. Jesus Himself set us this example in His prayer in the Garden of Olives : *Eumdem sermonem dicens*—He repeated the same words.

VII. THE HOLY ROSARY, A METHOD OF PRAYER

There is one practice, dear to every Dominican soul, which has gradually absorbed and assimilated the very best of all that we have been considering in private prayers, with their vocal and bodily accompaniments, in the various forms of holy meditation, the contemplative especially, and even in the ejaculatory prayers themselves. I refer to the Rosary.

It might easily be set down as a purely vocal and mechanical devotion. And yet the Dominican Constitutions do not hesitate to declare that the Rosary, recited in common, may occupy at least a part of the time which the community must devote to mental prayer. As a matter of fact, if properly understood, the Rosary is a perfect method of prayer. It was fully recognized by Romeo of Livia, a Friar whom St. Dominic himself trained to the religious life, and of whom Bernard Gui said that " he glowed with the fervour of his devotion to the Virgin Mother of God, and to Jesus the fruit of

---

[1] Many souls have followed this practice in our Order. *Cf. L'Année Dominicaine*, January, pp. 36, 40-41, 45, and February, pp. 288-291 ; etc.

her womb." He used a knotted cord to number all the
Aves he recited every day whilst he " ruminated " on the
Christian mysteries in his soul. He died in 1261, " grasp-
ing his instrument of prayer tightly in his hands, and
urging upon the friars this devotion to Our Lady and
to the Child Jesus."

" At the beginning, in the middle or at the end of all
his sermons he had spoken of it ; sometimes indeed it
constituted the subject-matter of his entire discourse."
If Our Lady said to St. Dominic and his Order : " Go
and preach my Rosary," Blessed Romeo was one of the
first who are known to have recommended and practised
this devotion under a form very similar to that now in
use. To-day, Dominican religious, both men and women,
wear at their side beads of hard wood, connected by a
cord or a little metal chain, which take the place of
Blessed Romeo's knotted cord. And by means of the
Rosary Confraternity our Order tries to initiate all
the pious faithful into the life of prayer.

We take into our hands these Rosary beads blessed
by the Church, this instrument of devotion to Our Lord
and His Mother. Even if we are so tired that we can
do nothing more, the religious gesture is in itself a
significant and eloquent attitude before God. When
Fr. Cormier, of pious memory, allowed himself to be
photographed, he always took his Rosary between his
fingers so that he should be represented in this devout
posture.

But this instrument, expressly designed for prayer,
moves the person who handles it to prayer. These beads,
which the Church's blessing has loaded with graces,
stimulate the soul. They slip through our fingers, and
as they do so we duly recite a *Pater* and ten *Aves*, then
another *Pater* and another decade of *Aves*. . . . The
Rosary includes as many *Aves* as there are psalms with
which to praise God in the liturgical Office. On the

beads it is easy to keep count of our salutations, so that we can be certain, when they are told, that the full number has been completed.

Surely, however, someone may object, this must be one of those prayers condemned by Our Lord in the gospel as only vain babbling. Not at all. Long discourses, in which we set forth our spiritual and material wants to the Heavenly Father Who knows everything, may quite conceivably degenerate into mere words. These short reiterated salutations call for no absorbing effort on our part : they leave us quite free to upraise our soul devoutly to God. They even help us to do so. By setting up automatically what is tantamount to a barricade between ourselves and the outside world, they begin by promoting recollection which is the condition of all true prayer. And then, by directing us repeatedly to the Holy Virgin and the divine fruit of her womb, they carry us along and end by fixing us in their presence.

We can picture Jesus and Mary in their different states : living on earth at Nazareth, at Bethlehem, at Jerusalem —suffering the great dolours of the Passion and the Compassion—glorious finally after the Resurrection, the Ascension and the Assumption. The Rosary bids us contemplate them in the mysteries which they once enacted, the graces of which they would impart to us. The whole work of salvation is there : in the redemption which they wrought for mankind by this series of mysteries, and in the communication to each one of us of the graces of these mysteries. What better preparation for receiving the grace of salvation than that of one who, as he considers the joyful, sorrowful and the glorious mysteries through which Jesus and Mary passed and by which they draw us after them, visualizes those mysteries again in spirit and is thrilled in turn with heartfelt joy, grief and hope ? The successive feasts of the liturgical year have no other aim than to establish us in this favourable state. With the Rosary it is the whole liturgical year that one sums up weekly if one performs the minimum required of Rosarians, and daily if one wishes to be a fervent Dominican Tertiary.

Have we too little time? We must remember that according to the Rule the Rosary may replace the Canonical Office. It can even do the double duty of the Office and mental prayer. Since we are also allowed to separate the decades, the busiest of us can find the two minutes required for a decade at odd times during the day—on the way to work and back, perhaps, or at the rest hour. In the morning, and, more particularly still, in the evening—the time so favourable for prayer—we shall no doubt be able to devote more than two minutes to this exercise and thus make it more fruitful.

The last mention of Our Lady in the Holy Scriptures occurs in the passage of the Acts which says that, after Our Lord's Ascension into Heaven, all His disciples with one spirit persevered in prayer with certain women and Mary the Mother of Jesus. We may see in this a foreshadowing of the practice of the Rosary. The Blessed Virgin Mary is present, the only witness in some cases and at all times the best witness, of the great mysteries of Jesus in which she participated. Her very presence, when she is not telling the story, recalls all that took place, all that she went through. And the disciples, gathered round about her, pray as they think it all over, and as they eagerly anticipate the consummation of the mysteries. Have we not here all the essentials of the Rosary? It is indeed a wonderful devotion! Let us say it in common, as it was said by the little primitive Church and as it is said every night in all Dominican communities to this day.

"Daughter," said the Blessed Virgin one day to a child who was afterwards to become the Venerable Agatha of the Cross, a Dominican (1546–1621), "Recite the Rosary. . . . When you repeat this prayer, meditate carefully upon the mysteries of the Life, Passion, Death and Resurrection of my Son."

From that moment Agatha applied herself particularly to reciting the Rosary, but, so great was the relish and the light she derived from it, that sometimes, after beginning the *Our Father*, she would dwell on the first two words, and could say nothing else for two or three days. Her spirit and her heart swam in the light and joys of a blissful contemplation.

She had perfectly attained to that contemplation towards which the Rosary uplifts the soul, and she could cease reciting it and meditating upon it. But here is a very exceptional case. For most souls, however well advanced, and indeed for herself at normal times, the Rosary has ever proved a means of entering into contemplation and of remaining in it.

Another Dominican Tertiary of the seventeenth century, Marie Paret, wrote in a letter : " After my Rosary I recite scarcely any vocal prayers : I find myself inclined rather to rest in the presence of God." [1] Other vocal prayers are often a hindrance to this devotion of simple recollection in God. The Rosary, far from hindering, actually fosters it.

For mystical souls, especially if they are naturally expansive, like our Blessed Father St. Dominic, the Rosary will also furnish an outlet for those intense emotions which sometimes flood the soul. The exuberance of their sentiments will find expression in a clause from the *Pater*, the *Ave* and the *Gloria*, or in the names of Mary and Jesus, pronounced with devotion.

If, on the other hand, the soul finds itself in dryness, incapable either of meditating on the mystery or of contemplating the gospel scene, it will at least be able to fall back upon those *Aves* and will take shelter in them, instead of allowing itself to be swept away by the whirlwind of distractions.

Those who are accustomed to use one of the other methods of mental prayer we have described, and are sometimes distressed at their lack of success, will do well

---

[1] Brémond, *Histoire Littéraire du sentiment religieux*, Vol. VI, p. 417.

on such days to take up their Rosary. It is better to tell one's beads and to recite *Aves* in an attitude of devotion than to say and do nothing at all for God.

I may even be quite unable to attempt anything else. Too many duties and occupations may engross my mind for me to be equal to assembling my ideas and recollecting myself. Or I may be obsessed by one idea, a violent temptation to lust or anger, to jealousy or vengeance, unbelief or despair. More often still, I am simply tired out, harassed at the end of a hard day's work, or else ill in bed and unable to collect my thoughts. In all those circumstances the Rosary is the best means of calming my soul in the presence of God.

Let us all and always bless the Holy Virgin for giving to St. Dominic and his Order this matchless method of prayer !

FOURTH SECTION

TOWARDS PERFECT CONTEMPLATION

WE are all contemplatives by vocation. The most gifted, the most privileged, will never, here below, get beyond imperfect contemplation. But God calls all, without exception, to perfect contemplation—to behold Him face to face and to enjoy His love throughout eternity.

Quiet and free souls, you who have both the leisure and the inclination to recollect yourselves in lofty thoughts or in the sweetness of pure love, rejoice as you look forward to the splendid destiny of seeing all truth immediately, and of enjoying the divine friendship to your heart's content.

And you others, bustling people, always busy, engrossed in a thousand things, involved in affairs and worries rather by necessity perhaps than by choice, think of the eternal rest that awaits you. It will not be inactivity, but a noble, orderly, beatifying activity. Your most excellent faculty, your intelligence, in its most excellent act, pure intuition, will fix itself upon the most excellent of all objects, God Himself unveiled at last, and there will ensue perfect felicity in which all your other faculties, each in its appointed order, will find their share of bliss. "There we shall be at rest and we shall love, we shall behold and we shall praise. . . . We shall see God unendingly, we shall love Him untiringly, we shall praise Him unwearyingly. That will be the duty, the wish and the employment of all."

This, then, is our common end. Whoever we may be, we ought to say with the Psalmist : " One thing have I asked of the Lord and this will I seek after ; that I may

dwell in the house of the Lord all the days of my life,
that I may see the delights of the Lord."

But this goal will be reached only in Heaven, and
according to the merits obtained upon the earth. If it
is permissible to say that we inaugurate here below, in
the state of grace, our state of eternal glory, it is necessary that it should be on the same plane. We have
already indeed certain titles to the divine heritage, but
we shall not, strictly speaking, taste the first fruits of
that beatific estate. What are these titles and what gives
them their value ? What is the source of our merits ?
It is Charity, that love which over-rules and directs
towards God all the activity of our soul. " If any one
love Me," said Jesus, " My Father will love him, and I
will love him and will manifest Myself to him. . . ."
We shall see God in Heaven, according to the degree in
which we have attained to loving Him at the moment of
our death. The charity which we have then in our heart
will regulate the degree of our eternal contemplation.

Charity manifests its vigour in the works it produces,
and these works themselves increase its strength. Hence
the importance of these works, not only to teach us where
we stand in relation to our last end, but also to bring us
gradually nearer to it. Everything invites us to put our
charity into practice.

There are two great methods of doing this. God, Who
is the object of our love, may be sought in Himself or
He may be discovered in our neighbour. In Himself,
where He lacks nothing, all that we can do is to contemplate Him with complacency. What more could we
do ? Our love is satisfied that our divine friend should
be perfect and infinitely happy, and we delight in
dwelling upon that thought. But in our neighbour He
appeals to our benevolence. There God is to be found,
as it were, in need ; and our more or less pressing duty
is to devote ourselves to His service. And so charity
urges us to do our utmost in that direction.

We see here two very different ways of life : the contemplative life with its holy leisure, *otium sanctum*, as St. Augustine called it, and the active life with its rightful work, *negotium justum*. Christians are drawn to one or the other of these two lives, according to their tastes and their vocation. In the Order of St. Dominic there is a multiplicity of branches, some of which are contemplative and the rest active.

Notice particularly that the same virtue of charity intervenes in every case. Charity acts, manifests itself, in all these works, outwardly so different, and charity increases through the one and through the other. So truly is this the case that by following the one road or the other we can attain to Christian perfection, which is only the perfection of charity. Indeed, I even go so far as to assert that by the one as by the other, one can arrive at that mystical union which we spoke of in connection with infused contemplation, and which is its fundamental element. Those who are perfect in the active life, like the perfect in the contemplative life, will experience the vivid sense of the reality of God in that interior impulse which drives the soul towards Him, or even permits her to relish His presence. If there is anywhere on earth a foretaste of eternal contemplation, it is there and there alone.

But we cannot hope to attain to this unless our works are genuinely the fruits of charity. Perhaps we are aspiring after the contemplative life, and are content to quote St. Thomas's statement to the effect that " taking things in themselves, there is greater merit in loving God than in loving one's neighbour. Consequently what arises from the love of God is more meritorious than what comes from loving one's neighbour. Now the contemplative life does proceed directly and immediately from the love of God." [1]

Very true ; but is it really, is it always, the love of God which animates you ? How if a certain amount of indolence is mixed up with it, if there is a great deal of

[1] IIa IIae, q. 182, a. 2.

egoism on your part, a hankering after a peaceful life
for which you have a natural taste, some intellectual
curiosity which finds satisfaction in reading and study,
a tendency to do like others, or even an element of snob-
bishness ? Such a thing is by no means impossible. I
doubt whether the love of God is the great motive of
your life if you are indifferent to your neighbour and his
necessities, if you are lacking in kindliness and devotion
towards those around you in your peaceful home, if
you are not doing penance and are not praying for the
poor sinners who are in the world. Because true charity
absolutely entails that twofold current of love, and if the
one is markedly absent the other is only apparent. St.
John does not hesitate to say so repeatedly in his epistle :
" If any say, I love God and hateth his brother, he is a
liar. For he that loveth not his brother whom he seeth,
how can he love God Whom he seeth not ? And this
commandment we have from God, that he who loveth
God loveth also his brother." [1]

And those who devote themselves to the works of the
active life, do they not also require some words of warning?
Yes, their natural tastes or the exigencies of their life
may suffice to explain their comings and goings, the
trouble they take over a particular affair, their devotion
to certain people. We may be burning with fever
after a strenuous day's work, we may give all our goods
in doles and yet be lacking in charity, St. Paul tells us.[2]
In that case all our doings profit us nothing unto everlasting life. Charity abides only where the work is done
for God. Do you sometimes feel a desire, a craving, to
think upon God, and do you think about Him whenever
you can ? If so, then I can believe that you are spending
yourself out of love for Him. That very longing reveals
the charity which inspires you. Moreover, unless your
attention is at least intermittently riveted upon God,
how can your intention to act only for Him continue

[1] John iv. 20–21. *Cf.* iii. 17.
[2] 1 Cor. xiii. 3.

to preside over all your activity? If only for that reason, a minimum of the contemplative life is incumbent upon all men. A general commandment bids us dispose ourselves sometimes to meditate upon God. *Vacate et videte quoniam ego sum Deus.*

A true Dominican ought to make a special point of doing this, even if he is only a member of the Third Order and a prey to all the cares of secular life. Let him make use of every leisure moment to upraise his spirit and his heart to God. "It may well happen," says St. Thomas, "that a person will acquire, in the works of the active life, merits superior to those earned by another in those of the contemplative life. If, for instance, out of a superabundance of divine love, and in order to fulfil the will of God for God's glory, he is prepared to forgo for a season the sweetness of divine contemplation." [1] From that very fact he merits a more perfect contemplation in eternity.

[1] IIa IIae. q. 182, a. 2.

CHAPTER VI

ON CONFORMING OUR WHOLE LIFE TO THE TRUTH

FIRST SECTION

THE TRUTH OF LIFE

IT is of very little use to study truth and to make it the subject of our meditations if we rest content with contemplating it as mere dilettanti, without " regulating our life according to what we know." " We must do the truth in charity," St. Paul tells us, and St. John insists that " we must walk in truth." St. Dominic seems to be borrowing the beloved disciple's terminology when he says : " I have no greater joy than to learn that my children are walking in the truth." [1] All his life our Father set us a wonderful example of that course. But before we consider it, I want you to hear what St. Thomas has to teach us about Truth of Life.

I. THE GREAT PART PLAYED BY THE VIRTUE OF PRUDENCE

A Dominican soul, even more than others, must shun falsehood and dissimulation. What could be more illogical than a lack of truth on the part of one who displays *Veritas* as his motto and claims kinship with St. Dominic, of whom Blessed Jordan of Saxony declares that in him was never seen the faintest shadow of deceit or dissembling ? Simplicity, straightforwardness, frankness, sincerity, these must be the characteristics of our conduct. In a Dominican soul they should spring up as from their very source. Our danger will probably lie elsewhere, and we shall rather need to take care that humility and charity temper what may easily become an exaggeration of those qualities. Sincerity must beware of being self-assertive. Frankness must avoid degenerating into a harshness which is wounding to the feelings of others.

[1] Eph. iv. 15 ; 2 John 4 ; 3 John 4.

" Tell the truth courteously," was the advice given to
a penitent by Fr. Antoine Chesnois (1685). " Tell it
without heat, without dealing out blame ; and renounce
every form of self-love. We must uphold sweetly the
truth for which Jesus Christ died, and this we must do
for the love of God Who cherishes it, and for the love of
our neighbour, to whom it is useful."

If veracity is a moral obligation we owe to others, it
is also, and primarily, a duty of fidelity to oneself. We
are endowed with reason, that is to say, designed for the
truth by our very nature ; we owe it to ourselves to act
accordingly, to be true. Now this fidelity to reason is
not limited to our relations with others, as, for instance,
when we are speaking to them or when we assume some
significant attitude before them. Always and everywhere
our life must bear its stamp. Through our reason, reinforced by faith, we are in a position to know the principles
which regulate life, and therefore under the obligation
of conforming our whole conduct to them. If we do
this we shall live aright. If we do this we shall walk in
the truth.

Do I seem to be setting my readers on a road opposed
to the one along which I was leading them before ?
In the earlier part of this work it was definitely stated
that all perfection consists in charity. We have heard
St. Paul reduce to this primary virtue the sum total of
the Christian virtues : to his eyes they appeared only as
divine manifestations of charity in a soul. Has not the
love of God a sort of instinct which discerns what ought
to be done and deters from evil ? *Ama et fac quod vis.*
Love, and do as you will !

Yes, charity is the starting point for everything in
Christian conduct ; it is the foundation which nothing
can replace. But with St. Thomas we must definitely
maintain that it does not suffice. One cannot abandon
oneself exclusively to general inspirations of the love of
God.

Moreover, is it so very certain that such and such an

inspiration is the outcome of charity? It is for our reason to discriminate between the genuine inspirations of divine love and those natural instincts which are its counterfeits. How often human passions are mixed up with divine inspirations, and even simulate them in order to supplant them. Some day there will come One Who, as His forerunner has told us, will have a fan in His hand to winnow the grain from the chaff. But the divine Judge has endowed us with reason to enable us to exercise that judgment beforehand on ourselves.

Thanks to Him, our reason is qualified through the supernatural gift of prudence, not only to exercise the necessary discernment, but also, and herein lies its chief rôle, to organize and direct all the powers for good which God has given us. It is our faculty of government. It is impregnated with the tendencies communicated to it by divine love. It sees everything from the point of view of God Whom it seeks to please in all things. It strives ever to maintain itself on a high plane, beyond the reach of spurious forms of prudence, carnal prudence, worldly prudence, natural prudence. And this supernatural prudence of ours, itself regulated by charity, will endeavour unceasingly by its injunctions to bring all our conduct into conformity with charity. It is the means through which the good impulses of divine love are realized in the details of daily life. *Veritatem facientes in caritate.* In charity, it says to us, let us do the truth.

To that end it seeks the happy medium between the extremes to which our human passions are ever tending.

Do not be afraid that the happy medium implies mediocrity. For the ends are ever in view, those magnificent ends which charity prescribes. Prudence selects the means of attaining those ends. To be proportioned to their supernatural goal they must necessarily transcend the natural means which will satisfy the sage of this world. What a difference there is between the temperance of a Greek philosopher or of an ordinary plain

man and the life of that disciple of Christ who " chastises
his body to bring it into subjection," who practises
perpetual virginity.

And yet even in the use of the very best means exaggeration is quite possible. Here again our reason will
find the happy medium, whilst never losing sight of the
end to which all these means are subordinate. " The
excellence of a religious rule," writes St. Thomas,[1]
" lies not in the rigour of the observances practised, but
in the perfect adaptation of these observances to the
end aimed at. Take poverty for instance : what constitutes its religious value is the release it gives from
earthly anxieties and the consequent facility it affords
for concentration on divine and spiritual things. Poverty
is therefore not necessarily the better for being more
strict, seeing that it is not good in itself, it is not our goal.
Holy poverty is but a means ; its value depends upon the
measure of its success in freeing us from anxieties and
thus making us better disposed to practise our contemplative and apostolic charity." For the same reason
the ideal does not mean wearing oneself out by mortifications and prolonging pious exercises to an extraordinary extent. All that should be regulated by the
holy virtue of prudence.

It is not always easy to apply these principles. To do
so successfully in the various cases in which we become
involved will require much reflection on our part.
Rectitude is essential, but by itself it is not sufficient.
We shall recall personal experiences, happy or unhappy,
in the past. If necessary we shall seek advice, and this
is where spiritual direction has its place. It would be an
abuse to be for ever running after a director and to expect
him to make all our decisions for us. But often, especially
in the early stages of the spiritual life, he will assist our
deliberations so that we shall be able to judge and decide.
If we think we have obtained the light of the Holy Spirit
without having reflected very much, we must most

[1] IIa IIae, q. 188, a. 6, ad 3 ; III *C. Gent.*, C. 133, vel 134.

certainly submit those inspirations to scrutiny, because
they may quite possibly have no such exalted origin.

We must then decide upon our course of action, taking
special care not to allow any prejudice, any movement of
passion to cloud that singleness of vision mentioned in
the gospel and thus warp our judgment.

Finally, when once our decision is taken, we must
insistently and constantly school ourselves to bring about
its practical realization.

These are, all of them, intellectual acts. Of course,
charity is always necessary ; it is necessary at the outset,
as we have seen, and it remains essential to the very end,
because if we lacked the fervour of love we should neglect
to take the decision and to abide by it, in spite of all the
excellent reasons which support it.   Prayer and communion, which stimulate prayer, are also of a primary
importance.   But it is by the acts of prudence that we
are enabled to introduce truth into our life.

Let us every morning foresee and plan our day ; let
us relentlessly watch and control our behaviour throughout the day ; and at night, in a final examination of
conscience, let us review the past hours to judge them
and to make the necessary amends.[1]

II.   UNDER THE GUIDANCE OF PROVIDENCE

Enough has now been said to put the soul upon her
guard against the dangers of illuminism.   But there is,
in quite a contrary direction, another peril which also
must be avoided by those who wish to abide in trueness
of life.   I will call it a practical rationalism.

If we dwell overmuch on the doctrine that has just
been set forth we may be tempted to fancy that all
perfection depends upon our personal conceptions, our
systematic efforts, our well-ordered self-examinations.
But we should then be forgetting that our reason is not
the sovereign master.   We should be forgetting that

[1] *Cf.* Gardeil, *La vraie vie chrétienne.*   On self-control, personal and
supernatural.

above our personal prudence there is a higher prudence which has foreseen everything from all eternity and which unceasingly provides for everything. It is called divine Providence. That limited little providence of ours, our prudence, is subject to the designs of divine Providence. Otherwise we should be like masons who worked without reference to the plan made by the architect. Nay, we should be more foolish still, because the mason may have good ideas and may possess a forceful personality apart from the architect. Whereas we, apart from God, are utterly non-existent.

Here, again, let us live in the truth. The force which our personal being represents has to reckon with the great forces which impregnate it before it can act effectually in any way whatever. It must first reckon with the superior force which enfolds and penetrates all the rest, God, without Whom nothing exists, nothing can act, nothing succeeds. Never let us work as though all depended on us alone. Even if we proceed to add that one should pray as though all depended upon God we shall not be correcting our mistake, and the practical consequences of that error are disastrous. We must not say " as though everything depended upon God." Everything *does* actually depend upon God in the first place.

He and He alone has foreseen everything, and although He is pleased to make use of secondary causes, it is He Who, in the first instance, provides for all. His Providence embraces all beings without exception. He holds in His indefatigable power the whole human race and each one of the individuals who compose it. He penetrates the depths of our being, all the gamut of our faculties, together with the acts in which they are utilized, the voluntary acts even more than the involuntary, and the supernatural still more than the acts of the natural order. For the measure of true being in anything is also the measure of the intervention therein of God, Who is the only source of all being.

If He has given us our nature and our faculties, it is still more certain that it is with His help we pass from power to action, because we are richer in being when we act than when we do not act.

If our activity has the privilege of being exercised with that perfect mastery, that sovereign indifference which characterize a free being, it is necessary that our Creator should act yet more intensely within us to safeguard and make actual our liberty as creatures, because this spontaneity of our action, this independence of our will, is a higher kind of being, which can emanate only from the Supreme Being.

And should this free act become supernatural and worthy of eternal life, that is to say, in some sense divine, there will be all the more reason for recognizing that God is its only source.

Because this act is free and meritorious, do not imagine, superficial theologian, that when we perform it we are at God's side as a little auxiliary cause whose consent is added to grace in order to make it efficacious, like a child who puts his small hand into his father's to help him lift a burden. In this latter case the force that raises the load is the resultant of two forces applied from two distinct sources. But God is the unique source of all works of grace, and they proceed from us only as from a secondary cause, subordinate to the first cause, entirely penetrated by its influence, moved entirely by its efficacy. That is what St. Thomas has explained to us, and we of the Order of St. Dominic are proud of being Thomists even in these deep waters. We are not afraid that the Almighty Creator will hamper the freedom of our will at the very moment when He enables it to realize itself fully ; and we are well satisfied to see our salvation committed into the hands of God, instead of being left to us.

It is only when we give way to evil and fall into sin that we alone are responsible, and that is because we are escaping from the creative force : our failure is a descent towards not-being. But nothing that is good in our activity is exclusively ours; everything comes from God Himself.

If that is so, if God is the sole first cause of all the good that is wrought in the world, if He has in view a supreme end to which everything is subordinated and must infallibly tend, then the secondary causes which He, in His goodness, invites to participate freely in the execution of His designs, have no other part to play than to fall in with His plan and to adapt themselves to the movement of His grace.

I need a better simile than that of the mason working under the directions of an architect. Look at an agricultural labourer engaged in that old-time occupation dictated and approved by the experience of centuries; watch him as he stands there with his two feet planted solidly on the ground which is the fulcrum of his physical strength. Gently he raises his body, lifting the heavy mattock aloft at arm's length; and then tool, arm and body descend together towards the earth, which attracts them and receives the blow. You townsfolk who are looking on marvel at the amount he dislodges in one solid piece after such a slight human effort, you who give yourselves such an infinity of trouble to cultivate a small garden, and often to so little purpose. The fact is that you deal innumerable small ineffectual strokes, whereas that man strikes only once, but he strikes true. You act as though everything depended upon your labour. The labourer inserts his humble effort into the movement of universal gravitation. He makes use of the whole cosmos to till his field.[1]

The same kind of thing happens with the sowing of seed. Note this example, because it is one which was used by St. Dominic. The wise husbandman awaits the right moment in the rhythm of the seasons, he reckons with the rain and with the temperature, he

---

[1] Though this method of digging may not be familiar to us, the force of the illustration will not be lost.

considers the sun, he even consults the course of the moon. And if the seed has been sown at the right moment the sower can go quietly to his home. Whether he sleeps or whether he wakes, the grain germinates, the plant grows. The good husbandman has performed in due season the act requisite for turning to advantage the world forces which foster life, whereas your various sowings will be fruitless if you disregard those forces. In vain will you betake yourself to your garden day after day. Nothing will grow there. You will get neither flowers nor fruit.

Instead of taking the initiative for ourselves in great spiritual enterprises and of flinging ourselves into them with the ardour of a conqueror whom nothing can resist, let us seek first to keep ourselves in a state of profound humility, always remembering that we are nothing in ourselves, and that of ourselves we can do nothing. But with this mistrust of ourselves we must always combine confidence in God, Who will save us from faint-heartedness and will make us magnanimous in spite of everything. Let us lean upon that infinitely wise, infinitely good, infinitely powerful God Who holds our destiny in His hands. The Lord leads us and upholds us, what then shall we fear? We should observe the ways of Providence with attentive faith, and cherish all the signs it gives us. " As the eyes of servants are upon their master's hands . . . even so are our eyes upon the Lord our God until He have mercy upon us." Detached from everything, indifferent to all except the will of God, let us cleave to it beforehand in faith and love it in the mystery in which it lies shrouded. Let us go on loving it and acquiescing in it continually, as from day to day it is revealed to us. Let us offer ourselves to be ruled by it. Whether it be smooth or rough, let us yield ourselves to it with a holy surrender which knows no restriction or limit. This can only be accomplished by an almost continual prayer which places us in harmony with God, prayer being, as we have said, not an influence exerted over God to bring Him round to our ideas, but an upraising of our soul towards Him to establish us in a disposition to receive His graces.

It is when they are thus steeped in prayer that the thoughts, judgments and counsels of our prudence will be fruitful, because the sap of grace will flow into them. Let us waste no time fretting vainly over the past or being over-anxious about the future. But let us from day to day adapt ourselves to the designs of God, and follow the movement of His grace without attempting to antici-pate or to delay, and let us co-operate with it and follow it until its purpose has been achieved.

III. ST. DOMINIC SURRENDERED TO PROVIDENCE

As it was written of Our Lord, so it might be said of our Order : *Coepit facere et docere.* What our great doctor taught with such authority our Patriarch had already fulfilled. We shall now contemplate in St. Dominic a marvellous illustration of the Thomist doctrine.

If anyone ever adapted himself to grace, without anticipating it, but without delay, it was our holy Patriarch.

He certainly did not anticipate. For thirty-four out of the fifty-one years of his life he was not even aware of the great work which God would require of him. But he was standing at attention, ready to put into act God's idea. For God had a special use for him and He fore-shadowed it in the celebrated dream He sent to her who still bore the infant in her womb. Jane of Aza herself did not understand at once the meaning of the black and white dog who was to set the world ablaze. Never-theless, she was enacting her part in God's plan by training her little Dominic in the love of Jesus and Mary and by instilling into him a great pity for those in distress. It was she who had imparted to him that sym-pathy with the poor which led the young professor to sell his beloved books to buy bread for the hungry, that compassion for miserable sinners which afterwards troubled the sleep of the Canon of Osma and was the psychological foundation of his vocation to the apostolate. "From the time he was a child," said Brother Peter Ferrandus, " his compassion had never ceased to increase. He took to himself all the sorrows of others. . . . " Rodriguez of Cerrat remarks that this sympathy seemed to have passed into him by a natural transfusion from the heart of his mother, for she was extraordinarily tender-hearted. The example and the lessons she gave the child, as he grew up beside her, completed the work already begun in his own tender heart.

No one could foresee that it was the future founder of the Preachers whom God was shaping through the instrumentality of the priest-uncle, the worthy arch-deacon of Gumiel, to whose care his mother entrusted him between the age of seven and fifteen. Living beside his pious kinsman in the presbytery and in the church, the boy received a religious influence which permeated his youthful mind. These eight years left a permanent stamp upon him ; Dominic would always be most at home in a church, spend as much time as possible in the sanctuary and near the altar, and often pass whole nights there.

Again we see the future Father of the Preachers in the young man who is sent to Palencia, at that time the only centre in Spain for higher study. He is expected to become a priest like his two brothers, Antony and Mannes, but it had occurred to no one to provide them with special instruction. Dominic obeys, he applies himself strenuously to intellectual work, and when he becomes a professor he still continues to learn. The taste for study which he retained all his life—persevering study of the things of God—will form an essential part of the Dominican vocation.

Dominic is thirty years of age. Certain providential circumstances lead him to take up his residence in the cloister of the cathedral of Osma, of which he is now a canon. He remains there until he is thirty-four, enjoying the liturgical life which he loves ; but the sobs which escape him at night as he thinks of souls in peril seem to suggest that he has not yet found his full vocation. " Unceasingly and insistently," says Peter Ferrandus, " he besought the Divine clemency to pour into his heart the charity necessary to enable him to work effectually for the salvation of his neighbour. He was obsessed by the example of Him Who had given Himself entirely for our salvation." Nevertheless, he would always remain a canon, and his Order would be partly canonical. But of this Order of Preachers and of its ramifications he has at present no idea. God has the idea and that is enough. Dominic allows himself to be led by Providence.

He allows himself to be led, when his bishop Diego takes him across Europe on a long journey undertaken by command of the King of Castile, who wishes to marry his son to a Danish princess. The marriage is arranged. They come back, and then start off again to fetch the bride. When they reach their destination they find that the little far-away princess is dead. She had played her part in the destiny which is being prepared. She had been the providential reason for two years of travel across Christendom. Dominic, as he crosses and recrosses central Europe, has seen for himself the spiritual misery and the terrible distress in which the Church is plunged. The interest of bishops and clergy centres mainly in lawsuits over earthly possessions ; they do not know how to preach the truths of religion. Immorality is everywhere triumphant, and, more deadly still than sins of the flesh, heresy is eradicating from men's minds the faith which is the very root of justification.

The Pope is obliged to appeal to Cistercian monks in their retirement to make what was to prove an unavailing effort to save those poor souls. It will be for Dominic to create the new Order which will succeed where the Cistercians fail. But Dominic does not yet know it.

He is actually contemplating something quite different. On their way back from Denmark he persuades his bishop to go to Rome to ask the Pope to allow them to start off together to evangelize the savage tribes of the Cumans. If ever there was in Dominic's soul anything of the nature of an overweening desire, an insistent idea, it was this ambition which he was never to be allowed to realize in person. The Pope refused his sanction. Don Diego was well satisfied to obey. As for Dominic, he submits without hesitation and without a murmur, but it is a terrible blow to him. As he treads the road to Spain it seems to him that all his highest aspirations have crumbled. He is dispossessed of all that he stood for— as it were emptied of himself. All is over ! . . . His life is a failure ! . . .

On the contrary, everything was only just beginning, and history can scarcely point to any other career so fruitful. His utter detachment, his complete malleability, his self-surrender to God, had made him a fit instrument for great works.

All unknowingly he has been preparing himself for thirty-four years by his obedience to the guidance of Providence to be a useful tool in the hands of the Almighty. Now the hour has come for that tool to strike the earth with a blow which will stir it to its depths : now the time is at hand for a marvellous sowing of seed.

A combination of unforeseen circumstances stopped our travellers on their homeward way at Castelnau, not far from Montpellier. There it is that Dominic discovered his true vocation.

IV. ST. DOMINIC'S PRUDENCE IN ACT

The Abbot of Citeaux and the Pope's legates were in conference. They had almost decided to stifle heresy in blood, since other measures had failed. " What is your opinion ? " they asked the two Spanish prelates. The answer was the outcome of their meditations during their two years of travel, and it was expressed in words suddenly inspired by divine grace. " Send away all these sumptuous equipages and retinues that surround you, discard your costly apparel and let us keep only the books we need. Poor in all other respects, we shall then be able to preach with authority to the people who are estranged by the ignorance and the wealth of the clergy." Dominic was the first to carry out his proposal. Soon he was to be left to do so alone. Old Don Diego returned to his bishopric to die there. The Cistercians were on their way back to their secluded abbeys, away from the turmoils of the world. But Dominic sees his way clearly before him and sets to work.

Can you picture the man as he haunted the roads round Fanjeaux, the stronghold of heresy? Already he embodied in himself the whole of the future Order of Preachers.

Of medium height, slight and sinewy, clad in a white tunic and a black cloak, he speeds about, book in hand as at the University of Palencia, sometimes singing a hymn in his beautiful melodious voice, sometimes reciting a psalm as he had formerly done in the cathedral of Osma; but now, poor and dependent henceforth upon alms for his daily bread, the son of the Guzmans practises an asceticism which exceeds that of the heretical "*perfecti*," so greatly admired by the people; and as he goes about he is mainly engaged in evangelizing work, in preaching the true doctrine and in destroying the heresy which infests the souls of men. He accosts those he meets—the harvesters, for instance, who are working on a Sunday. He challenges the heretical leaders to public discussions, in which he shows himself to be a marvellous controversialist, indefatigable and irresistible. The little books in which he summarizes his teaching are irrefutably logical, and their truth is confirmed by miracles. He teaches poor people to know God as He has revealed Himself to us in the flesh He assumed in that Incarnation which heresy will not accept, and which the world, nevertheless, so badly needed; he makes them contemplate all the life of Jesus, His death and His resurrection, in the company of His Mother, the Blessed Mary. He bids them greet her devoutly, repeat to her

the Angel's *Ave* in order that she may help them to understand and to imitate the divine Exemplar. In short, he
institutes the Rosary.

That is how Dominic, lending himself to the grace of
God, laboured and sowed when the right time had come.
He soon became celebrated. He was offered a bishopric.
" No," he said, " I have to look after my new plantation
of preachers and of nuns at Prouille ; that is my work
and I shall undertake no other." What was that plantation ? A very humble cloister where some of his women
converts prayed. Beside it, a poor little house in which
he stayed in the intervals between his preaching tours,
alone at first, and then, a few years later, with five or six
companions. It was called " the holy preaching community of Prouille."

After ten years Dominic has only fourteen friars.
But the Pope wrote him the following prophetic words :
" In consideration of the fact that the Brothers of your
Order will be, in the future, the athletes of the faith, we
confirm your Order." Trusting in the grace of God,
which he felt to be with him, and encouraged by the
approbation of the Vicar of Jesus Christ, Dominic, who
had inculcated in his brethren his own grand ideal, judged
that the time had come to disperse them over the world.
His resolution was taken. Vainly do Simon de Montfort and the Bishop of Toulouse endeavour to deter him.
" Never," says Jordan of Saxony, " did the man of God
revoke a decision once definitely made." And how right
he was, seeing that he had arrived at that resolution in
circumstances which we can infer and which are actually
those whose rules St. Thomas has prescribed in his
treatise on prudence.

The evangelical sower understood that the right season
had come. As one casts grain into the earth at seed-time,
so Dominic dispersed his sons. He himself used this
illustration. And Jordan also uses it to describe another
dispersion which our Father afterwards effected at
Bologna.

He sent half their number, that is to say seven, to Paris, the great university town, " to study, to preach and to found a convent." Only one religious accompanied him to Rome, where he expected to find fresh subjects. Four went to Madrid and two remained at home in Toulouse. From Rome, where he dwelt near the Pope, Dominic encouraged his children from afar. Several months elapsed, and after having recruited fresh vocations, he founded a friary at Bologna, the chief university centre after Paris. Then, a year later, we find him travelling over Europe : he visited the convents, he founded others in suitable places, he restored courage, he prevented or corrected 'any aberrations which might warp the ideal of the Preachers. He travelled quickly, walking forty, fifty or sixty kilometres a day. One morning he left Orleans, and the next day he was in Paris, after having covered one hundred and twenty kilometres on foot. In order to re-conquer Europe for the faith, priories soon arose at all strategical points.

Then the old desire reasserted itself more insistently than ever in the heart of Dominic : he wanted to carry the gospel beyond the limits of Christendom to the pagan Cumans and to die amongst them as a martyr. So imminent was his departure that he allowed his beard to grow. But he fell ill and died, only six years after the foundation of his Order. His sons, who inherited his spirit, were to be missionaries in his stead. Soon they were to cover the whole world, and their habit be taken by a young man known to us as St. Thomas Aquinas. With him came the fulfilment of the Pope's prophecy to St. Dominic. Thanks to that radiant sun who sheds his lustre over our Catholic schools, the Order of Preachers had indeed become the light of the world, and even if no single Dominican were left upon the earth, the immortal books of the Angelic Doctor would suffice to merit for our Order, until the end of time, the glorious title which Honorius had prophetically bestowed upon it. I may add that there are still some Dominicans in the world and that a modern Pope, Benedict XV, has paid them the following tribute in a letter to the Most Reverend Fr. Theissling : " The Order of Preachers is deserving of praise, not so much for having trained the Angelic Doctor, as for never afterwards having deviated from his doctrine by so much as a hair's breadth."

That is what St. Dominic brought about through faithfully following divine grace without anticipating it or delaying to correspond with it. May his example, no less than the teaching of St. Thomas, be of service to all his sons ! Those of us who are already advanced in years have undergone spiritual experiences, some happy, others unhappy, which will bear out what we have briefly set forth. Let us look back over our lives. Is it not true that whatever good has been wrought through our agency has been entirely thanks to God, Who disposed of us according to His good pleasure and often against our own wishes ? Is it not also true that our folly, our indecision, our inconstancy, have frequently been responsible for nipping in the bud the fruit to which divine grace was leading ?

All the souls whom St. Dominic has begotten in the spiritual life and whom St. Thomas has nourished with his doctrine ought to have a persevering determination to realize in all its fulness this trueness of life. Thomist theologians have proved experts in setting forth the theory. The humblest sisters have often rivalled them in its practice. Of one of them, whom I have selected almost at random, it has been written : " Her great maxim was that there is not a single moment of our life in which God has not a special and particular design for the sanctification of His elect, with a view to increasing their merits, and that we must in every one of our actions work in accordance with the full measure of the grace that is in us." [1]

[1] The Ven. Mother Anne Raviol of the Convent of St. Catherine of Siena at Dijon (1604–1677).

SECOND SECTION

AUSTERITY OF LIFE

" THE Secular Third Order of the Friars Preachers, or the Order of Penance of St. Dominic "—those are the words with which our Rule begins. Those who bear such a family title and who are genuinely anxious to be loyal must feel in duty bound to make their lives tally with that description.

Moreover, unless penance is joined to the supernatural prudence which formed the subject of the last section, we are not walking in the truth. Constant fidelity to reason cannot be maintained without the mortification which enables us to rule our senses according to reason's dictates and to counteract their excesses. Grace, which is providentially bestowed upon us and to which our prudence must always submit, is normally crucifying, inasmuch as it is an inflowing of the very grace which Jesus received in its fulness and which led Him to the Cross. Those are the principal reasons for penance. And in deciding upon the manner in which it should be practised, we shall have the help of Providence and prudence, acting in collaboration.

This being our subject, the section we are commencing is really a continuation of the last; and both belong to the same chapter because they are both concerned with conforming our whole life to the truth.

I. THE RELATIONSHIP OF GRACE AND OF THE CROSS

Death is repugnant to life; natural life recoils with all its might from the Cross. But what of the supernatural life? The same thing holds good of the supernatural life in the state of innocence. In Adam it had no affinity with the Cross. Grace was then performing its great function of communicating the divine life to man. Through grace he lived in the name of the Father, of the Son and of the Holy Spirit, and gave glory to the Trinity, Whose presence he already enjoyed in faith whilst he looked forward to the bliss of beholding it in clarity of vision. This enjoyment of God in faith is poetically represented by the divine visits paid to man by God in the cool of the evening which we read of in Genesis. Grace, therefore, is not in itself crucifying.

But the Christian grace, which is derived, as its name implies, from Christ Himself, the only kind of grace that is available to us, is closely bound to the Cross. Whilst, like the grace of Adam and of the angels, it animates us and unites us to the Trinity, it mortifies us and separates us from the things that make one body with us. Our characteristic formulary : " In the name of the Father and of the Son and of the Holy Ghost," is completed by the sign of the Cross.

Before we consider this grace in ourselves, let us look at it in Jesus Christ, the Head of our regenerated humanity. In the grace which resided in all plenitude in Our Lord, there was what our great spiritual teacher of the seventeenth century, Louis Chardon, described as " an inclination towards the Cross, a gravitation to the Cross." [1]

St. Paul tells us that Jesus Christ came into the world saying : " Father, behold I come as a Victim." That saying was no more audible to human ear than is the sound of the Eternal Word, but it is none the less an expression of the very truth. The saying was not invented by St. Paul. Since divine grace is adapted to every man's vocation, and since the vocation of the Incarnate Word was to die upon the Cross, His grace must necessarily have urged Him towards it.

His mission might have been a different one. But it

---

[1] The Abbé H. Brémond has introduced the public to the sublime teaching of Chardon in Vol. VIII of his *Histoire Littéraire du sentiment religieux en France*, and Fr. Florand has studied it in the light of the doctrine of St. Thomas (*La Vie Spirituelle*, 1935).

was actually this.   It was to this end that Jesus was
consecrated substantially by the hypostatic union.   The
same union that raised Him above all men as their
Head was the source of that fulness of sanctifying grace
with which His human nature was endowed to enable
it to play its part.

Read the gospel, and you will see that Our Lord was
dominated by the thought of the Cross.   He has, if I
may so play upon the words, a passion for His Passion.
He resembles, if I may use the illustration, those princes
in the old fairy tales whom nothing could divert from
the great love they had conceived for a beggar maid.
St. Luke shows Him surrounded by a crowd eager to
hear Him.   Interrupting the flow of His discourse,
Jesus suddenly exclaims, at the thought that He is to
shed His blood :   " I have a baptism wherewith I am
to be baptized.   Alas ! the hour has not yet come !
How am I straitened until it be accomplished ! "

When, after many months of life lived in common and
in familiar intercourse, He at last leads His disciples
to confess that He is the Son of God, He proceeds forthwith to show them that he must inevitably suffer ; for
that cause the Son of God became incarnate.   A few
days later, as we are told by three of the evangelists, He
was on the summit of Mount Tabor.   Revealing what
had been hidden, He participated visibly in celestial
glory, which transfigured His body and even His garments.
But of what did He speak ?   What does He yearn for ?
Listen to Him, Peter, James and John, ye whom He has
brought to this manifestation.   Hear Him ! . . . It is
the awful voice of Jehovah Himself that bids you listen.
. . . He sighs for His Passion, and He constrains Moses
and Elias to talk with Him about the death He is shortly
to accomplish in Jerusalem.   It seems like an echo—
in time and on this our earth—of the great eternal decree
revealed in a sentence of St. Paul's : *Proposito gaudio,*
sustinuit crucem.   Joy was offered Him. . . . But it was
the Cross which He wished to bear.

" Get thee behind Me, Satan," He said to Peter, who
wished to stop Him on the road to Calvary, but to Judas,
who pointed Him out and betrayed Him to the executioners
He said " Friend " ! The following day, as He is dying
upon the Cross, He exclaims : " *Consummatum est !* "
All that He had come to accomplish is finished. There
is nothing more for Him to do here below.

That is what grace effected in Jesus. Now the grace
which sanctified Him is identical with the grace that
overflows from His soul into ours ; our grace is His.
In the opening chapters of *The Cross of Jesus* Chardon
explains (following Cajetan and St. Thomas) that by
grace " holy souls are one mystical person with Jesus."
It is as our Head that He died upon 'the Cross, and it
is to that crucified Head that we members are subject.
If they are to form part of a well-constituted body, the
members must be in conformity with the Head. Therefore " the inclination that the soul of Jesus has for the
Cross extends to the holy souls who compose His mystical
body." And again : " Crosses are distributed to holy
souls according to the measure of grace which is given to
them."

Is not that precisely what Jesus proclaimed from the
very first day that He disclosed His intention to suffer ?
" If anyone will come after Me," He immediately added,
" let him deny himself and take up his cross daily."
The Cross ! The instrument of torture which was familiar
to everyone in those days, and which served no other
purpose. There were no ornamental crosses, or crosses
of honour, such as we have to-day, but only the crosses
which criminals bore to the place of execution. And every
Christian must bear his cross in like manner daily in
order to die upon it daily in ceaseless mortification.

Is not that the teaching which St. Paul repeated and
which we find developed in the works of St. Thomas
when he comments upon the Apostle or when he expounds
the *Summa* of Christian doctrine ? " We have been
grafted into Christ like a branch into the trunk, but it is

into His Passion that we are grafted," they tell us. " Man is crucified with Christ by the fact of his baptism."

This means, of course, primarily that baptism applies to us the merits of the Passion endured by our Head, an application which the other sacraments will renew or amplify. But there is more than that. The sacraments incorporate us into Christ on the Cross, so that we may take part in the sorrowful reality of His Passion. That is why baptism, which has the virtue of removing all penalties, does not do so during the course of this present life. The community of life established between Christians and Christ, as between members and the head, requires that Christians should bear the cross themselves and should suffer with Christ before sharing His glory.[1]

II.   THE MOTIVES FOR MORTIFICATION

If we seek to discover the ultimate motive for mortification we shall discover that it lies in sin. It was in order to repair the sin which has sullied the entire human race that the grace of Christ received that tendency towards the Cross, which it retains when it passes into us. It is the more bound to retain that tendency because we personally are stained by the sin of the whole race and by our individual sins. Like the thieves who were crucified with Jesus, we can say that we receive what we have deserved, whereas He had committed no sin.

Having taken upon Him the sin of humanity, He set Himself the duty of making reparation for it. Sin is an offence which is in some sense infinite, because it attacks the infinite goodness of God. Such disorder Jesus regarded with a deep abhorrence to which His divine personality gave an infinite value, and we have seen Him enduring in His Passion all the propitiatory penalties which sin merited. How intense was the suffering

---

[1] *In Rom.* vi. 4–5 ;   IV *Gent.*, LXXI ;   IIIa, q. 69, a. 3 ;   IV *Gent.*, LV ;   IIIa, q. 49, a. 3, ad 3.

of our Saviour in His humanity ! It was His wish to make
expiation in His body and in His soul for the sins of the
world. And His satisfaction was not merely sufficient
to counterbalance them all ; it was superabundant.

By sin we had turned away from God and had attached
ourselves to creatures. In that paltry good we vainly
sought our happiness, which can only be found in God.
The penalty incurred by such a fault is, on the one hand,
eternal privation of divine bliss resulting logically from
our culpable desertion of God, and, on the other hand,
the positive penalty corresponding to the forbidden
pleasures we have sought from creatures.

The former penalty, being infinite, is expiable only by
the Redemption of the God-Man. It is He Who saves
us from eternal damnation. The divine Head, with
Whom we form but one mystical person, applies to His
members the satisfaction which He wrought upon the
Cross.

But the other, the penalty of the senses we must share
with Him. Since the disorder is within our own sphere
of things it is only proper that we should collaborate in
repairing it, and the grace of Jesus invites us to do this.
So incumbent upon us indeed is our duty of making satisfaction, that if we fail to do it here below we shall be
condemned to it in the world to come. We shall attain
bliss only after passing through Purgatory, where we
shall pay our penalty.

" It is certainly just," says St. Thomas, " that he who
has yielded over much to his own will should have to
endure what is contrary to his will : moral equilibrium
will thus be restored. Hence the saying in the
Apocalypse : ' As much as she hath glorified herself
and lived in delicacies, so much torment and sorrow
give ye to her.' " Sufferings accepted will atone for the
forbidden pleasure we have snatched.

Several of the saints and beatified members of our
Order, who had been converted from a worldly and
sinful life, inflicted severe penances upon themselves

during the remainder of their lives to expiate sins which, like Jesus, they abhorred, but the penalties of which, like Jesus, they embraced.

A far greater number, who preserved their innocence, our Father St. Dominic, for instance, and St. Catherine of Siena, never had occasion to bewail other than venial sins. But for these defects, which the coarser eyes of our conscience could not even detect, they punished themselves unmercifully.

Moreover, they were mindful also of the sins of others, of the sin of the whole world. Since it is a fact that we form, all of us together, only one single mystical body of which Jesus is the Head, it is fitting that all, more especially those who are intimately linked with Christ, should participate in His expiatory sorrow for human sin of every kind. And so we see St. Dominic, after praying on his knees with his hands clasped round the foot of the crucifix and his eyes upraised to Christ—in the attitude depicted by Fra Angelico—rise suddenly to his feet and discipline himself until the blood flows. He scourged himself first for his own sins, then for sinners in general, and finally for the souls in Purgatory. And, like Christ in His agony, he cried aloud in anguish because there was nothing he could do for the souls of the damned.

Even if perfect reparation could be made for all the sins that had ever been committed, mortification would still be necessary to prevent their recurrence. Sin, because it is a disorderly pursuit of creatures, has produced in the soul a certain disposition which may become a habit, if the act has been frequently repeated. After the fault has been remitted, these tendencies may remain, weakened indeed by grace so that they no longer control us, but still sufficiently strong to make it necessary for us to be watchful.

Those who have not sinned personally are likewise

bound to mortify themselves. As the result of the Fall
our sensibility is normally unruly. God had given this
sensibility to our reason as a means of helping it in its
task, by warning it against evil to be avoided, and by
directing it towards good to be accomplished. When
our appetites are very sensitive to the slightest attraction
of the good or to the slightest touch of evil, they are ful-
filling their preordained office. The trouble is that in
our fallen nature they have become unduly quickened :
they arrogate to themselves a wholly unwarranted independence, and even try to dominate the reason which
they would fain compel to be the industrious slave of
the senses. How many men have fallen in this way to a
lower level than that of the beasts ! It is our duty to
impose upon our passions the rule of reason, the supernatural rule. If we do not mortify our craving for
pleasure and our fear of pain, by constant austerity, our
soul will lose control over the body it animates, and the
spiritual harmony which should prevail in our human
constitution will be liable at all times to serious
disturbance.

" I am as distrustful of my body to-day, when I am
sixty-eight, as though I were only twenty-five," said
Venerable Fr. Hyacinthe de la Haye (1671). " I regard
it as a bad servant whose insubordination, disloyalty and
resentment I fear the more because I have beaten him
well and fed him ill."

These two reasons alone should suffice to inspire us
to self-renunciation from the earliest stages of the interior
life. But gradually a third motive will supervene. We
must assuredly continue to make reparation for the past
and safeguard our perseverance, but what will appeal to
us more and more, if we are faithful, will be to participate
in the sufferings of our beloved Christ. We shall want
to be always with Him Whom we love, and since it is
on the Cross that He dwells here below, since He becomes

actually present in our earthly temples only by renewing mystically His sacrifice of Calvary, it will be on the Cross that we shall meet Him until we go to Heaven. " I desire in this life to be conformed to Thy divine Passion," said St. Catherine of Siena to Jesus, when He gave her the choice between a golden crown and a crown of thorns ; " my happiness will always lie in suffering with Thee." And Catherine de Ricci : " O my Spouse, my Love, Thou sufferest for me, and I am not even on the Cross ! But see, Lord, how ready I am to suffer for Thee ! "

We have here the key to that thirst for martyrdom which consumed St. Dominic. He is overjoyed when hired assassins threaten to kill him on the road between Prouille and Fanjeaux. " All I would ask of you," he says to them, " is to kill me, not at one blow, but little by little, cutting off my limbs one by one and setting them before me ; to tear out first my right eye and then my left, and to leave me thus, a shapeless trunk bathed in my own blood." The assassins were stupefied. " What is the use of playing his game for him," they exclaimed to one another. And so they left him unmolested.

Why, except to be like the suffering Christ, did our saints so persistently seek sufferings similar to his, and embrace them so eagerly ? From St. Dominic to Père Lacordaire they used the discipline freely. When Henry Suso was enduring the scorn of men, an interior voice said to him : " Remember that I, Thy Saviour, did not turn away My countenance from those who were spitting in My face." St. Rose of Lima rested a heavy wooden cross on her tender shoulders, already lacerated by much scourging, and she carried it by night along the paths of her father's garden. She also spent hours fastened to the cross in her cell, uniting her prayers to those of our dying Lord. And when, for fifteen years, she suffered a mysterious agony which drew from her the great plaint : " My God, why hast Thou forsaken me," where but in her union with Christ does she find the strength to say : " Thy will be done ! "

This union of love underlies those extraordinary phenomena of spiritual participation in the Passion, and of corporal stigmatization which was granted to so many of our saints. The Order of St. Dominic counts the greatest number of stigmatics of any Order amongst its members. As many as a hundred have been reckoned, some twenty of whom belonged to the Third Order. The Church has, in several cases, investigated and approved the facts, and the Order observes the Feast of the Stigmata of St. Catherine of Siena on April 1st.[1]

Yes, Jesus is still in agony in those dear members of His mystical body who visibly continue upon earth His redemptive Passion, and thereby fill up what is lacking for the whole body, which is the Church. Brothers and sisters of all those stigmatics, let us at least in spirit relive the sufferings of Jesus, and let us dwell upon them lovingly and continually. The Rosary helps us to do this because, out of the fifteen mysteries it offers for our contemplation from the Incarnation to the entry of the saints into glory, no less than five are consecrated to the Passion.

For these various reasons, we members of the Order of Penance must be very much upon our guard against the prevalent pagan spirit which encourages us to live our life according to our inclinations, as though the Cross had never been set up on this terrestrial globe.

We must also beware of a practical naturalism which falsely claims to find support in the principles of St. Thomas. Our doctor certainly does teach that nature is not destroyed by grace. Grace grafts itself upon nature to perfect it. But if our nature can thus adapt itself to grace because sin has not affected it in its essential principles, yet the fact must be recognized that in the development of its activities it is afflicted with an evil bias. It is thrown off its axis. The sign of this is that man no longer has a natural affinity for his final

---

[1] R. P. Alix, *Manuel du Tiers-Ordre*, p. 153, and *Année Dominicaine* (April), with regard to the Stigmata of St. Catherine of Siena.

goal. He has to overcome the difficulty he finds in submitting to God and in upraising himself towards the Creator. He has to resist his tendency to be alarmed or seduced by creatures. Grace consequently demands and effects some very painful readjustments in our nature.

Finally, on the ground that " the religion of our Father St. Dominic is wide and joyous," let us not forget that compunction lies at the root of that religion. " What do you ask ? " was the question we were asked in the first instance, and we replied : " God's mercy and yours." Like the beatitude promised by Our Lord in the Sermon on the Mount, Dominican joy is born only of trust in divine mercy and of readiness to make the requisite renunciations.

" How can any Christian give himself over to vain joys," asks St. Lewis Bertrand, " when he is aware that he will have to appear before God's tribunal and knows neither the day nor the hour ? " An ejaculatory prayer of St. Augustine's was particularly dear to him and to Blessed Peter of Jeremias, as indeed it has been to many other Dominican souls : " Lord, burn, cut, and do not spare me here below, provided Thou spare me in eternity."

III.   THE PRACTICE OF PENANCE

Have I been guilty of the weakness I am tempted to criticize in the biographers of our saints, by seeming to attach too much importance to certain extraordinary penitential practices ?

I do not think so, because I have only mentioned these macerations in order to emphasize the spirit which inspired them, and the motives which led holy penitents to mortify themselves. These motives we must make our own, absolutely.

As for the rest, it is obvious enough that one cannot, in a moment of spiritual exaltation, set about imitating at haphazard one or other of those practices. With respect to those that form part of the regular observances of a community no danger is to be apprehended. They afford little scope for pride or conceit. And the Superiors keep a watchful eye to prevent all excesses.

Outside these limits there is a grave risk that the heart may indulge in vain glory. There is also the danger that one may lose one's health or become incapable of carrying out the duties of one's state of life. There is even the possibility, as St. Vincent Ferrer once pointed out, that after having erred by excessive austerity, a man may come to regard himself as justified in no longer mortifying himself at all.

And here I will borrow from Père Petitot, and commend to your consideration a remark of his which was inspired by St. Teresa of Lisieux : " Except in the case of a special vocation, of graces verified as far as possible by several authorized, experienced and prudent directors, all exceptional mortifications such as discipline to blood, iron chains, and suchlike practices of any kind not prescribed by the Rule, must be absolutely prohibited, especially in these days when ill health is so much on the increase."

This advice was nothing new in our Order. It will be remembered that St. Teresa of the Child Jesus referred particularly to the history of Blessed Henry Suso, of whom we shall have more to say presently. St. Dominic appeared in person to Blessed Benvenuta, who was in the habit of scourging herself with an iron discipline three times during the night, as he had done. Our Blessed Father reprimanded her severely for not having mentioned this practice to her confessor. When the confessor was informed, he at once took away Benvenuta's instruments of penance.

Is it because he was afraid lest injudicious use might be made of the holy Patriarch's example that Blessed Jordan of Saxony, unlike many hagiographers who revel in such details, says not a single word about St. Dominic's terrible disciplines in his account of our Father's life ? [1]

---

[1] We know from the testimony of John of Spain for the process of canonization that three times during the night St. Dominic used to scourge himself until the blood flowed.

It is a remarkable fact that in his letters to Blessed Diana and her sisters in the Convent of Bologna he never makes the least allusion to this particular form of penance. He speaks only of fasts, abstinences and vigils. To these he frequently recurs. But why? . . . To guard against exaggeration in those young religious, so full of fervour but lacking experience.

He is seriously apprehensive of the actual excesses into which such exaggeration may lead them. But his concern has a deeper root. Their lack of moderation troubles him because it is a sign that his daughters are wanting in that great virtue of discernment, for which every true Dominican ought to have special esteem and devotion, the virtue of prudence.

"Many times have I exhorted you, in speech when I was with you, by letters when I have been absent, to refrain from excessive and indiscreet mortifications : and therefore if, after so many warnings, any one of you should be so imprudent as to outrun due restraint, she would be guilty of still more reprehensible negligence."

This virtue of prudence must, moreover, as we know, rely on the direction of divine Providence. Its part is not to precede but to follow, not to take the initiative but to receive the divine suggestion and faithfully to correspond to it. Jordan is grieved to see that Diana and her sisters have not yet entered into the spirit of which our Blessed Father was so perfect an incarnation and of which St. Thomas was soon to expound the principles. He writes to Diana : " I will not have you hasten your end by excessive compunction and immoderate mortification. As Solomon says : ' He that runneth too fast, stumbleth,' and that is why I exhort you not to run so hard, lest you faint by the way. If you run, it should be with the moderation recommended by the Apostle to those who would win the prize. And may our God deign so to draw us after Him that we may quietly and joyously run in the fragrance of His sweetness ; may He lead us according to His will ! In all humility, in all patience, know how to wait. Cultivate your souls without emaciating your bodies, while, like the labourer patiently awaiting the precious fruit of the earth, you patiently wait for the precious fruit, the blessed Fruit of the Womb of the glorious Virgin Mary."

Does Blessed Jordan want to stifle a taste for mortification in his daughters ? No, but he wishes to direct it to the serene acceptance and patient endurance of the exterior and interior trials which their life brought them under the guidance of divine Providence. After alluding, in one of his letters, to the things he had to suffer, long separation from those dear to him, repeated attacks of fever, the loss of an eye, he assures Diana, who is distressed at them, that " the divine Workman knows the refining required by His handiwork ; what we have to do is to submit in all things to His will and to surrender into His hands the guidance of our lives." [1]

After Blessed Suso had spent a long time undergoing terrible mortifications, he was one day told by God to throw all his penitential instruments into Lake Constance. " Thou hast been long enough in the lower schools. . . . I will take thee to the highest school which is to be found in this world. . . . The highest school and the craft that is taught there consist simply in an entire and perfect detachment from self. . . . Look within, and thou wilt see that self is really still there, and thou wilt perceive that notwithstanding all thy outward practices . . . thou art yet undetached from self in respect to contradictions at the hands of others." Then, when the Servitor was rejoicing at the prospect of leading for the future a tranquil and peaceful life, he was told : " Thou wilt have to fight harder than ever. . . . Hitherto thou hast struck thyself with thine own hand and hast left off striking when thou wouldest. Now I Myself will take hold of thee and give thee into the hands of strangers. . . . Thou shalt suffer the loss of thy good name. . . .

---

[1] *Cf.* the letters of Blessed Jordan edited by M. Aron, and the notice devoted to them by Fr. Lemonnyer in *L'Année Dominicaine*, June, 1926.

In thy past mortifications thou wast held in high esteem
. . . now thou shalt be abased in the sight of all. . . .
Thou art of an affectionate and love-seeking nature.
Now, in the very quarter where thou wilt look for special
love and fidelity, thou shalt encounter unfaithfulness,
sufferings and afflictions. . . . Open the window of thy
cell : look and learn. (There was a dog in the middle
of the cloister worrying a piece of carpet.) As the carpet
suffers itself to be ill-treated in silence, even so do thou."

Whether it be a case of grievous physical pains and of
great mental sufferings like those described above, or
whether the difficulties to be overcome are only those of
our normal daily life, in them we shall find our primary
penance. It will exercise all the moral virtues required
by our condition. Hugh of St. Cher aptly compared
penance to a lyre, all the strings of which must be well
tuned in order that from the instrument may rise up
to the Lord a harmony without a discordant note.

It is absolutely essential that we should practise such
mortifications as are necessary to restrain us from the
sins to which we are inclined by our own temperament
and by our relations with other people. " We are, one
and all, poor frail beings," said St. Augustine, " and we
carry vases made of clay. We walk with difficulty and
are always getting into one another's way. We must be
patient with ourselves, indulgent to our brothers and
very careful to avoid all occasions when they would
make us fall."

The faults we have committed in the past and those
we commit every day bring upon us many annoyances,
much humiliation. Prone as we naturally are to murmur
at the consequences, forgetting their cause, let us on the
contrary view our faults with detestation and accept
in reparation all the troubles that have come from them.
This is our bounden duty : it is simply indispensable.

The duties of our state of life entail a certain amount of
strain and fatigue. Here is another form of penance to
be daily endured.

Finally, let us remember that we must never allow pleasure to be the ultimate end of any of our activities. It may accompany them and may even help us to accomplish a duty. But we must never act for the sake of pleasure. On that fundamental principle we must base the austerity of our life. It is assumed in the Rule and it underlies the injunction that Tertiaries should refrain from attending places of worldly amusement, notably dances and frivolous entertainments (IX. 38).

Besides these mortifications, members of the Third Order will observe those that are definitely specified in the Rule (VIII. 37) : three fasts in preparation for the three great feasts of Our Lady of the Rosary, St. Dominic and St. Catherine of Siena. Furthermore, in order if possible to remain faithful to the ancient Rule, they are exhorted to fast, if they can, every Friday of the year. A vague reference is made to other practices which the brethren may observe, subject to the approval of the Director or of a discreet confessor. Rising at night to recite Matins on special days and in Advent and Lent was obligatory in the ancient Rule. Early rising to attend daily Mass before starting on the day's work is still very urgently recommended (VII. 33).

If a dispensation is obtained from the fasts and abstinences which the Church commands under pain of grave sin, that dispensation naturally extends to the penitential ordinances of our Rule. But in the case of these, as in the case of those which are prescribed by the Church, an intelligent and fervent soul will at least observe as much of them as is consistent with health and the duties of one's station. For instance, if unable to fast, such a one will take care to substitute privation of some other sort.

In this connection, when commenting upon the ancient Rule whose austerity appals us to-day, Père Rousset added the following judicious words : " We do not lack strength for the service of the world ; and, not to mention the compulsory fasts of the poor, the privations of the working man, the labours and vigils of the ambitious, to what numberless painful mortifications do not delicate women submit every day for the world and for vanity ! Yet no sooner does a confessor attempt to impose upon them a mere fraction of such mortification for the service of God than they exclaim that it is too much and impossible ; and those healths which have withstood so many sleepless nights spent at entertainments, balls and theatres cannot, without being seriously impaired, bear to sacrifice half an hour's rest to be consecrated to prayer and to meditation."

One might enlarge on this subject and add a few more details. How much discomfort is endured by those who wish to be dressed in the latest fashion and to preserve a slim figure ! But when it comes to wearing at all times the white woollen scapular and thereby sacrificing a little elegance, to renouncing for its sake the low-cut gown of the woman of the world—alas ! must we own it ?—there are Tertiaries who have not the courage to do it.

But between these degenerates and the glorious phalanx of our martyr and of our ascetics, there is, thank God, a host of men and women who, by their life of simple austerity, do honour to the Order of Penance and are recognized by St. Dominic as his true children.

THIRD SECTION

THE FRUITFULNESS OF LIFE

WHAT Dominican will imagine that it suffices merely to possess the truth oneself, to let it permeate simply one's own conduct and for this end alone to make all the sacrifices which are asked? We are not isolated here on earth. As members of a family, of a profession, of a parish, of a nation, of the human race, we know very well that no one is a stranger to us. In proportion to their nearness to us we must be concerned with all. " Do not say : I want to save myself ; but say : I want to save the world ! " cried Père Lacordaire. We shall therefore do our best to make the saving truth shine forth both in our immediate circle and to the uttermost parts of the world. We shall use the truth for the exercise of our charity. The forms of this charity are manifold, as we shall see. But its spirit is everywhere the same, as we shall also see.

I. MANIFOLD WORKS

" The Order from its earliest days was specially instituted for preaching and the salvation of souls," the primitive constitutions of the Friars Preachers declare ; " the efforts of its members must be directed primarily, fervently and absolutely to being of service to their neighbour." St. Dominic wished to make " holy preaching " general, to evangelize all souls in every possible way.

Now " the Third Order of St. Dominic shares in the religious and apostolic life of the Order of Friars Preachers." Our Rule tells us so in its first paragraph. " The object of the Third Order," it goes on to say, " is

the sanctification of its members and the salvation of
souls."

Amongst the means proposed to that end, and following
upon " assiduous prayer and the practice of mortification," the efficacy of which on behalf of others we already
know, we find . laid down " apostolic and charitable
works for the Faith, according to each one's particular
state or condition in life " (I. 1–3).

Prayer and penance are the special province of the
purely contemplative sisters who reinforce the Friars
Preachers in that direction. In the matter of works
of the apostolate and of charity, it is for us Tertiaries to
bring our contribution to the Order.

Before ever they can even be admitted to the Third
Order postulants must give evidence of their apostolic
zeal (II. 8). Once they have entered the family of the
Preachers, " following the example of the Apostolic
Patriarch Dominic and the Seraphic Virgin Catherine
of Siena, Tertiaries should be animated with an ardent
and generous desire for the glory of God and the salvation
of souls " (XI. 40).

The forms of apostolate in the First Order were various
from the outset. They have been multiplied by the
invention of printing and the needs of our own times.
The Third Order has permitted in the past and is ever
permitting more and more the inclusion of fresh means,
both the Third Order regular and more recently the
secular Third Order.

Works have lately been published upon the Dominican
congregations of the Third Order regular.[1] In France
alone the number of such congregations is astonishing,
as is also the diversity of the needs to which they minister.

Some of them are engaged in various works of mercy.
Others are more specialized. Several arose to meet
requirements which were felt at the same time in different
localities.

[1] There is a book with this title by R. Zeller (*Letouzey*) ; another,
entitled *Les Dominicaines*, by M. M. Davy (*Grasset*).

When the State educates the young without any religious principles, giving them only vague moral counsels devoid of spiritual foundation, how can we do otherwise than pity Catholic children ?   The daughters of St. Dominic come forward to help anxious parents to give their children the full instruction they need to enable them to face life worthily and to tackle all their duties.

Then there are hapless orphans or poor little foundlings whom their parents have abandoned. For them many Dominican homes have been opened. With the sisters they find the holy family that will care for them and give them a good upbringing.

Several other convents exist as refuges for young girls whose abnormal disposition and precocious tendencies necessitate a moral and religious re-education.

Others require a real rehabilitation. Dominican Sisters devote themselves to this task. To those who have fallen and whom the world scorns, after having been the cause of their lapse, to those who have been in prison, they open their house of refuge. There, the penitent Magdalen gradually raises herself. She shares the life of her sisters who have not failed, and after several years may wear the same religious habit and lead the same religious life.

But it was not moral ills alone that moved the heart of St. Dominic. And the daughters of him who sold his beloved books to help the poor become hospital nurses to tend the sick. They even specialize in the care of those afflicted with such grievous infirmities as blindness and leprosy.

They also go forth to nurse the sick poor in their homes, to do the housework for the invalid mother, to look after the children and to prepare the working man's meal.

Others have opened hostels, clubs for working girls, convalescent homes in which souls as well as bodies find the repose, the nourishment and the comfort they require. These are good halting places on the road of life.

For a long time past they have made themselves assistants to the clergy by teaching the catechism and forming play-centres, especially in the towns. More recent foundations aim at making up for the shortage of clergy in country places where the same priest cannot look after five or six parishes. Thanks to them, the Holy Sacrament can still be adored in the tabernacles, children are instructed in their religion, the sick prepared for the sacraments, and everything is ready when the priest comes to say Holy Mass. And I have not mentioned those who follow the apostles into distant missions.

In our days, when the feminine spirit has new requirements and when the part played by women in the world approximates more and more to that of men, the Dominican tree naturally puts out new shoots ; and we now have sisters who attempt to reproduce as nearly as possible the studious life and the apostolate of the Friars Preachers themselves.

The various branches of this complex tree will live in fraternal harmony, each one bearing the fruit St. Dominic expects of it. As between the Fathers, occupied in various works, all of them under Dominican inspiration and complementary to one another, so amongst the different congregations there must be a readiness to understand, to sympathize and to collaborate. . . . To none is it permissible to be so puffed up with the sense of their particular vocation as to regard with scant sympathy or to depreciate another work which has received the same sanction as their own.

Anna de Wineck, a contemplative of the monastery of Unterlinden, would have liked to be also a nursing sister. As this was impossible, she made three hospices in her heart—one for sinners, one for the dying and the third for the souls in Purgatory.

What the contemplatives cannot accomplish by themselves can be done through the Sisters of the Third Order regular. And the Tertiaries also can co-operate in their own special way. Mingling as they do in the

world to an extent impossible to the religious of both
sexes who are more or less withdrawn from it, the Seculars
of the Third Order are entrusted with the office of acting
as the good leaven which penetrates into the dough and
transforms it.

In no circumstances whatever may Tertiaries neglect
any of their home duties on the fallacious plea of performing those of the Third Order.   To do so would show
complete misapprehension and would scandalize the
very souls they were specially bound to edify.   There is
no better way of being faithful to the Tertiary profession
than by the perfect fulfilment of all family duties, no
better means of honouring the Order of Penance than
forgetfulness of self and readiness to make sacrifices
for one's own kith and kin.

But may Tertiaries rest content with doing their duty
to the family ?   No, they must not stop short there.
The Rule requires that in order to remain " mindful of
the traditions of our forefathers " they should place
their activity and their words at the service of the truth,
of the Catholic faith, of the Church and of the Roman
Pontiff, proving themselves their valiant defenders in
everything and always.   Let them also assist in apostolic
works, especially those of the Order.   They should devote
themselves as far as possible to works of charity and of
mercy.   And finally they should give good help to their
Parish Priest (XI. 41–43).

Such is the programme laid down in the Rule we have
professed.   This is what St. Dominic expects of the Third
Order.

In the course of time this ideal may have become somewhat obscured.   Indeed, it would seem to have been
reduced to a collection of individual practices for isolated
Tertiaries, and to have entailed, for the rest, nothing
further than meetings which result in no religious influence
or social efficacy in the outside world.   This must not

continue. As our Master General, the Most Reverend Fr. Gillet, has repeatedly said : " Our programme must not be based upon pretence ; it must actually realize the ideas of the Patriarch from whom we descend, and the injunctions of the Rule which determines our conduct."

Our Holy Father, Pope Pius XI, who reckons nothing as " dearer and more precious " than the lay apostolate in the form of Catholic Action, reminded the Tertiary Congress in Rome on March 6th, 1935, that St. Dominic, in founding his Third Order, had already called laymen to collaborate in the apostolate. He also pointed out that even in the primitive Church precursors of Catholic Action are to be found in the persons of those active Christians whose names have come down to us in the Epistles of St. Paul.

After we had been born into the Christian life in the sacrament of baptism, were we not made adults by the sacrament of confirmation and endowed with power and grace with which to defend our faith and do battle for it ? As long as there existed amongst Christians a sufficient number of men possessed of priestly powers, it was not thought necessary to call upon those who only had a very limited measure of such powers. These were exercised only exceptionally and in individual cases. But in view of the present shortage of priests, and of the difficulty such priests as are available experience in obtaining access to certain centres, it has become neces-sary to ask for the help of the lay people, and to urge them to organize themselves into groups to render such help efficacious. Leo XIII, Pius X, Benedict XIV and, above all, Pius XI have made provision for this. From henceforth it is the duty of laymen to organize themselves so that they may co-operate with all their might in the apostolate and evangelize those around them. Each one at his post, they will fight to re-christianize social cells lost in the heart of a pagan world. Of course, they remain subject to the Catholic hierarchy and receive its guidance, but they form their own groups, and their leaders are laymen. Such are the conditions in which, at the wish of Pius XI, Catholic Action has been instituted. Our Holy Father the Pope went so far as to say to Canon Cardijn : " Catholic Action is not *a* dominant thought but *the* predominant thought of our Pontificate." He had previously declared : " We have defined it consciously and deliberately—not, as we believe, without divine inspiration." From henceforth, then, " the participation of the laity in the hierarchical apostolate " must be regarded as an essential part of the constitution of the Church.

The Third Order is not, in itself, an organ of Catholic Action. Only exceptionally, when a fraternity is especially organized for such a purpose, as might happen in certain large towns, will it be possible for it to dedicate itself corporately to such action. But in any case, who will be better prepared than a Tertiary of the Militia of Jesus Christ to become a soldier of the lay apostolate ? All true Catholics, all those who have been confirmed, should join some group of Catholic Action. All cannot be expected to pledge themselves specially, like the Tertiary, to a particular mode of life which facilitates the Christian perfection postulated by the sacramental character of Confirmation, and postulated also by the exercise of the apostolate which derives from that character. Similarly one cannot expect all priests to take the three vows of religion, although these latter are in some sense called for by their priestly character and would place them in a position to fulfil their duties better. But when priests do so bind themselves by entering an Order, by becoming in some way or another real religious, the Church rejoices and benefits by it. Catholic Action will benefit in like manner by the affiliation of its members to the Third Order, especially when that Third Order combines, as does ours, a special mission for the apostolate with concern for personal perfection. No doubt amongst the protagonists of Catholic Action there are souls who, without belonging to the Third

Order, surpass many Tertiaries in personal sanctity and apostolic influence, just as there are secular priests who are undeniably better than some religious ; but it is none the less true that the vows of religion and, to a lesser degree, the Tertiary profession, establish the soul in a favourable position for resisting the evil which is so prevalent, for keeping steadily in view the one thing needful and for diffusing the true Christian spirit. The Third Order is thus fitted to supply Catholic Action with much of the strength required to make it the advance-guard of the Church which is always struggling to pene-trate into human society.

The Third Order is therefore a power-house for Catholic Action. Although the actual apostolate is exercised outside, yet it is within the Order that our Tertiaries will renew their strength in order to become, each one in his own circle, real combatants. They decide for themselves the field in which to display their zeal, and how they can best enlist for that work in the army of Catholic Action. But they can always obtain in the Order, and from the Director of the Fraternity, advice to help them when they need guidance. Indeed, at the National Congress of the Third Order held at Bologna in May, 1935, the Master General wrote in the margin of the resolutions : " Let the Prior of each Chapter make a point of placing himself in communication with the Director of Catholic Action for the better utilization of the spiritual energies of the Chapter to meet local requirements, and also to avoid the dissipation of forces and the overlapping of activities."

There are no geographical limits to the apostolate of our Tertiaries. At the same National Congress of Bologna, the Most Reverend Father " prescribed that there should be each year a Missionary Day organized by Tertiaries, and that in all Chapters a special delegate should be nominated, charged with the duty of co-ordinating the activities of the Chapter in the interests of Missions."

II. ONE SPIRIT

Whatever the work may be in which they exercise their charity, Dominican Tertiaries will carry them out in the spirit which must equally inspire it all, the spirit which characterizes the entire Order. We know what that spirit is—zeal to communicate the Truth to the world ; that is the spirit, identical in all, which must guide this manifold work.

The more immediately and directly the work tends to communicate the Truth, the more does it approximate to the Dominican vocation. But if, for personal reasons or in response to special needs, it should prove desirable to undertake other work which is only remotely connected with the communication of Truth, the Dominican soul will be devoted to it in exactly the same spirit. With those who appear to be unable to do anything, the poor invalid lying helpless in his sick-room or the nun in her enclosure, the yearning to spread the truth must be ever alive and active in their heart, like a yeast which tends to raise the world.

He who never experiences any sentiment of this kind has reason to doubt whether he has the true Dominican spirit. By virtue of his vocation, the true Dominican is eager to spread the truth which he possesses and which he contemplates with love. That belongs to the very essence of his vocation. The essence of a thing remains everywhere the same and is eternal. Circumstances may arrest or modify their development, but cannot fundamentally change them. Under all skies and in all countries, in its root, in its vigorous trunk and in its branches, the oak is always the oak, and the Dominican soul is always apostolic.

One of Dominic's sons can never enjoy the truth in peace as long as there are still in the world men who do not possess the truth which is necessary for salvation. How can anyone cheerfully sit down to a well-served table and enjoy a good meal when he sees about him

poor people who have no bread ? Our holy Father felt
this pity for the poor who hungered for material food,
and he felt it even more deeply for infidels, heretics and
sinners. We remember his heartfelt sighs when he
emerged from the nocturnal contemplations which were
preludes of the eternal vision of the divine Truth :
" And sinners ! What is to become of sinners ?—of poor
lost souls eternally deprived of the Truth ? " . . . We
know how, after a tiring journey, he spent a whole night
without sleep in order to convert the heretical innkeeper
of Toulouse. . . . And we remember his constantly
recurring desire to carry the gospel to the infidel Cumans.

The Dominican contemplative in her convent, the
Dominican Tertiary whom sickness or some other
disability has reduced to inactivity, will remember that
their Father, by his aspirations, his prayers and his
sufferings, effectually assisted in spreading the truth
throughout the world. Our Lord said : " If I am in the
world, it is to bear witness to the truth." Does anyone
imagine that He forgot this purpose of His incarnation
during the thirty years of His hidden life and especially
during the day of His silent Passion ? On the Cross He
was dying for the Truth and to draw all souls to it.
Since His coming and because, as our Head, He unites
to Himself all the members of His mystical body, any
of those members can work by self-sacrifice for the redemption of the rest. The Communion of Saints is not a
meaningless term.

" Weep not for Me but for yourselves and for your
children," said Jesus on the way to Calvary to those who
were grieving over His bodily suffering, and who did
not realize that the lot of their dear ones, severed from
the saving Truth, was far more grievous. . . . When he
is helpless and sick, the Dominican who is faithful to
his vocation forgets his own suffering to consider the
infinitely greater misfortune of people he knows personally, or can imagine, who are heading for an eternity
of unhappiness. And his heartfelt concern for sinners,

coupled with his aspirations, his prayers and the oblation of his sufferings to God on their behalf, will earn for those erring souls graces of light and conversion.

And it is not merely great sufferings or heroic sacrifices that can have this efficacy. " Lord," said a Dominican sister of that monastery of Toss which was so celebrated for its fervour in the thirteenth century, " Lord, I am firmly convinced that Thou wilt give me a soul for each thread I spin."

And therefore, whoever we may be and however humble the work in which we spend our days, we must firmly resolve to devote to the apostolate all the merits we can acquire. Surely the thought that we can thus co-operate effectively in such a work ought to make us more careful to do all things well. However hidden our life may be, it acquires by this means apostolic value.

We are none of us so obscure that our influence is not felt. The nuns, who are hidden behind the great walls of their enclosure, are shut up there by their own free will. People in the world know it ; they have some idea of their occupation, and it is for them a light and an encouragement to know that these religious are logical enough in their faith to draw from it these conclusions and to sacrifice everything to the one thing needful. Unseen and unheard, they sound a trumpet-call to Christians who are absorbed in temporal affairs and are in danger of forgetting what their faith demands of them. They provoke, even in the conscience of unbelievers, the question of the ultimate destiny of man.

More in the public eye and therefore more expressly edifying will be the life of the Tertiary who, in the surroundings in which Providence has placed him, leads the excellent Christian life to which he is pledged.

Unlike his brothers of the First Order, he does not preach : perhaps he is not even able to take part in works directly connected with the apostolate, but, to quote

U*

the words of Abbé Huvelin, " a man does much less by what he says than by what he is." A Tertiary is a follower of Christ ; his example takes the place of precepts. The spiritual realities which his soul experiences are embodied in his attitude, and become apparent to all in his very gestures. He does not perform his duties like other people. Virtue goes out from him, the very virtue of Christ penetrating through that visible member who is so intimately linked to Him. None of those who live near him escapes his beneficent influence. The soul of the true Dominican Tertiary illuminates all the souls who are round about him.[1] This is looked upon as natural enough and just what is to be expected. But grave scandal is caused by a Tertiary who fails to diffuse that influence amongst the members of his family, or his neighbours, and in the exercise of his profession.

Merely by their conduct during a religious ceremony, Tertiaries can do a great deal of good. " Let them behave with great reverence in Church, especially during the celebration of the divine Office, and be an example to all the faithful " (VII. 38).

By their modesty, their obvious purity, their goodness, gentleness, patience, by their spirit of self-sacrifice and their sense of duty, the humblest member of our Third Order can prove that the Truth is in them, since it produces such fruits ; and their conduct will be a living argument to carry conviction to souls assailed by doubt.

---

[1] " I have been told of the case which occurred recently of a young girl of twenty, a Tertiary and a Jocist, who as she lay day after day in hospital, tortured by a terrible disease of the spine, exercised the most fruitful apostolate. Without even speaking, without teaching the truth in words, simply by lying there, holy, surrendered to God, radiant in her suffering, preaching the crucified truth, she was a Preacher of our Order—as was also, but many years earlier, Blessed Mary Bartholomew Bagnesi, whom we commemorate on May 28th. And even as the obsequies of the Dominican *Beata* were a triumph attracting the entire city of Florence and almost leading to a riot because everyone wished to approach her holy relics, so this little Dominican Tertiary from a Paris suburb drew together on the day of her funeral a multitude of souls, those of her brother and sister Dominicans, of her brother and sister Jocists—all of whom, by a common and spontaneous impulse, broke forth in church into the singing of the *Magnificat* " (P. B., *L'Année Dominicaine*, May, 1936, p. 164).

Professors who have the Dominican spirit may be teaching only mathematics or geography, but they will do it with such a religious sense of duty, such sympathy with the souls of their pupils, that these young souls will be touched, moved and attracted, and their spiritual life will receive a permanent impress.

Some nurses have a Dominican manner of tending the sick. Their charitable ministrations proceed from a soul illuminated by the truth, and through the body they seek for souls to whom to impart the light. The poor patient may be tempted in his distress to doubt God and to blaspheme His justice and goodness : the arrival of the little sister, who looks after the sick-poor, checks the oath and restores belief in a good God. Sickness and the approach of death bring home to the human mind the vanity of bodily life and of earthly possessions : the little sister comes at the right moment to pass on to that liberated mind the eternal truth which overflows from her own.

Pius II wrote in the Acts of Canonization of our Mother, St. Catherine of Siena : " No one who drew near to her ever failed to be the better and the wiser for having been with her."

St. Catherine of Siena was not satisfied with praying and doing penance in her little room, with ministering to material wants and sufferings in the way we have described ; she also exercised the gift of teaching the truth which God had given her in so large a measure. By her words, her letters and her books, she was a Sister Preacher in the fullest sense of the term. Every Tertiary must examine himself as to how much he can do in that direction. Our Most Reverend Father General once wrote in an encyclical letter to the Brothers and Sisters of the Third Order : " A Tertiary will not fully have apprehended his mission unless he exercises the apostolate to the best of his ability ; very often he will find that ability greater than he had suspected. . . . In the family circle to begin with. . . . Without self-assertion, with all deference to the liberty due to every soul, he can make the life of the Order known, he can quietly help others to build up their faith and piety on the solid foundations which he thanks God for having given to himself. This he can sometimes do in the course of conversation, or perhaps by reading aloud passages from a book to provoke interest in its further perusal or possibly by arranging an interview with a Father. How often a parent could avert or mitigate a painful family crisis by resorting to one or other of these means ! They will enable the light to shine in spirits obscured by the heady fumes of youth and by the sophisms of the world."

At the National Congress of Bologna in 1935 our Master General also expressed this wish : " Let every Tertiary who is head of a family restore in his home the excellent habit of reciting the Rosary in common every evening, and let him suggest to his friends and sub-ordinates that they should do likewise." Even if only one Rosary were said during the course of the week, what a doctrinal apostolate one might exercise by recalling and considering all the great mysteries of our faith ! One form of " preaching," which lies within the reach of the very humblest Tertiary of the Order of Friars Preachers, is to spread the practice of the Rosary, to win souls for the Rosary Confraternity, and to inscribe them either in the Living Rosary or in the Perpetual Rosary.

" In the parish," the encyclical goes on to say, " every-one is free to select the good works that specially appeal to him ; but except it be a case of something which is in danger of collapsing without their help, Tertiaries should reserve themselves particularly for works which are definitely apostolic, such as instructing children and adults in the catechism, either in groups or individually. One single soul is a large audience, Père Lacordaire once declared. Or again, there will be conferences of various kinds, some specifically Catholic in character, others on some more general subject, calculated to attract the indifferent, to whom a few apostolic words may be addressed in the course of the meeting. The indifference which is so widespread in our days is to be met with amongst women as well as amongst men.

" Let no one excuse himself on the ground that he is not sufficiently well instructed in the truths of religion or that he is unable to expound or explain them ; he must learn, and then he must turn his knowledge to good account."

The Father General also calls attention to the more modest and more self-effacing part that one can play in these good works by practical co-operation in their organization and administration.

There is no one who could not at least labour to make known the various publications by means of which our Fathers seek to spread the Truth.

Finally, outside the limits of the parish the whole world lies open to our action. " Possessed of the truth and of charity ourselves, and secure in our possession of the one and of the other, we are in duty bound to propagate them wherever they ought to reign, that is to say, every-where : in public life, in social life, in economic life, in international life."

But all this presupposes that the truth and the charity within us are genuine. That we should possess them is essential. They may find different modes of expression according to the various forms of the apostolate we have been considering, but no true Dominican can be devoid of them if he wishes his life to be fruitful.

Now, as regards authoritative truth, it is from God that we receive it. Our divine Master has revealed it to humanity, and He gives to each one of us faith for assimilating His divine science. This faith, which St. Catherine compares to a supernatural pupil in the eye

of the intelligence, allows us to believe the truth which
God beholds. A true Dominican must value his faith
more highly than his bodily eyes. Our Order has had
its inquisitors who were jealous for the orthodoxy of the
faith. Several of them, Peter of Verona at their head,
died for it, rejoicing to subscribe their Catholic *Credo*
with their blood. Our duty is to make within our own
hearts the inquisition necessary to preserve the purity
of our faith amid the prevailing atmosphere of modernism
in which so many heresies thrive to-day. We must
imitate our Blessed Father whose numerous journeys led
him alternately in opposite directions, to Rome, as being
the residence of the infallible depository of revealed
religion, and then from Rome to radiate to the ends of
the earth, and to sow broadcast the seed of approved
doctrine. The Rule, in more than one passage, directs
us expressly to follow the example of our Blessed Father
(II. 8 and XI. 41).

None of our Tertiaries, none of our combatants and
certainly none of our priests, should be unacquainted
with the pontifical encyclicals which appear from time
to time to reiterate the great truths of our faith, to make
pronouncements on questions which are exercising the
Church and to give timely and definite direction to our
apostolic activity.

But the teaching which the Church gives on behalf
of God to the faithful requires our serious study if we
are to assimilate it sufficiently to be in a position to
communicate it to others. It was because St. Dominic
never ceased studying and pondering Christian doctrine
day and night, at home and abroad, that he was always
ready to preach it to good effect. When Blessed Jordan
of Saxony was asked what Rule he professed, he replied :
" That of the Friars Preachers : it consists in living
virtuously, in learning and in teaching." The great
theologian Cajetan, who became Master General of our
Order, went so far as to assert that a Friar Preacher
who did not study for four hours a day could scarcely

be held to escape the guilt of mortal sin. Priests of
our Order and also we Tertiaries will do well to meditate upon this assertion which, although perhaps too
sweeping, affords food for serious reflection. The
Dominican Father who directed Blessed Clara Gamba-
corta, advised her " to let no one induce her to neglect
study." And he added this solemn warning : " Remember that in our Order very few persons have become
saints who have not also been scholars." The devil
must be aware of the fact. We are told that he was so
much incensed at the sight of St. Rose of Lima absorbed
in the works of St. Lewis of Granada that he tore the book
from her hands and tried to destroy it. The lives of the
early Fathers of the Order describe analogous incidents
in which the demon is depicted as striving, on specious
pretexts of poverty or religion, to divert the Friars from
their studies.

This study cannot be carried equally far by all.
Between St. Rose of Lima, meditating upon Lewis of
Granada, and Cajetan commenting on St. Thomas's
Summa, there is a wide margin. But through translations
of the *Summa*, published in handy volumes with doctrinal
notes and technical explanations, professors of our Order
have placed within the reach of the educated public the
subject-matter of our great commentators. And for
those to whom Lewis of Granada himself or our more
modern spiritual authors are not available, there are
the conferences given at the monthly meetings of the
Fraternity, in which the Father Director aims at impart-
ing to all the doctrine necessary for the apostolate as
well as for our individual sanctification. Clearly, we
have travelled far from the conception of persons coming
to such meetings merely to do a little needlework for
the Fathers, to cull the latest news about the Order and
to recite a few prayers together. These are excellent
things in their way, but they are not sufficient.

If, in our Order, such importance is attached to studying the truth, it is out of charity, out of love for our God

Whom we wish to know better in order to contemplate Him in His beauty ; it is also out of love for souls to whom we wish to make Him known so that they may attain to contemplating Him with us in eternal life. Where it is only a case of our personal contemplation, although it is undoubtedly desirable for us to deepen our study of God we have little to gain from encumbering ourselves with other knowledge. Souls who are purely contemplative will avoid intellectual curiosity as a distraction detrimental to their interior recollection. But those who are to exercise an effective apostolate amongst doubters and unbelievers will be obliged to extend their studies, especially in the direction of apologetics, exegesis and history, in order to carry out St. Paul's injunction and exhort in accordance with sound doctrine as well as refute those who gainsay it.

We are told that St. Dominic once tried to sell himself as a slave to the Moors to obtain the release of a prisoner. The same charity impelled him to devote himself to the study of sacred science, and every true Dominican, as far as he can, dedicates himself to it in perpetuity, with a view to saving unhappy souls whom the devil holds fast-bound in ignorance and error. Theirs is the worst form of distress because it may become eternal if we do not work to deliver them from it. Before all other forms of charity, we are bound to dispense to them the charity of Truth. There is no finer philanthropic work. And in any case we are pledged by our vocation to that particular kind of almsgiving.

Study, if it is understood in the sense we have described, is a means of enriching oneself to be in a position to give to others. But the book we must study first—the book which will encourage us to pursue the other studies unremittingly and to turn them to good account, is the book of charity. " My son," said St. Dominic, " I have made my chief study in the book of charity : it teaches everything."

APPENDIX

THE DOMINICAN COLOURS

LIKE their brothers and sisters of the First Order, Tertiaries are entitled to a white and black habit. If they are established in the regular life, they can wear it continuously. If they remain in the world and wear only a rudiment of that habit in the form of the little white woollen scapular,[1] nevertheless the complete habit retains for them its symbolic value, which they must daily endeavour to realize. And that is why they may be clothed after their death in the complete habit of the Order (III. 12–16).

The two colours, black and white, are so dear to certain Tertiaries that they keep to them even in their ordinary attire.

Others elect to wear on an outer garment, marked only by simple good taste, the little black and white cross which is characteristic of our Order.

To one and all I wish to say a few parting words which may be applied more or less literally, according to circumstances. They will take the form of a sort of address at a clothing, and while calling attention to the significance of our colours they will summarize in a few pages the teaching of this book.

You are clothed, first of all, entirely in white wool. Then a black cloak is thrown over that whiteness. Why? There are many reasons for it. Theodoric of Apolda mentions a few in his book on St. Dominic, and Blessed

[1] A plenary indulgence is gained by those who die with the habit or at least with scapular—whether they are wearing it or whether it lies upon their bed.

Raymund of Capua expatiates on them in his life of St. Catherine of Siena.

White is universally regarded as the symbol of innocence. When a catechumen has been thoroughly cleansed by the grace of baptism, he is given a white garment to indicate that he is perfectly free from all taint of sin. *Accipe vestem candidam.* Formerly neophytes used to wear their white baptismal robe for eight days —from Holy Saturday until *Dominica in albis*, Low Sunday.

In your case the white habit will be worn until your death. But over your white tunic will be placed the black cloak which the Church does not give to the newly baptized. Why are you invested with that mantle? Because it is practically impossible to spend upon the earth the eighteen years, which must precede admission into Dominican life, without any stain on the baptismal robe. The black cloak symbolizes penance, without which perfect innocence cannot be regained. In the hope of regaining it permanently, you enter St. Dominic's Order, one of the great characteristics of which is penance.

If, not satisfied with your Tertiary profession, you one day make your religious profession which St. Thomas and all tradition regard as a second baptism—even on that very day in which your soul sees herself purified from all sin and from all penalties due to sin, you will still continue to wear over your white robe the black cloak.

Your white robe also suggests a special anxiety which will inspire you to avoid for the future all taint of sin. A man wishing to embark upon a piece of work likely to soil his clothes does not dress himself in white. The slightest spot would show and would be offensive to the eye.

All those who attach importance to the whiteness of their habit will therefore avoid contact with anything

that could sully it. Do you know the legend of the white
ermine that figures in the arms of Brittany ? I tell it
the more willingly because Albert de Morlaix in his
history of Brittany asserts that St. Dominic was descended
from a Breton lord, and that the cross on our shield is
formed of four ermines gardant.   It seems hardly credible.
Be that as it may, the pretty story of the ermine runs as
follows :

For hours she had been eluding the hunter. Slipping
through the undergrowth, she was gradually out-distanc-
ing him when she came to a bog. Nothing could be
easier than to cross it and so ensure her safety. That
meant, of course, that she would have to soil her beautiful
fur. But—to save her life ! No—better to die. And so
the little ermine remained on the brink of the swamp,
where she was soon overtaken by the hunter and trans-
fixed by his arrow. *Potius mori quam foedari.* Death
before defilement ! That is the motto of Brittany, and
it must be yours. " Those white garments of salvation,
keep them pure and spotless."

But lay to heart this essential point which the black
cloak may help you to remember : your anxiety to
remain pure of all stain must always, if it is to be really
serious and efficacious, be associated with an equally
strong anxiety for mortification. As I have already told
you, penance is necessary to expiate past sin. Mortification is indispensable to prevent sin in the future. The
black mantle tells of death. It is the evil tendencies
which are ever ready to revive in your soul that must be
relentlessly and incessantly mortified, that is, put to death.

Have trust and be of good courage ! For your habit—
particularly that part of it which is white, stands for the
graces of purity which the special protection of the Blessed
Virgin will dispense to you. It is she who, in memorable
circumstances and before the eyes of St. Dominic himself,
cured Blessed Reginald and showed him the " complete

habit " he was to wear. The scapular which had hitherto been lacking became " the most important part of our habit, the mother's pledge from Heaven of the love which the Blessed Virgin Mary bears towards us. Under her wings and mantle you will find a shade from the heat and a bulwark and defence in death from all dangers both of body and soul."

Let us reflect upon this all-powerful protection which our habit is constantly enlisting. And let us never allow ourselves to be hypnotized by dangers and by our weakness. Our Heavenly Mother is there, the true valiant woman who has woven our white habit for us. It is she who has made our saints, men and women alike, so pre-eminent in purity. Have you ever noticed what stress is laid in the Office upon their signal virginity? That is Mary's gift.

Remember the story of a pious woman of Lombardy which is told in our old chronicles. It was in the first days of the Order. She had seen, for the first time, two of these new religious, " clad in a habit very clean and beautiful." Doubts regarding their virtue arose in her mind, and she said in herself, " They will never be able to maintain their purity." The following night the Holy Virgin appeared to her, looking very stern : " You have offended me in the person of those religious who are my children," she said. " Do you suppose that I cannot take care of them ? " And half opening her mantle she showed her a great company of friars, including the two travellers of the preceding day.

Every morning as you clothe yourself again in the white habit, say respectfully to the Holy Virgin : " *Monstra te esse Matrem, fac ut monstrem me esse filium tuum*—Show thyself to be my Mother, and enable me to show myself to be thy son." Then kiss your scapular with something of the veneration you would bestow upon the holy seamless coat which Mary wove for her Son. You also, like the saints, have received the habit from her. But if you wish to have the benefit of Mary's active protection, you must remain humble, very humble indeed. *Humilibus dat gratiam.* It is to the humble that grace is given. The black cloak will be a perpetual reminder of the humility which is indispensable. " Receive the black cloak, a symbol of the humility that befits you." If ever you allow yourself to forget that your purity is Mary's gift and begin to take the credit of it to yourself, you will very soon lose it altogether.

It is interesting to notice how insistent the Fathers of the Church are upon this virtue of humility in the various sermons to Christian virgins which have come down to us. If you have any comprehension of the language of symbols, your black cloak will constantly impress upon you what St. Ambrose and St. Augustine preached to the Christian virgins of old.

Our habit has yet another signification, and one which is more essentially Dominican. The whole ideal of our Order has been summed up in the single word *Veritas* and in St. Thomas's terse phrase : " *Contemplari et contemplata aliis tradere.*"

How well our white habit typifies not only that candid truth to which the Order of St. Dominic is pledged, but also the light of contemplation and the enlightening beams of apostolic zeal. It has the same meaning as the dazzling star which was seen to shine on our Blessed Father's brow.

Only there are certain conditions which must be fulfilled if we are to keep our faith pure, if we are to have a deep knowledge of the truth, if we are to contemplate that truth in love, and if we are to succeed in spreading round about us the light of truth and the influence of a good example. Those conditions are symbolized by the black cloak. Whereas white is the most diffusive of colours, black is the most absorbent. It is absolutely essential that our spirit should, in the first instance, absorb the light which comes to it from God the author of revelation, from the Church which propounds it to us on His behalf, and from our masters who explain it to us. It is necessary also that our faculties should themselves be absorbed in prayer, in study, in pondering and in assimilating the truth. And to succeed in this we must of necessity guard against distractions, restrain our senses and know how to recollect ourselves. And all this is covered by the symbolism of the black cloak.

You are familiar with that charming painting in which Fra Angelico represents St. Dominic as a very young man, seated with a book on his knees. He is wrapped in the black mantle. His chin rests lightly on his right hand while he reads, he meditates and he contemplates. His face is aglow ; a halo surrounds his head ; the star glitters above his forehead. It will be quite otherwise when he rises to speak to men about God. His arms will be outspread in an eloquent gesture, displaying to the eyes of all the whiteness of his tunic until then in a great measure hidden under the black cloak. After having absorbed the light, he will diffuse it round about him. . . .

All in our own way—even the Sisters Preachers—we must imitate our Father in diffusing the truth round about us by our words or by our example, and we must make the preliminary preparation for it in recollection and in the necessary austerities.

One last aspect of this manifold symbolism I will try to set before you. White garments signify joy. It is so here below, and it would seem to be the same on high. On the day of the Transfiguration, to give His disciples some idea of His glory and of his eternal beatitude, Our Lord revealed Himself clothed in a garment of dazzling whiteness. No fuller could rival it. Snow itself is not whiter. And St. John in the Apocalypse described a procession of white-robed figures whom he saw following after Our Lord in Heaven. Who are those and from whence do they come ? At the beginning of the feast of all our

Dominican saints, our liturgy borrows from St. John the question : *Hi qui amicti sunt stolis albis, qui sunt et unde venerunt ?* Those whom we commemorate on this day in the whiteness of their garments, who are they and whence do they come ? The answer is evident. There is no need to elaborate it. They are those who in time past received the white robe of St. Dominic—the symbol here below of everlasting joy.

Of that celestial bliss did they not receive a foretaste on earth in the charity which the holy observances of their Order helped them to exercise, in the contemplation of the divine beauty, wherein their charity delighted, and in the assurance, following from that contemplation, that their God, Whom they loved so well, was infinitely perfect, and that all was being realized according to His good pleasure ? That was the source of the joy which, as Blessed Jordan says, illumined the face of our Blessed Father. Sister Cecilia has left it on record that he always seemed happy and smiling. St. Catherine of Siena asserts that " his religion is all joyous : it is a garden of delights." To some novices whom he had just admitted into the Order and who broke out into hysterical laughter during Compline, Jordan of Saxony said : " Laugh, dear brothers, laugh ! " and he reproved an old friar who sought to repress their levity.

Let us see to it, nevertheless, that we keep a veil of melancholy over our Dominican joy—like the black cloak which covers our white tunic.

Sister Cecilia, whose whole life was a joy to her Blessed Father, adds a qualifying clause to her statement that he usually looked radiant when he visited the convent : " Except," she says, " when he was moved to compassion by the afflictions of others." Now this was often the case, and it was the more liable to happen because our Blessed Father's soul knew how to appreciate at their true value the various forms of affliction and sensed especially the ills of the soul. The persistent faults of his religious daughters themselves crucified

him, we are told. When he saw in the distance the
crowded roofs of a town, the thought of the miseries of
men and of their sins plunged him in sorrowful reflections which clouded his countenance. He shed bitter
tears by night over the sins of mankind.

St. Catherine also suffered from the sorrows of the
world. She actually regarded herself as the cause of all
those ills and used to end her prayers with the words :
" I have sinned, Lord, have pity upon me." She continually recommended to her disciples this knowledge
of themselves and of their pitiable condition, warning
them at the same time never to separate it from their
knowledge of God's mercies. She composed a whole
treatise upon tears, and it has been said that " her spiritual
sons were trained in a school of tears ; sorrow, Christian
sorrow, is the family characteristic of those who were the
children of her vows and of her prayers."

If Blessed Jordan of Saxony approved of laughing
novices, it was because of the motive which he regarded
as underlying their merriment : " You may well laugh,
because you have escaped from the devil who formerly
held you in bondage." And Gerard de Frachet ends
this little episode by saying : " The souls of the novices
were greatly comforted at these words, but it came to
pass that from that moment all untimely laughter
became impossible to them."

In a word, Blessed Jordan had established them in the
truth. And this truth which implants joy in our hearts
also tempers it with compunction. Although we are
delivered from the devil we retain the recollection of
having been in his hands : there is still the possibility
that we may fall into them again, and we know, alas !
that an incalculable number of our fellows remain in
his keeping. United to God we happily are indeed, but
in the shadows of faith. We do not see Him, we know
Him ill, and we participate only very imperfectly in
His felicity. Our joy is more especially a joy of hope,
as St. Paul says : *spe gaudentes*.